TIME
ANNUAL

The Year in Review 1998

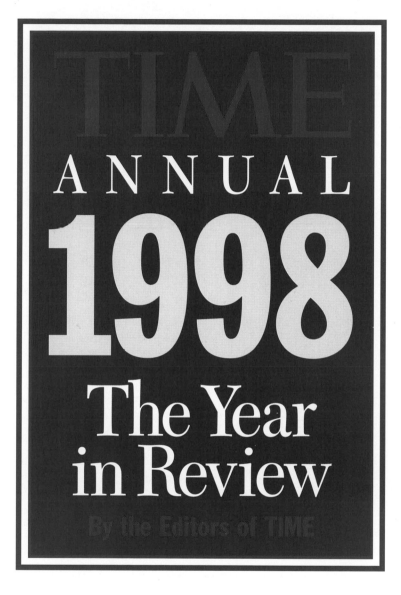

TIME

ANNUAL

1998

The Year
in Review

By the Editors of TIME

TIME ANNUAL 1998

22

54

77

THE YEAR IN REVIEW

97

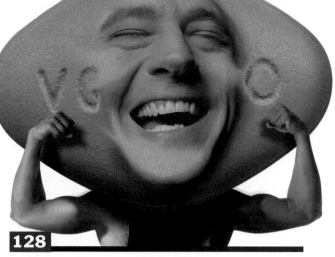

128

150

TIME ANNUAL 1998

MANAGING EDITOR	Kelly Knauer
ART DIRECTOR	Ellen Fanning
PICTURE EDITOR	Patricia Cadley
PRODUCTION EDITOR	Michael Skinner
RESEARCHERS	Valerie Marchant, Denise Lynch, Leah Shanks Gordon
COPY EDITORS	Bruce Christopher Carr, Ellin Martens, Bob Braine
PRODUCTION DIRECTOR	John Calvano
TIME SPECIAL PROJECTS EDITOR	Barrett Seaman

TIME INC. HOME ENTERTAINMENT

PRESIDENT	David Gitow
DIRECTOR, CONTINUITIES AND SINGLE SALES	David Arfine
DIRECTOR, CONTINUITIES & RETENTION	Michael Barrett
DIRECTOR, NEW PRODUCTS	Alicia Longobardo
GROUP PRODUCT MANAGERS	Robert Fox, Jennifer McLyman
PRODUCT MANAGERS	Christopher Berzolla, Roberta Harris, Stacy Hirschberg, Kenneth Maehlum, Daniel Melore
MANAGER, RETAIL AND NEW MARKETS	Thomas Mifsud
ASSOCIATE PRODUCT MANAGERS	Carlos Jimenez, Daria Raehse, Dennis Sheehan, Betty Su, Niki Viswanathan, Lauren Zaslansky, Cheryl Zukowski
ASSISTANT PRODUCT MANAGERS	Victoria Alfonso, Jennifer Dowell, Meredith Shelley
EDITORIAL OPERATIONS DIRECTOR	John Calvano
BOOK PRODUCTION MANAGER	Jessica McGrath
ASSISTANT BOOK PRODUCTION MANAGER	Jonathan Polsky
BOOK PRODUCTION COORDINATOR	Kristen Travers
FULFILLMENT DIRECTOR	Michelle Gudema
ASSISTANT FULFILLMENT MANAGER	Richard Perez
FINANCIAL DIRECTOR	Tricia Griffin
FINANCIAL MANAGER	Amy Maselli
ASSISTANT FINANCIAL MANAGER	Steven Sandonato
MARKETING ASSISTANT	Ann Gillespie

THE WRITING OF THE FOLLOWING TIME STAFF MEMBERS AND CONTRIBUTORS IS INCLUDED IN THIS VOLUME:
Bernard Baumohl, Jonathan Beaty, Lisa Beyer, Jay Branegan, Massimo Calabresi, Margaret Carlson, James Carney, Howard Chua-Eoan, John Cloud, Jay Cocks, Adam Cohen, James Collins, Richard Corliss, Michael Duffy, Philip Elmer-DeWitt, John F. Dickerson, Daniel Eisenberg, Christopher John Farley, Andrew Ferguson, Jeff Galbraith, Nancy Gibbs, Frank Gibney, Elizabeth Gleick, Frederic Golden, Christine Gorman, Paul Gray, John Greenwald, S.C. Gwynne, Bruce Handy, Barry Hillenbrand, Margot Hornblower, Robert Hughes, Walter Isaacson, Pico Iyer, Daniel Kadlec, Jeffrey Kluger, Michael Krantz, Nadya Labi, Richard Lacayo, Erik Larson, Michael Lemonick, Belinda Luscombe, J.F.O. McAllister, Terry McCarthy, Johanna McGeary, J. Madeleine Nash, Bruce W. Nelan, Stacy Perman, Eric Pooley, Paul Quinn-Judge, Joshua Cooper Ramo, Romesh Ratnesar, Christopher Redman, Richard Schickel, Joel Stein, Chris Taylor, Mark Thompson, Karen Tumulty, Douglas Waller, James Walsh, Richard Zoglin

SPECIAL THANKS TO:
Gerry Abrahamsen, Ames Adamson, Ken Baierlein, Robin Bierstedt, Sue Blair, Andy Blau, Anne Considine, Urbano DelValle, Dick Duncan, Elena Falaro, Brian Fellows, Linda Freeman, Marti Golon, Arthur Hochstein, Kin Wah Lam, Joe Lertola, Alex LeVine, Amy Musher, Rudi Papiri, Ken Smith, Michele Stephenson, Miriam Winocur, Anna Yelenskaya

We welcome your comments and suggestions about TIME Books. Please write to us at:
TIME Books • Attention: Book Editors • PO Box 11016 • Des Moines, IA 50336-1016

If you would like to order any of our hard-cover Collection Edition books, please call us at 1-800-327-6388, Monday through Friday, 7:00 a.m.–8:00 p.m. or Saturday, 7:00 a.m.–6:00 p.m. Central time.

COPYRIGHT 1999 BY TIME INC. HOME ENTERTAINMENT

Published by TIME Books • Time Inc., 1271 Avenue of the Americas, New York, NY 10020
ISBN # 1-883013-61-5; ISSN# 1097-5721

Printed in the United States of America

▶**1998** **A year when one man gave us a thrill just by getting back to where he once belonged ...**

GEORGE SHELTON—NASA

THE YEAR IN REVIEW

HATS OFF!
"Big Mac"—Mark McGwire—cracks his record homer No. 62, as Sammy Sosa takes a bow

Jed Jacobsohn—Allsport

Jonathan Daniel—Allsport

▶1998 And two men dragged us into a

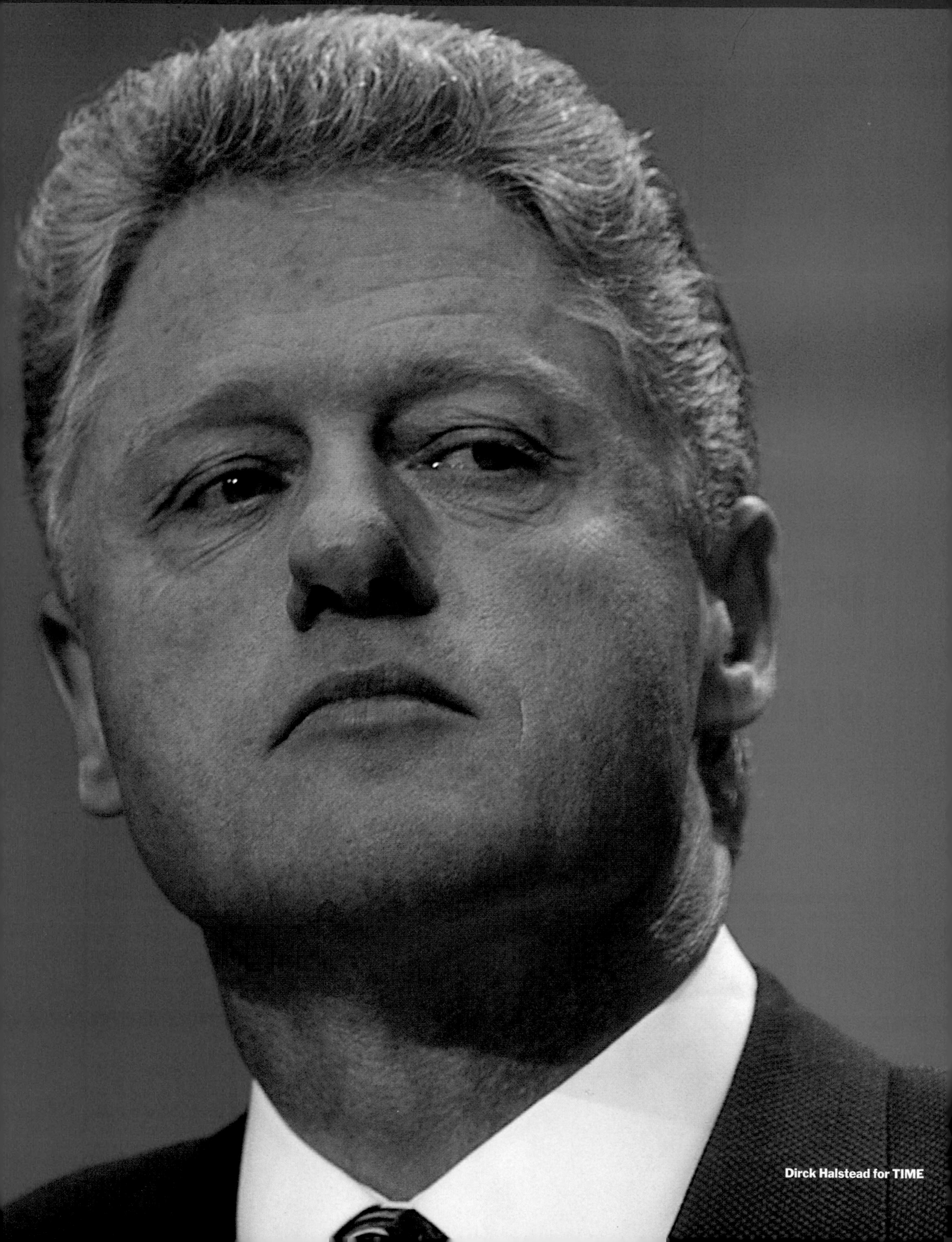

Dirck Halstead for TIME

DON'T GO THERE!
But Kenneth Starr did—
revealing every detail of Bill
Clinton's affair with a White House
intern in a report to Congress

Chuck Kennedy

LEAP OF FAITH
Pope John Paul II, an old foe of communism, accepted Fidel Castro's invitation and made a historic pilgrimage to Cuba

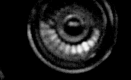

BIENVENIDO SU SANTIDAD Juan Pablo II

TRAGEDY IN WYOMING
A bouquet honors Matthew Shepard, a 21-year-old gay man who was beaten, tied to this fence and left to die

Steve Liss for TIME

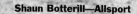

A REALLY BIG SHOW
Sumo wrestlers strut their
stuff during the opening
ceremonies of the Winter
Olympics in Nagano, Japan

HILLARY CLINTON

She won a scarlet letter—oops!—purple heart for standing by her man

TUSSLING TITANS

Safe at home! Mogul Murdoch got L.A.'s Dodgers, though mogul Turner objected

TOM HANKS

We're goin' in! Forget the pillboxes— America's box offices soon surrendered

TONY BLAIR

He got the Irish to stop fighting? Put him on the global-warming task force!

TINA BROWN

Eustace Tilley cries tears of relief as Mistress Buzzworthy goes Hollywood

BILL CLINTON

Visiting Jiang's China, Chairman Bill urged: Let a billion dollars blossom!

KIM JONG IL

Now North Korea's boss has a missile. But his people need bread, not ballistics

LEONARDO DiCAPRIO

Sinking feeling? Hardly. A voyage on Cameron's Titanic floated his boat

OPRAH WINFREY

The TV queen outsteered the Texas beef barons who said she dissed their meat

MONICA LEWINSKY

The victim got a book deal … posed for Vanity Fair … and hates Linda Tripp

JERRY SEINFELD & CO.

The masters of their domain exited—but they closed with a whimper, not a bang

JESSE VENTURA

The ex-pro wrestled the governorship of Minnesota from the usual suspects

BOB DYLAN

The eternally-touring sphinx of folk-rock got a Grammy—and so did son Jakob

SLOBODAN MILOSEVIC

"Out, damned Kosovar!" The Butcher of the Balkans earned his title again

PAULA JONES

O.K., her case was thrown out of court, but she got $850,000—and a new nose

GEORGE BUSH

"Subpoena! Duck!" He opposed Secret Service testimony in Clinton's case

STEVE CASE

Acquiring Netscape and its Navigator, the AOL boss set a course for Gatesland

MARK McGWIRE

Yes, he took a muscle builder, but as one player noted, he still had to hit the ball

"Is the Senate smart? Not if it has an alternative."
—TRENT LOTT, Senate majority leader

"Because I'm drunk."
—GRANGER DAVIS on why he was breaking California's new law against smoking in bars

"Look, I won! I'm back!"
—BOB DOLE, a neighbor of Monica Lewinsky's at the Watergate apartments, upon seeing the huge press stakeout

BRAD MARKEL—GAMMA LIAISON

"I'm not willing to preside over people who are cannibals."
—NEWT GINGRICH on stepping down as Speaker of the House

"If you can't ride baked, you shouldn't be riding."
—SEAN ("Chavez") HOLMES, a snowboarder in Whistler, B.C., where Olympic gold medalist Ross Rebagliati lives and trains

"I've never had champagne before!"
—SAMMY SOSA, delirious, after the Chicago Cubs beat the San Francisco Giants to make the playoffs

"It's like paying to see Elvis and getting

"I started off with short dresses, which I knew I wouldn't get to wear. But I looked a lot better in a short dress, to be perfectly honest."
—MICK JAGGER on his role as a cross-dresser in the movie *Bent*

"I thought his only enemy was Captain Hook."
—HENRY STERN, New York City parks czar, on the theft of a Peter Pan statue from a city park

"Sorry about the crowding, but welcome to coach class."
—SENATOR MIKE DEWINE of Ohio welcoming the heads of seven airlines to a single Senate hearing table

"Who put Viagra in the thermometer?"
—Houston car-wash sign, during Texas' long, hot summer

EXPRESS NEWSPAPERS—ARCHIVE PHOTOS

"I do not have a personal relationship with a computer."
—JANET RENO, Attorney General, frustrated with her office technology

"I survived Vietnam. I survived being married to a redhead. I'll survive this."
—RICHARD WILSON, North Carolina resident, on Hurricane Bonnie

"What will we do without Newt there?"
—A White House official after hearing Gingrich would resign

CARLOS OSORIO—AP/WIDE WORLD

"I have to be who I am. I can't go out and gain weight... in order to be a better role model."
—CALISTA FLOCKHART, *Ally McBeal* star, on rumors that she is anorexic

"It is a great drug."
—ELIZABETH DOLE, whose husband Bob was in the test group for Viagra

"I'm going through eye-exercise therapy, strengthening my eyes. I'm supposed to ... like, rest them."
—MARTHA STEWART explaining why her eyes were shut during an Al Gore speech, reported by the New York *Times*

"There were an awful lot of people against the automobile too."
—RICHARD SEED, physicist, on the reaction to his plan to clone babies for couples that are infertile

a garage band instead."
—JOHN MABRY, life-size St. Louis Cardinal, after getting booed for filling in for a resting Mark McGwire

"The unemployment numbers are down to the lowest in 25 years ... The principal credit goes to Janet Reno, who continues to appoint special prosecutors."
—DICK ARMEY, House majority leader

EVAN AGOSTINI—GAMMA LIAISON

"Don't blame them for being dull. That's how they've been chosen as high-ranking politicians."
—TAKASI INOGUCHI, Tokyo political science professor, on the blandness of Japanese leaders

"Let's be blunt: yesterday's Evita is today's Velveeta."
—MR. BLACKWELL, placing Madonna third on his worst-dressed-women list

"I'd rather have a hot poker in my eye than an airport named after him."
—RANDY SCHWITZ, of the National Air Traffic Controllers Association, on plans to rename Washington's National Airport after Ronald Reagan

"I buy expensive suits. They just look cheap on me."
—WARREN BUFFETT, billionaire investor and down-home Nebraskan

LIST-O-MANIA!

End of the century coming? It's time to take inventory! Here is our list of some of the year's best lists. Warning: guaranteed to start arguments, divide families and boost Blockbuster profits

The Random House list of the 100 Most Influential Novels of the 20th century

James Joyce

LIPNITSKY, PARIS

1. ULYSSES by James Joyce
2. THE GREAT GATSBY by F. Scott Fitzgerald
3. A PORTRAIT OF THE ARTIST AS A YOUNG MAN by James Joyce
4. LOLITA by Vladimir Nabokov
5. BRAVE NEW WORLD by Aldous Huxley
6. THE SOUND AND THE FURY by William Faulkner
7. CATCH-22 by Joseph Heller
8. DARKNESS AT NOON by Arthur Koestler
9. SONS AND LOVERS by D.H. Lawrence
10. THE GRAPES OF WRATH by John Steinbeck
11. UNDER THE VOLCANO by Malcolm Lowry
12. THE WAY OF ALL FLESH by Samuel Butler
13. 1984 by George Orwell
14. I, CLAUDIUS by Robert Graves
15. TO THE LIGHTHOUSE by Virginia Woolf
16. AN AMERICAN TRAGEDY by Theodore Dreiser
17. THE HEART IS A LONELY HUNTER by Carson McCullers
18. SLAUGHTERHOUSE-FIVE by Kurt Vonnegut
19. INVISIBLE MAN by Ralph Ellison
20. NATIVE SON by Richard Wright
21. HENDERSON THE RAIN KING by Saul Bellow
22. APPOINTMENT IN SAMARRA by John O'Hara
23. U.S.A. (trilogy) by John Dos Passos
24. WINESBURG, OHIO by Sherwood Anderson
25. A PASSAGE TO INDIA by E.M. Forster
26. THE WINGS OF THE DOVE by Henry James
27. THE AMBASSADORS by Henry James
28. TENDER IS THE NIGHT by F. Scott Fitzgerald
29. THE STUDS LONIGAN TRILOGY by James T. Farrell
30. THE GOOD SOLDIER by Ford Madox Ford
31. ANIMAL FARM by George Orwell
32. THE GOLDEN BOWL by Henry James
33. SISTER CARRIE by Theodore Dreiser
34. A HANDFUL OF DUST by Evelyn Waugh
35. AS I LAY DYING by William Faulkner
36. ALL THE KING'S MEN by Robert Penn Warren
37. THE BRIDGE OF SAN LUIS REY by Thornton Wilder
38. HOWARDS END by E.M. Forster
39. GO TELL IT ON THE MOUNTAIN by James Baldwin
40. THE HEART OF THE MATTER by Graham Greene
41. LORD OF THE FLIES by William Golding
42. DELIVERANCE by James Dickey
43. A DANCE TO THE MUSIC OF TIME (series) by Anthony Powell
44. POINT COUNTER POINT by Aldous Huxley
45. THE SUN ALSO RISES by Ernest Hemingway
46. THE SECRET AGENT by Joseph Conrad
47. NOSTROMO by Joseph Conrad
48. THE RAINBOW by D.H. Lawrence
49. WOMEN IN LOVE by D.H. Lawrence
50. TROPIC OF CANCER by Henry Miller
51. THE NAKED AND THE DEAD by Norman Mailer
52. PORTNOY'S COMPLAINT by Philip Roth
53. PALE FIRE by Vladimir Nabokov
54. LIGHT IN AUGUST by William Faulkner
55. ON THE ROAD by Jack Kerouac
56. THE MALTESE FALCON by Dashiell Hammett
57. PARADE'S END by Ford Madox Ford
58. THE AGE OF INNOCENCE by Edith Wharton
59. ZULEIKA DOBSON by Max Beerbohm
60. THE MOVIEGOER by Walker Percy
61. DEATH COMES FOR THE ARCHBISHOP by Willa Cather
62. FROM HERE TO ETERNITY by James Jones
63. THE WAPSHOT CHRONICLES by John Cheever
64. THE CATCHER IN THE RYE by J.D. Salinger
65. A CLOCKWORK ORANGE by Anthony Burgess
66. OF HUMAN BONDAGE by W. Somerset Maugham
67. HEART OF DARKNESS by Joseph Conrad
68. MAIN STREET by Sinclair Lewis
69. THE HOUSE OF MIRTH by Edith Wharton
70. THE ALEXANDRIA QUARTET by Lawrence Durell

Saul Bellow

The Sporting News list of the 100 Greatest Baseball Players of the 20th century

1. Babe Ruth
2. Willie Mays
3. Ty Cobb
4. Walter Johnson
5. Hank Aaron
6. Lou Gehrig
7. Christy Mathewson
8. Ted Williams
9. Rogers Hornsby
10. Stan Musial
11. Joe DiMaggio
12. Grover Cleveland Alexander
13. Honus Wagner
14. Cy Young
15. Jimmie Foxx
16. Johnny Bench
17. Mickey Mantle
18. Josh Gibson
19. Satchel Paige
20. Roberto Clemente
21. Warren Spahn
22. Frank Robinson
23. Lefty Grove
24. Eddie Collins
25. Pete Rose
26. Sandy Koufax
27. Tris Speaker
28. Mike Schmidt
29. Napoleon Lajoie
30. Steve Carlton
31. Bob Gibson
32. Tom Seaver
33. George Sisler
34. Barry Bonds
35. Shoeless Joe Jackson
36. Bob Feller
37. Hank Greenberg
38. Ernie Banks
39. Greg Maddux
40. Yogi Berra
41. Nolan Ryan
42. Mel Ott
43. Al Simmons
44. Jackie Robinson
45. Carl Hubbell
46. Charley Gehringer
47. Buck Leonard
48. Reggie Jackson
49. Tony Gwynn
50. Roy Campanella
51. Rickey Henderson
52. Whitey Ford
53. Roger Clemens
54. Harry Heilmann
55. George Brett
56. Willie McCovey
57. Bill Dickey
58. Lou Brock
59. Bill Terry
60. Joe Morgan
61. Rod Carew
62. Paul Waner
63. Eddie Mathews
64. Jim Palmer
65. Mickey Cochrane
66. Cool Papa Bell
67. Oscar Charleston
68. Eddie Plank
69. Harmon Killebrew
70. Pie Traynor
71. Juan Marichal
72. Carl Yastrzemski
73. Lefty Gomez
74. Robin Roberts
75. Willie Keeler
76. Al Kaline
77. Eddie Murray
78. Cal Ripken Jr.
79. Joe Medwick
80. Brooks Robinson
81. Willie Stargell
82. Ed Walsh
83. Duke Snider
84. Sam Crawford
85. Dizzy Dean
86. Kirby Puckett
87. Ozzie Smith
88. Frank Frisch
89. Goose Goslin
90. Ralph Kiner
91. Mark McGwire
92. Chuck Klein
93. Ken Griffey Jr.
94. Dave Winfield
95. Wade Boggs
96. Gaylord Perry
97. Rollie Fingers
98. Dennis Eckersley
99. Paul Molitor
100. Early Wynn

Joe DiMaggio

The Ladies' Home Journal list of the 100 Most Important Women of the 20th century

Eleanor Roosevelt

ACME—CORBIS-BETMANN

Activists & Politicians

Jane Addams
Madeleine Albright
Mary McCleod Bethune
Carrie Chapman Catt
Hillary Rodham Clinton
Marian Wright Edelman
Indira Gandhi
Ruth Bader Ginsburg
Emma Goldman
Anita Hill
Dolores Huerta
Maggie Kuhn
Golda Meir
Rigoberta Menchú
Sandra Day O'Connor
Jacqueline Kennedy Onassis
Rosa Parks
Alice Paul
Frances Perkins
Eva Perón
Jiang Qing
Eleanor Roosevelt
Phyllis Schlafly
Gloria Steinem
Daw Aung San Suu Kyi
Mother Teresa
Margaret Thatcher

Writers & Journalists

Maya Angelou
Hannah Arendt
Rachel Carson
Agatha Christie
Simone de Beauvoir
Anne Frank
Betty Friedan
Ann Landers
Margaret Mead
Margaret Mitchell
Toni Morrison
Dorothy Parker
Sylvia Plath
Gertrude Stein
Barbara Walters
Laura Ingalls Wilder
Virginia Woolf

Doctors & Scientists

Virginia Apgar
Helen Caldicott
Marie Curie

Rosalind Franklin
Jane Goodall
Grace Hopper
Melanie Klein
Mary Leakey
Barbara McClintock
Lise Meitner

Entrepreneurs

Coco Chanel
Julia Child
Elsie de Wolfe
Katharine Graham
Ruth Handler
Estée Lauder
Jean Nidetch
Mary Quant
Martha Stewart
Oprah Winfrey

Artists & Entertainers

Marian Anderson
Lucille Ball
Margaret Bourke-White
Maria Callas
Isadora Duncan
Ella Fitzgerald
Jane Fonda
Greta Garbo
Martha Graham
Katharine Hepburn
Billie Holliday
Janis Joplin
Frida Kahlo
Dorothea Lange
Madonna
Marilyn Monroe
Georgia O'Keeffe
Mary Pickford
Leni Riefenstahl

Athletes

Nadia Comaneci
Babe Didrikson
Gertrude Ederle
Sonja Henie
Billie Jean King
Suzanne Lenglen
Wilma Rudolph

Pioneers & Adventurers

Nancy Brinker
Helen Gurley Brown
Diana, Princess of Wales
Amelia Earhart
Betty Ford
Helen Keller
Maria Montessori
Jane Roe
Margaret Sanger
Valentina Tereshkova

Margaret Thatcher

SVEM SIMON

Sixty of TIME's 100 Most Influential People of the century (40 to come in 1999)

Leaders & Revolutionaries

Teddy Roosevelt
V.I. Lenin
Margaret Sanger
Mao Zedong
Winston Churchill
Franklin Delano Roosevelt
Eleanor Roosevelt
Adolf Hitler
Mohandas Gandhi
David Ben-Gurion
Ho Chi Minh
Martin Luther King
Ayatullah Ruhollah Khomeini
Margaret Thatcher
Lech Walesa
Ronald Reagan
Mikhail Gorbachev
Pope John Paul II
The Unknown Rebel
Nelson Mandela

Builders & Titans

Henry Ford
David Sarnoff
Charles Merrill
Willis Carrier
Lucky Luciano
William Levitt
Leo Burnett
Ray Kroc
Pete Rozelle
Sam Walton
Louis B. Mayer
Amadeo Giannini
Stephen Bechtel
Walt Disney
Juan Trippe
Walter Reuther
Thomas Watson Jr.
Estee Lauder
Akio Morita
Bill Gates

Artists & Entertainers

Pablo Picasso
Martha Graham
Le Corbusier
Igor Stravinsky
Coco Chanel
James Joyce
T.S. Eliot
Louis Armstrong
Charlie Chaplin
Marlon Brando
Rodgers & Hammerstein
Frank Sinatra
Lucille Ball
The Beatles
Bob Dylan
Aretha Franklin
Jim Henson
Steven Spielberg
Bart Simpson
Oprah Winfrey

The American Film Institute list of the 100 Most Important Movies of the 20th Century

1. CITIZEN KANE (1941)
2. CASABLANCA (1942)
3. THE GODFATHER (1972)
4. GONE WITH THE WIND (1939)
5. LAWRENCE OF ARABIA (1962)
6. THE WIZARD OF OZ (1939)
7. THE GRADUATE (1967)
8. ON THE WATERFRONT (1954)
9. SCHINDLER'S LIST (1993)
10. SINGIN' IN THE RAIN (1952)
11. IT'S S WONDERFUL LIFE (1946)
12. SUNSET BOULEVARD (1950)
13. THE BRIDGE ON THE RIVER KWAI (1957)
14. SOME LIKE IT HOT (1959)
15. STAR WARS (1977)
16. ALL ABOUT EVE (1950)
17. THE AFRICAN QUEEN (1951)
18. PSYCHO (1960)
19. CHINATOWN (1974)
20. ONE FLEW OVER THE CUCKOO'S NEST (1975)
21. THE GRAPES OF WRATH (1940)
22. 2001: A SPACE ODYSSEY (1968)
23. THE MALTESE FALCON (1941)
24. RAGING BULL (1980)
25. E.T. THE EXTRA-TERRESTRIAL (1982)
26. DR. STRANGELOVE (1964)
27. BONNIE AND CLYDE (1967)
28. APOCALYPSE NOW (1979)
29. MR. SMITH GOES TO WASHINGTON (1939)
30. THE TREASURE OF THE SIERRA MADRE (1948)
31. ANNIE HALL (1977)
32. THE GODFATHER PART II (1974)
33. HIGH NOON (1952)
34. TO KILL A MOCKINGBIRD (1962)
35. IT HAPPENED ONE NIGHT (1934)
36. MIDNIGHT COWBOY (1969)
37. THE BEST YEARS OF OUR LIVES (1946)
38. DOUBLE INDEMNITY (1944)
39. DOCTOR ZHIVAGO (1965)
40. NORTH BY NORTHWEST (1959)
41. WEST SIDE STORY (1961)
42. REAR WINDOW (1954)
43. KING KONG (1933)
44. THE BIRTH OF A NATION (1915)
45. A STREETCAR NAMED DESIRE (1951)
46. A CLOCKWORK ORANGE (1971)
47. TAXI DRIVER (1976)
48. JAWS (1975)
49. SNOW WHITE AND THE SEVEN DWARFS (1937)
50. BUTCH CASSIDY AND THE SUNDANCE KID (1969)
51. THE PHILADELPHIA STORY (1940)
52. FROM HERE TO ETERNITY (1953)
53. AMADEUS (1984)
54. ALL QUIET ON THE WESTERN FRONT (1930)
55. THE SOUND OF MUSIC (1965)
56. M*A*S*H (1970)
57. THE THIRD MAN (1949)
58. FANTASIA (1940)
59. REBEL WITHOUT A CAUSE (1955)
60. RAIDERS OF THE LOST ARK (1981)
61. VERTIGO (1958)
62. TOOTSIE (1982)
63. STAGECOACH (1939)
64. CLOSE ENCOUNTERS OF THE THIRD KIND (1977)
65. THE SILENCE OF THE LAMBS (1991)
66. NETWORK (1976)
67. THE MANCHURIAN CANDIDATE (1962)
68. AN AMERICAN IN PARIS (1951)
69. SHANE (1953)
70. THE FRENCH CONNECTION (1971)
71. FORREST GUMP (1994)
72. BEN-HUR (1959)
73. WUTHERING HEIGHTS (1939)
74. THE GOLD RUSH (1925)
75. DANCES WITH WOLVES (1990)

Lawrence of Arabia

COLUMBIA PICTURES

76. CITY LIGHTS (1931)
77. AMERICAN GRAFFITTI (1973)
78. ROCKY (1976)
79. THE DEER HUNTER (1978)
80. THE WILD BUNCH (1969)
81. MODERN TIMES (1936)
82. GIANT (1956)
83. PLATOON (1986)
84. FARGO (1996)
85. DUCK SOUP (1933)
86. MUTINY ON THE BOUNTY (1935)
87. FRANKENSTEIN (1931)
88. EASY RIDER (1969)
89. PATTON (1970)
90. THE JAZZ SINGER (1927)
91. MY FAIR LADY (1964)
92. A PLACE IN THE SUN (1951)
93. THE APARTMENT (1960)
94. GOODFELLAS (1990)
95. PULP FICTION (1994)
96. THE SEARCHERS (1956)
97. BRINGING UP BABY (1938)
98. UNFORGIVEN (1992)
99. GUESS WHO'S COMING TO DINNER (1967)
100. YANKEE DOODLE DANDY (1942)

▶ Day after day, month after month, like a 600-lb. gorilla, the White House sex scandal hunkered down in our living rooms, on our front porches, in our brains, dominating the news. "God, I'd like to forget all this," said House Judiciary chairman Henry Hyde. Henry, we hear you.

THE FRONT PORCH IN CRISIS
It may be August on Martha's
Vineyard, but the summer air
is tense as Bill Clinton admits
he misled the American people

Brooks Kraft—Sygma

A POLITICAL AFFAIR

TO IMPEACH

ON SATURDAY, DEC. 19, 1998, WILLIAM JEFFERSON CLINTON, the 42nd President of the United States, became only the second President in American history to be impeached by the House of Representatives—which was reeling from the events it had been called upon to absorb in a few short days. All the same, as votes were cast on the four articles of impeachment,

A sordid sexual liaison shames Bill Clinton—and imperils his presidency

the mood that the strange year of 1998 was always supposed to invoke but seldom did—sober-minded, even abashed—finally settled across the capital. In a passionate floor speech before the vote, House minority leader Richard Gephardt cried, "May God have mercy on this Congress!" It was the one sentiment that might have received bipartisan approval.

Within hours, the House approved two of the four articles of impeachment against the President. It was the climax of a tumultuous year—and of an unnerving week in which the incoming Speaker of the House, Bob Livingston, resigned, and the air over Baghdad exploded with a U.S. and British attack. So did the air over Washington, where the unremitting outcry over sex, lies, desperation and hypocrisy created an atmosphere of venom and mayhem.

The journey to impeachment began in January 1998, as the details of a sex scandal involving President Bill Clinton and a young White House intern, Monica Lewinsky, began to seep into the media. By year's end, the scandal would touch every American's life, and the media's saturation coverage would be derided as "All Monica, All the Time." But finally, the sad tale

December 1995 she took a full-time job with the White House's Office of Legislative Affairs. In April 1996, when Pentagon spokesman Kenneth Bacon was seeking an assistant, the White House sent her name to Bacon, and she was hired.

But by then the young woman had begun a sexual affair with the President. According to Lewinsky's eventual testimony to the grand jury, her flirtation with Clinton began during the government shutdown in the fall of 1995, when the interns had the run of the West Wing. Lewinsky bumped into the President in the hall on her way to the ladies' room. She lifted her jacket to show him her thong underwear. He asked if she wanted to see his private office. And an affair was born.

According to Lewinsky's testimony, the affair included phone sex and mutual groping—and some 10 acts of oral sex performed on the President by Lewinsky in the vicinity of the Oval Office. Lewinsky dreamed of a blossoming emotional relationship, but her account portrays the President as a varsity cad who had his first lengthy conversation with her after their sixth sexual encounter. She also claimed he held out the prospect of a life together after the White House.

was the story of three people: Bill Clinton, Monica Lewinsky and Whitewater independent counsel Kenneth Starr.

MONICA AND BILL Monica Samille Lewinsky arrived in Washington in 1995 at age 21, fresh out of college, with a prized Capitol asset: connections. Her mother, Marcia Lewis, a socialite and writer, lived at the Watergate apartments. Through a Democrat friend, she wangled Monica a summer internship at the White House, where Lewinsky soon became known to staff members as starstruck by the President. In

Lewinsky's account brought into focus the second character in the scandal: Bill Clinton, 52. Reckless and arrogant, the President chose to carry on heated sexual encounters under the eyes of his staff members and security detail with an employee half his age who was immature and indiscreet, sending mushy notes by messenger and telling her mom, her friends and her therapist that she had bagged the Big Guy.

Moreover, Clinton was already under intense scrutiny. Kenneth W. Starr, 52, a former U.S. Solicitor General, had

INDISCREET COUPLE: Bill Clinton embraces Monica Lewinsky at a Washington Democratic fund-raising event in October 1996

been investigating the First Couple's dealings in the Whitewater real estate deal in Arkansas since 1994. The conservative Republican was a highly controversial figure: Democrats saw him as conducting a politically inspired vendetta against Clinton; Republicans saw him as a high-minded investigator with the country's best interests at heart. Starr's team had already looked into allegations of sexual infidelity by Clinton when he was Governor of Arkansas. Just as perilous for a President who had famously admitted in a 1992 TV interview to having "caused pain in my marriage," Clinton was also being sued in a civil trial by Paula Jones, a former Arkansas state employee. Her suit, funded by Republicans, accused Clinton of an uninvited sexual advance in a Little Rock hotel room in 1991.

MONICA, LINDA AND LUCIANNE Monica Lewinsky was sent to the Pentagon to keep her out of the President's way. But once there she befriended Linda Tripp, then 48, another former White House aide, who had joined the Bush Administration as a secretary and later ran afoul of the Clinton team. Tripp was no friend to the President. Before leaving the Clinton White House, she had seen a volunteer named Kathleen Willey outside the Oval Office; Willey's makeup was smudged and her blouse was untucked. She told Tripp that Clinton had made a sexual advance,

but Tripp felt Willey's mood was more pleased than angry.

In the summer of 1997, *Newsweek* ran a story based on Tripp's account; lawyers for Paula Jones saw Willey and Tripp as character witnesses against Clinton and aimed subpoenas at them. Anticipating that she might be asked about Lewinsky, in August 1997 Tripp sought the advice of a friend, New York City literary agent Lucianne Goldberg, a Republican and former Nixon operative who specialized in dealing personal dirt on politicians. Goldberg had approached Tripp months before regarding a book on former White House lawyer Vincent Foster; Tripp had been the last to see him before his suicide. The women had become close, and Tripp followed Goldberg's counsel on what to do about Lewinsky: she bought a tape recorder.

Gradually Lewinsky began to tell Tripp about the affair: how she would go to the White House, usually in the late afternoon or evening, and be cleared in by the President's personal secretary, Betty Currie. As Lewinsky later testified, Clinton broke off the affair in March 1996; it resumed, briefly, in February and March 1997.

THE JONES CASE In December 1997 Lewinsky was subpoenaed by Paula Jones' lawyers, and her subsequent phone conversations with the President took a different tone. She later told the grand jury that Clinton suggested she see his

ON THE ATTACK: Independent counsel Ken Starr is surrounded by a media pack as news of the scandal breaks in Washington

friend Vernon Jordan, and Jordan would help her out. She met Jordan and presented him with a list of public relations firms she'd like to work for. Jordan later confirmed that he had guided her toward several jobs in the private sector. Meanwhile, on Dec. 28, the President met Lewinsky for the last time, and Betty Currie went to Lewinsky's apartment to retrieve several gifts the President had given her.

By now Tripp and Lewinsky were discussing whether to lie under oath in the Jones case. Lewinsky apparently told Tripp she intended to deny the affair and urged Tripp to do the same. "I have lied my entire life," Monica told her. In her sworn affidavit in the Jones case on Jan. 7, 1998, Lewinsky denied a sexual relationship with Clinton.

In his sealed deposition on Jan. 17, Clinton denied having sex with Lewinsky—but based his denial on the definition of "sexual relations" put on the table by the Jones lawyers. Months later, even after he admitted to misleading people, Clinton would insist he had not perjured himself in this testimony. The next day Clinton met with Betty Currie; later he said they had met to review his relationship with

Lewinsky, but Starr would charge Clinton used the meeting to coach Currie to avoid detection of the liaison.

But Tripp had turned on Lewinsky: she had passed the tapes along to Starr. Tripp and Starr's team met on Monday, Jan. 12. The next day, she was outfitted with a body wire to tape a meeting with Lewinsky at the Ritz-Carlton in Pentagon City. With Tripp's concealed tapes rolling, Lewinsky again discussed her plans to cover up the affair, and her hopes that Jordan would help her land a good job.

"I'm really sorry ... and I hate Linda Tripp."—Monica Lewinsky

That Wednesday, Lewinsky offered Tripp a draft of "talking points," suggesting that Tripp dismiss Lewinsky as a fantasizing stalker of the President, in effect supporting Monica's sworn statement that there was no affair. Many suspected the document had been written by the President or a close adviser, but it turned out to be Lewinsky's work.

Tripp's secret tape recordings now afforded Starr evidence that would potentially support charges of perjury, suborning perjury and obstruction of justice against the President; Starr received permission from the Justice Department to expand his inquiry. But Lucianne Goldberg had already leaked the story of the tapes to a *Newsweek* writer, Michael Isikoff. When *Newsweek* called Starr to say it was preparing to run the first detailed account of the affair, he pressured the editors to hold off and allow him time to enlist Lewinsky's aid in stinging Jordan; they agreed.

When Lewinsky met Tripp at the Ritz-Carlton again on Friday, Jan. 16, she quickly found herself surrounded by FBI agents and prosecutors and taken upstairs. In a long showdown, Starr's team offered a deal: in exchange for immunity, Lewinsky would admit to the affair and wear a wire that might let Starr nab Jordan in an attempt to keep her quiet. If not, Starr had the tapes that would allow him to prosecute her for perjury. Lewinsky cried and asked for her mother. "My life is ruined," she said. Once notified of the trouble, Lewinsky's father in California reached a longtime family friend, a medical malpractice lawyer named William Ginsburg, who quickly tried to work out an immunity deal with Starr. When the two sides could not agree on terms, Starr's big squeeze tightened. Starr needed Lewinsky—and he needed corroborating evidence of obstruction of justice to head off a he-said/she-said battle.

Newsweek held its story, but it was leaked to cyberspace snoop Matt Drudge, who put it on his Drudge Report website on Jan. 21. The dam broke: the story was featured in the Washington *Post* and other mainstream sources. For the first time, Americans heard the allegations against Clinton and the names Monica Lewinsky and Linda Tripp. Dismayed parents found children turning from the TV to ask, "Mommy, what's oral sex?" Jay Leno and David Letterman began cracking jokes, all-news cable channels went to nonstop coverage, and TV anchors raced home from covering the Pope's visit to Cuba to report on the scandal.

STEPHEN SAVIOA—AP/WIDE WORLD

INNOCENT BYSTANDER? Betty Currie, after testifying to Starr's grand jury

Meanwhile, on Jan. 21 Clinton denied the affair three times: on National Public Radio, on TV's Public Broadcasting System and to the Capitol Hill newspaper *Roll Call*. On the 26th, he stood at a White House lectern, looked his audience in the eye, wagged his finger and firmly denied having "sexual relations with that woman, Miss Lewinsky." Still, details on the tapes continued to leak to the press. Starr's office was later charged with running a clandestine campaign against both Clinton and Lewinsky through leaks, but Starr denied such actions. Lewinsky herself was now a target of a criminal investigation. Starr began putting pressure on her to testify, issuing subpoenas and calling her friends to testify. He even called her mother before the grand jury; Marcia Lewis left in tears.

WILLEY AND JONES On March 15, Kathleen Willey, 51, appeared on *60 Minutes* and told her story of the President's having fondled her outside the Oval Office in 1993. But even though the former Clinton volunteer had a dignified manner that the President's other accusers often

PRESSURED: Lewinsky with first lawyer William Ginsburg

Starr's fell. But Starr's team was piecing together a story from White House records and the testimony of Lewinsky's mother and Betty Currie that corroborated many revelations in Lewinsky's own voice, captured on Tripp's tapes. Meanwhile, Monica posed as Marilyn Monroe for *Vanity Fair*—hardly helping her image as an innocent wronged.

A turning point came on June 2: Lewinsky abruptly replaced Ginsburg with Jacob Stein and Plato Cacheris, two veteran Washington lawyers. They quickly paid a courtesy call on Starr, and after 55 days—during which the two camps sent out careful feelers and held secret meetings—Starr announced on July 28 that Lewinsky would testify against the President in exchange for immunity. Monica also gave Starr a dark blue, high-necked dress that had long been the subject of rumors: stained with Clinton's semen, it offered scientific proof of the affair.

The deal came just after Starr had resorted to a last effort to get information: on Friday, July 17, he sent a subpoena to Clinton's lawyer, David Kendall. The President later agreed to appear voluntarily on Aug. 17 to give testimony in front of a TV camera in the White House, with his lawyers present. Starr agreed to withdraw the subpoena.

A DECISIVE DAY When he consented to testify before Starr's grand jury, Clinton had agreed to make three of the hardest speeches of his life: to his wife and daughter, to the grand jury and to the rest of America. On Thursday, Aug. 13, Clinton told Hillary the truth; on Sunday night the Rev. Jesse Jackson spent time with the First Family at the White House. The next day, when Clinton sat down in the White House Map Room, he had a statement for the grand jury that included a brief history of his relationship with Monica Lewinsky and gave dates and places of their liaisons.

lacked, there were questions about her account—including Linda Tripp's earlier statement that Willey was pleased, not angered by the advance—and the story faded.

Clinton found further reason to celebrate on April 1. In a stunning decision in Little Rock, federal Judge Susan Webber Wright threw out the Paula Jones sexual harassment case against the President as "lacking merit." Clinton got the news during a trip to Africa, and cameras captured him gleefully banging a drum in his hotel room.

In the months following the Jones decision, the scandal finally left the headlines. Without a star witness, the prosecuters hunted down bookstore receipts and credit reports in order to lend veracity to the tapes recorded by the politically suspect Tripp. Clinton's approval ratings—surprisingly high through the year—kept rising, while

> "It depends on what your definition of the word is is."—Bill Clinton

On most issues the President's account matched Lewinsky's. He admitted giving the young woman some gifts—a hatpin, a book of Walt Whitman poems and a T-shirt from Martha's Vineyard—that he had claimed not to recall in his Jones deposition in January. But he strongly repeated his claim that he had not perjured himself in that testimony.

THE DAM BREAKS

January 7, 1998
Lewinsky denies the affair in an affidavit in the Paula Jones case

January 12
Linda Tripp, left, hands over some 20 hours of secret tapes of Lewinsky to Ken Starr

January 16
Starr's investigators confront Lewinsky at the Ritz-Carlton hotel and suggest wiring her to catch Vernon Jordan as he urges her to perjure herself

January 17
In his sealed deposition in the Paula Jones case, Clinton denies having sexual relations with Lewinsky

January 18
Clinton and Betty Currie meet at the White House and review the details of Clinton's relationship with Lewinsky

January 20-21
The story leaks. First Internet snoop Matt Drudge, above, then the national media report Ken Starr is investigating the affair and possible perjury by the President

January 21
On NPR, the President denies having sexual relations with Lewinsky; five days later he repeats the claim on national television

A POLITICAL AFFAIR

EXODUS: As the House votes to impeach, Democrats walk out in protest of the process

even directly quoted Lewinsky's statement that no one had ever asked her to lie about it.

Weeks later, House Republicans played another card they believed would seal Clinton's fate: they released the video of his Aug. 17 testimony. The tactic backfired, solidifying opinion in Clinton's favor. Assuming the tape would be made public one day, the artful President had played to the bleachers, not to the grand jury; his approval ratings rose again.

THE ENDGAME Defying polls that showed most Americans favored censuring rather than impeaching Clinton, Republicans pressed ahead. On Oct. 8, reacting to the Starr referral, the House voted 258 to 176 to launch a full impeachment inquiry. But before hearings could begin, the election intervened—and both parties were stunned when the G.O.P. lost seats, barely holding its majority in the House. The election was widely perceived as a rebuff to the G.O.P.'s focus on the scandal rather than legislation, and when Speaker Newt Gingrich resigned, many felt the steam had gone out of impeachment.

They were wrong. On Nov. 9, the House Judiciary Committee convened to consider articles of impeachment. Presiding was chairman Henry Hyde, 74, an Illinois Republican; in September he had been "outed" by the online magazine *Salon* as having had an adulterous affair of his own. The first witness to address the committee was Ken Starr. His reception was highly partisan: after his testimony he was lauded by committee Republicans, grilled by the Democrats. A process that should have been deeply serious appeared tedious and illegitimate; few scandal-fatigued Americans even tuned in.

The only surprise came when Starr dropped the fact that he had found no evidence of wrongdoing by Clinton in two of his long-running investigations: the 1993 firing of White House travel-office employees and the improper collection of FBI files in 1993-94 by White House officials. Democrats quickly attacked Starr for waiting until after the midterm election before disclosing Clinton's inno-

At 10 p.m. Eastern time, the President addressed the nation in a four-minute speech from the Map Room. He admitted to a relationship that was "not appropriate" with Lewinsky and observed that "even Presidents have private lives." But he skipped right past the problem that the conduct he admitted to occurred not in his bedroom but off the Oval Office, with a much younger employee. Nor did he say he was sorry for what he had done. Seven months of lies and the famous finger-wag were passed off as giving "a false impression." The next day's editorial pages were blistering; even Democrats didn't rally round their man.

On Sept. 11, Starr unloaded his strongest artillery on Clinton, sending the House a 445-page summary, based on Lewinsky's testimony, of his findings about the affair. It was a trashy tale, a fetid blend of libido and legalese that shocked the nation with its unrelenting, clinical descriptions of the pair's sexual acts. When G.O.P. House leaders quickly published the report on the Internet, Clinton's lawyers thundered that its tawdry nature was meant to "humiliate the President and force him from office."

But the report's most shocking details had long been rumored, and its release only hardened previous positions. Clinton haters were revulsed by the President's behavior; Starr haters were revulsed that the independent counsel had included every sleazy detail of the affair—but had not

REVELATIONS

March 15
On *60 Minutes*, volunteer Kathleen Willey claims Clinton fondled her in the White House

April 1
Federal judge Susan Webber Wright dismisses Paula Jones' sexual harassment suit against the President in Arkansas

June 2
Lewinsky fires lawyer William Ginsburg in favor of politically astute Plato Cacheris and Jacob Stein

July 28
Lewinsky reaches a deal with Ken Starr to tesify in exchange for immunity and gives him a stained dress bearing Clinton's DNA

August 6
Lewinsky testifies to the grand jury, admits perjury and provides details of her affair with the President

August 17
Clinton testifies to the grand jury via TV, later admits to the nation for the first time a relationship that was "not appropriate," without conceding perjury

September 11
House releases complete 445-page Starr report, with racy details intact, on the Internet

October 8
The House votes, 258-176, along party lines, to approve a full-scale impeachment inquiry

THE STARR REPORT

The FINDINGS of INDEPENDENT COUNSEL KENNETH W. STARR *on* PRESIDENT CLINTON *and* The LEWINSKY AFFAIR

WITH ANALYSIS BY THE STAFF OF The Washington Post

cence. After Starr's testimony, the committee seemed to lose its way, taking up and then abandoning an inquiry into campaign-finance abuses and also devoting time to revisiting the Kathleen Willey charges.

With Newt Gingrich out and Speaker-elect Bob Livingston strangely aloof, G.O.P. whip Tom DeLay, a flinty former pest-exterminator from Sugar Land, Texas, began pushing hard for impeachment, arguing that the Constitution did not allow for a compromise like censure. DeLay and the White House were fighting for the crucial votes of some 30 G.O.P. House moderates, who were not beholden to the extreme Republican right. A brief Rose Garden speech by Clinton on Friday, Dec. 11, was meant to sway them, but it lacked substance and only angered people.

Less than 10 minutes after Clinton's speech, the Judiciary Committee began to vote on the first of four articles of impeachment; all passed in a vote along strict party lines. Clinton's position eroded over the next few days as moderate Republicans began announcing they would vote to impeach. But on Wednesday, Dec. 16, with the full House scheduled to vote on impeachment the next day, the President dropped a bombshell—ordering air strikes on Baghdad. Was the attack an attempt to postpone the vote? Senate majority leader Trent Lott said, "I cannot support this military action in the Persian Gulf at this time. Both the timing and the policy are subject to question."

Meanwhile the fires of scandal the Republicans had stoked were about to consume their own Speaker-elect, Bob Livingston. On Thursday night he informed his party caucus that he would soon be "outed" as an adulterer; they rewarded him with a standing ovation. The full House began debating impeachment Friday morning, with Republicans arguing that Clinton had broken the law and Democrats replying that even if he had, his low deeds did not rise to the level of impeachable high crimes.

On Saturday Livingston rose to call on Clinton to resign. Then—to the surprise of all—he declared he would resign his own House seat within six months. Lawmakers from both sides of the aisle stood and applauded. House minority leader Richard Gephardt then issued a plea for peace that rang across the city. "We need to start healing; we need to start binding up our wounds … The only way we stop this insanity is through the force of our own will."

But moments later, by a party-line vote of 228 to 206, the House adopted the first article of impeachment, accusing the President of lying under oath to Kenneth Starr's grand jury about his affair with Lewinsky. A second arti-

ENOUGH ALREADY!

MARGARET CUSACK FOR TIME

"You ever wanted to put one of those in the Oval Office?" —**Maria Shriver, NBC News correspondent, to Hillary Clinton, referring to a cot in Thomas Edison's lab**

"The statute of limitations has long since passed on my youthful indiscretions."—**Rep. Henry Hyde, 74, Chairman of the House Judiciary Committee, on his extramarital affair, which began when he was 41 and lasted several years**

"How come nobody ever thought I had an affair with anyone?"—**Former First Lady Barbara Bush**

"If I ever want to have an affair with a married man again, especially if he's President, please shoot me." —**Monica Lewinsky, to Linda Tripp**

"I was under that very desk 35 years ago, and I could tell you there's barely room for a three-year-old."—**John F. Kennedy Jr.**

cle, which accused Clinton of committing perjury in the Paula Jones suit, was rejected by a vote of 229 to 205. The House approved a third article, which accused Clinton of obstructing justice by coaching his secretary, Betty Currie, to lie about his relationship with Lewinsky, by a vote of 221 to 212. A fourth and final article, which accused Clinton of abuse of power for giving dismissive or evasive answers to some of a list of 81 questions put to him by the House Judiciary Committee, was rejected by a vote of 285 to 148.

After the House vote, the President and Mrs. Clinton emerged from the Oval Office. Hillary had her arm around her husband as the two of them, along with Vice President Al Gore and Gephardt, made their way to the Rose Garden, a bare magnolia tree behind them, a darkening gray sky above. Not a single speaker there, not even the President, uttered the word impeachment. Instead, Clinton vowed, with steel in his jaw, to serve until "the last hour of the last day of my term." With those words, the drama of 1998 ended. But the prospect of an impeachment trial in the Senate, or perhaps a bipartisan movement toward censure—or of yet another turn in the maddening, seemingly endless national nightmare—loomed on the horizon. ■

IN THE END

November 19
Ken Starr presents his findings in a 12-hour appearance before a House Judiciary Committee bitterly divided along party lines

November 27
Clinton responds to a list of 81 questions from the committee; Republicans say his answers are evasive

December 11-12
Chaired by Henry Hyde, below, Judiciary Committee votes along party lines to bring an impeachment vote to the full House

December 16
As impeachment looms, Clinton launches an air attack on Iraq

December 19
Led by G.O.P.'s DeLay, near right, House votes two articles of impeachment against the President; Senate trial is set for 1999; Speaker-elect Livingston, far right, resigns

Burning Down the HOUSE

When a fractious G.O.P. stumbles in the midterm election, it dumps a Speaker—then loses his successor

J.C. WATTS A football star at Oklahoma who became a Baptist minister, Watts is the first black G.O.P. House leader and a champion of the party's emerging "we care" message

DOUG MILLS—AP/WIDE WORLD

T O UNDERSTAND THE DEEP BEWILDERMENT THAT THE midterm election of 1998 visited on the Republicans, you had only to look at Senators Al D'Amato and Lauch Faircloth, two of Bill Clinton's sweatiest pursuers, making their baffled concessions. Or to hear Newt Gingrich, who had said in April that he would never give another speech without mentioning the White House scandals, complaining about how it was the media that had been obsessed with the whole nasty thing.

To understand the damage done to the party by the strict standards of sexual purity in public servants it had championed all year, you had only to look at the sad figure of Speaker-elect Bob Livingston announcing he would resign from the House, only two days after announcing he had committed adultery in his marriage.

Livingston's brief rise and fall and the G.O.P.'s surprising midterm election loss reflect the party's obsession with the President's sex scandal. American voters went to the polls thinking that the governing majority in Congress had done just about anything but govern. From the moment in January that Monica Lewinsky became as famous as Michael Jordan, official Washington and its media auxiliary were transfixed by the scandal. And for a while, who wasn't? But in time most people moved back to matters nearer at hand—getting ahead, getting settled, getting more sleep, anything but "that."

Somehow Congress did not hear. A federal tobacco deal collapsed; campaign-finance reform died; the pa-

tients' bill of rights was shelved. Through it all, the Republicans on Capitol Hill stayed on message. Too bad for them that the message was All Monica, All the Time. Though most candidates of both parties took pains to steer clear of the White House scandal, the G.O.P. leadership, in a campaign personally approved by Gingrich, brought it all up again in last-minute TV spots in districts around the country. Whatever else they cared about, people went to the polls with just a glimmer of a suspicion that Republicans were eager to drag them through the mess forever.

On Tuesday, Nov. 3, voters got the chance to send their own message to Washington. It was two words: Shut up! So

BOB LIVINGSTON
Speaker-elect for 32 days, he 'fessed up to past adulteries and resigned his seat the day President Clinton was impeached

KHUE BUI—AP/WIDE WORLD

DICK ARMEY
Though a key player in the policies that led to Gingrich's downfall, Armey survived a challenge in the caucus to retain his position as majority leader of the House

PABLO MARTINEZ MONSIVAIS—AP/WIDE WORLD

up. The Republican strategy was based on a 33% turnout, in which their base would have loomed larger.) Unions struggled successfully to get their members to the polls. And African-American leaders produced a turnout that saved Democrats in the South.

The stunning upset at the polls swiftly reverberated through the party, reshuffling the Republican leadership of the House. The shake-up began with the sudden departure of Speaker Gingrich and the ascension of Representative Bob Livingston of Louisiana; it ended—it seemed—with the election of G.O.P. House leaders in mid-November. Then it took a final surprising turn in December, when Livingston's fate became enmeshed in the gears of scandal.

Newt Gingrich took to the phones on the afternoon of Election Day still predicting that the President would be made to pay for his sins and that the Republicans would pick up six to 30 seats. But when the last returns came in, the C.O.P. had lost five seats—a setback not matched since 1822. "Well," said Gingrich when it was all over, "we all misjudged this one." The next morning he held a gripe session by conference call, letting others vent about the Republicans' utter absence of a message and the Democrats' lethally effective get-out-the-vote effort. Gingrich mostly listened. "He was in a state of shock," said a participant.

"You beat each other up, you eat your dead—and, you know, those standing will lead." —G.O.P. star J.C. Watts

It was different an hour later, during the "listen only" conference call with members. This time Newt talked a lot, but he made no sense. He blamed the election on the unions, on black turnout driven by scare-tactic radio ads, on the fact that the Senate had failed to take up the House's $80 billion tax cut, and of course on the media for hyping the Lewinsky scandal and blotting out the Republican message. Said a member who listened in: "He just doesn't get it. He's the problem. I don't see how you get over this bump in the road without getting rid of him."

It emboldens the princes to plot if they think the king has gone mad. Appropriations Committee chairman Livingston, who owed his position to Gingrich, was already calling members, testing out the idea that he might make a good Speaker. Four years earlier, Gingrich had hand-picked Livingston—at the time the fifth-ranking Republican on the Appropriations Committee—to become its chairman. Now Livingston, 55, would wield his clout as the guy who doles out the money to knife his benefactor. He called the Speaker on Wednesday and suggested in passing that he resign, but Gingrich did not seem alarmed. Meanwhile, conservative Steve Largent of Oklahoma and other ambitious Republicans began sniffing around in hopes of winning the other G.O.P. House leadership seats.

the election that was supposed to be another G.O.P. blowout ended with a gain of five House seats for the Democrats, no change in the Senate and the morning-after spectacle of dumbstruck Republicans pointing fingers at one another. They still controlled Congress, but with nothing like the headlong confidence they felt after their triumph in 1994, when they knew in their bones that they were the party with a direct channel to the majority will.

Even Republican leaders were praising the Democrats' shrewd campaign strategy. Instead of expensive TV advertising, Democrats stressed organization and turnout. (It worked. On Election Day 37% of all eligible voters showed

Winners & Losers

A surprising election yields tight races, new faces—and even pro wrestlers in high places

CHARLES SCHUMER

✓ In a major upset, the Brooklyn Democratic Congressman unseated Whitewater-probing New York Senator Al D'Amato after one of the election's most negative campaigns

✗ A constituent-friendly fixer who delighted in his can-do moniker, "Senator Pothole" lost his bid for a fourth term after he strongly attacked Schumer and committed a typical gaffe, describing his opponent as a "putzhead"—a Yiddish vulgarity

AL D'AMATO

GRAY DAVIS

✓ In a closely watched contest, the veteran California officeholder took a centrist stance on gun control and abortion and became the first Democrat to win the governorship in 16 years

✓ The Democratic California Senator—and in-law of Hillary Clinton—narrowly won a second term as she survived a strong challenger, Matt Fong

BARBARA BOXER

✗ In one of the few major races to go the G.O.P.'s way, the Illinois Senator—a favorite target of conservative Republicans—was ousted by challenger Peter Fitzgerald, despite the support of star campaigner Hillary Clinton

MOSELY-BRAUN

✓ Minnesotans—or at least 37% of the 61% of them who voted—gave the nation a smile by electing the former pro wrestler and current radio shock jock as their Governor

JESSE VENTURA

For the next 48 hours, the most important struggle within the party was not between right and left but loyalty and ambition. Everyone Gingrich called for support had a wish list. His original conservative allies said push impeachment to the wall, trim $100 billion in taxes, schedule an antiabortion vote, cut the International Monetary Fund loose. Moderates were seeking assurances that none of those moves would ever take place. Said Representative J.C. Watts of Oklahoma: "This is kind of the way Republican politics works. You beat each other up, you eat your dead—and, you know, those standing will lead."

The final piece of blackmail came from the crown prince himself: Livingston sent the Speaker a 16-point ultimatum calling on him to agree to its terms for ceding power to the Appropriations chairman "without exception." The letter was classic Livingston: stern, uncompromising, dictatorial and, it turned out, totally impulsive. A few hours after he sent it, Livingston called Gingrich and said, "Ignore it." But by 2 p.m. Friday, Livingston was announcing his own candidacy for the job, likening his great and good friend Gingrich to Winston Churchill—and then explaining why it was time for the Speaker to go.

By this time, even loyalists like Bill Archer, the chairman of the powerful Ways and Means Committee, were peeling away. By twilight on Friday Gingrich had gathered his troops to the phones to break the news. Only his departure, he said, would purge the poison from the party. He blasted the "cannibals" who would settle for nothing less than total victory and urged the troops to stay focused on 2000. "I am grateful to each and every one of you … I love all of you. Take care." No one tried to talk him out of it.

Bob Livingston, the Speaker-elect, was known as an effective legislator, devoted to budget cutting and trading favors. He had on occasion worked into his committee's bills such politically charged measures as curtailing federal funding for abortion and clean-needle distribution. But he had also resisted the right-wing line many times, arguing that ideological purity shouldn't keep the govern-

"We all misjudged this one," declared

ment from operating. Though admired as a straight-up dealmaker, Livingston was given to double-fisted gesticulations that made him look as if he were pulling pistols.

While Livingston was securing his new position, the Republicans were clawing at one another over whether they fumbled this election because they were too belligerent or because they were not belligerent enough. The fight was over moving to the center vs. mobilizing the base, "compassionate" vs. "principled" conservatism—and it was joined in the jockeying for the other G.O.P. leadership jobs in the House. In the G.O.P. caucus on Nov. 18, the members kept Representative Dick Armey of Texas as majority leader and retained Tom DeLay, the Texan who would later lead the drive for impeachment, as majority whip. Armey defeated the conservative Largent and moderate Representative Jennifer Dunn of Washington—the first woman to aim for a top leadership position—as well as Representative Dennis Hastert of Illinois, a middle-of-the-roader who was drafted by moderates but who ended up splitting the centrist vote with Dunn. G.O.P. conference chairman John Boehner of Ohio, a Gingrich ally, was replaced by rising star Watts, the only black Republican in the House.

With his new team in place, Livingston promised to concentrate on tax cuts, more money for defense and a new way of bookkeeping that would do away with the accounting trick of using Social Security money to mask budget deficits. But he kept his distance from the impeachment process, allowing DeLay to spearhead the drive to impeach Clinton without allowing a vote of censure. Livingston seemed to want to stay above the fray, and he did—until his sudden resignation on the day of Clinton's impeachment stunned his colleagues and dealt the Republicans yet another blow.

As House members dispersed from Washington in the wake of the impeachment, the newly powerful DeLay announced he would not seek the Speaker's chair and championed the more moderate and conciliatory Hastert for the post. Hastert, a six-term conservative, had served as DeLay's deputy whip. At year's end he seemed assured of election in the House vote, which was scheduled to take place when the new Congress convened in the first week of January, 1999.

Whoever fills the role, the new Speaker will face a party—and a House—divided. The members were split more deeply than ever along partisan lines by the impeachment process. The G.O.P. is divided as well. The religious conservatives complain that the party leadership offered no agenda in 1998 to bring them to the polls. But a good part of the agenda they have in mind—opposition to abortion, to gay rights and to legalized gambling—is not one that sells with most voters. In the early 1970s, the Democrats drifted into disaster after

Gingrich—as his assassins plotted

★ ★ ★ ★ ★ ★ ★ ★ ★ ★ ★ ★

they let the left wing of their party seize the wheel. Under Clinton they returned to the center; now the G.O.P. must do the same. For today's candidates, the two most frightening words in U.S. politics may be "activist base."

When the fall election was over, who could blame Minnesota voters if they thought Jesse ("the Body") Ventura was no less plausible as a leadership figure than Newt ("the Mouth") Gingrich or Bill ("the Libido") Clinton? The ex-wrestler who cruised to the governorship in the Land of 10,000 Lakes will find that running a state is a lot harder than running away with it, but he had one thing right: he said that no matter what else is on his plate, he was going to coach the same high school football team he's been coaching for a while. That alone should put him within earshot of what a real crowd is shouting about. ∎

★ ★ ★ ★ ★ ★

All in the Family

A dynasty takes shape as George Bush's sons hold the Governors' chairs in Texas and Florida

THE TRENDIEST PHRASE FOR REPUBLICANS IN 1998 turned out to be "compassionate conservatism"—Texas Governor George W. Bush's term for the crossover message that helped keep him in office with a resounding 69% share of the vote, including 6 in 10 women, 1 in 3 Democrats and almost half of all Hispanics. The victory sealed his place as the G.O.P.'s post-Gingrich guiding light and front runner for its presidential nod in the 2000 race.

HE'S GEORGE: The scion of the Bush clan smiles with wife Laura

HE'S JEB: The newly elected Governor rejoices with supporters

Driving the success of Bush, 52, was his emphasis on education. In the four years since he took office in 1994, the number of Texas students who passed all components of a state-mandated skills test has soared. Add his support for bilingual education and his refusal to bash illegal immigrants, and it's no wonder he scored highly with the state's Hispanic voters.

And for his running mate in 2000—well, how about his younger brother? Newly elected Florida Governor Jeb Bush, 45, won his race with 55% of the vote; along the way he dropped the hard-line tone that lost him the race four years earlier and adopted George W.'s more compassionate line. Jeb is already consulting some of the same thinkers as his big brother and is pushing an accountability program for schools that is based on the Texas plan.

Education is likely to emerge as a key issue in the next presidential race, and the Texas Governor's success on the subject stands in stark contrast to the dismal record that helped sink the G.O.P. in November. Says Diane Ravitch, a Democrat who worked in President George Bush's Department of Education: "[George W.] Bush is so far ahead of the national party that the people in Washington can't even see how behind they are." ∎

Doug Mills—AP/Wide World

HAIL AND FAREWELL
Gingrich and wife Marianne (in red) greet supporters in Washington after he resigned

Exit Newt

He came, he saw, but when he failed to conquer, Speaker Gingrich bailed out of his contract with the G.O.P.

NEITHER PRESIDENT BILL CLINTON NOR SPEAKER OF THE HOUSE Newt Gingrich could have predicted that the sex scandals surrounding Clinton's White House in 1998 would ultimately undo the Speaker rather than the President. Even as Gingrich set to sharpening the blade of the impeachment guillotine for the scandal-scarred Clinton, his adversary strove for peace in the Middle East, waved John Glenn back into orbit and watched the Dow follow close behind. By the fall, Gingrich had produced an impeachment spectacle that left voters gagging and a budget that drew the same response from his own party. When the routine midterm election became a humiliating setback for the Republicans, it was suddenly Gingrich whose judgment was challenged, his party mutinous, his tenure as Speaker numbered in days.

If Clinton has always had a gift for turning weakness into opportunity, Gingrich had a gift for turning opportunity into rubble. He was the one who made unbalanced budgets a thing of the past, but it was Clinton who got credit for it, hauled his own party toward a more sensible center and emerged strong from the midterm election. Gingrich had always been Clinton's best foil, the uglier alternative at whom Clinton kept pointing every time Americans got fed up with his own inability to stay focused. As scattered as Clinton can be, Gingrich was worse, talking about dinosaurs and space colonies and the perils of putting women in trenches.

And then there is the difference in their makeup. Clinton lied to the nation and his family, messed around with someone half his age and in 10 months never once showed any sign that he was thinking of resigning. Gingrich lost five seats and, within a few days, quietly stepped down.

In the spring Gingrich boasted to other G.O.P. leaders that they didn't have to do anything; instead, they merely had to wait for a crippled President to come to them. And sure enough, nothing resembling an agenda (or a budget) emerged from the Speaker's House. This guaranteed that Republicans would have little to brag about when they went home to their constituents, other than renaming Washington's National Airport after Ronald Reagan and passing a pork-heavy transportation bill that made fiscal conservatives shudder.

Gingrich finally decided to wrap all the unfinished budget business into one massive bill that raided $20 billion in "emergency funds" from the first U.S. budget surplus in decades to balance its books. When critics within his party blasted the bill, the Speaker called them "the perfectionist caucus." Just four years after the Contract with America was unveiled, his own followers had become the enemy. The field marshal was no longer leading his troops anywhere they were willing to go. ■

Blitz Over Baghdad

THE START OF IT WAS CHILLINGLY FAMILIAR: THE wail of sirens, the staccato blasts of antiaircraft fire, the tracers lighting up the night sky over Baghdad. Then came the crash of missiles in the distance, sending up an orange glow along the horizon. For four nights—beginning on Dec. 16, the eve of the scheduled impeachment vote against President Clinton in the House—waves of U.S. and British warplanes and missiles punished Saddam Hussein's outlaw nation. On the first night of Operation Desert Fox, Iraq was pounded by 280 American cruise missiles—almost as many as hit the country during the entire Gulf War in 1991.

When Washington announced an end to the bombing, it was clear that Iraq had been damaged. But there were other casualties, including the stature of the United Nations Security Council and the reputation of the U.S. in the eyes of some nations. It wasn't just Republicans who suggested that Clinton had ordered the assault in an effort to avert impeachment. That theory—though erroneous—echoed in Britain's Parliament, in French newspaper editorials and

throughout the Arab world. FOR MONICA'S SAKE, IRAQI CHILDREN ARE DYING read a sign waved during a demonstration at a Cairo mosque. From Russia and China came deep grumblings that the U.S. had overstepped itself. Among the more serious consequences of the action could be an erosion of the consensus for sanctions against Iraq.

Yet anyone who wanted to predict the timing of the air strikes merely had to consult Richard Butler's calendar. The head of the U.N.'s Iraq inspection team, known as UN-SCOM, had promised to give the Security Council a crucial report on Iraqi compliance by Dec. 15. Delivered on schedule, it showed that the Iraqis had been up to their usual tricks: concealing equipment that could be used to make bioweapons, blocking interviews with workers at suspicious sites, lying about sealed documents detailing the military's past uses of chemical agents.

The President needed no prodding for war. A month earlier, Clinton had ordered a meticulously planned assault and called it off at the last minute, when Saddam promised to cooperate with UNSCOM. At the time, Clinton declared

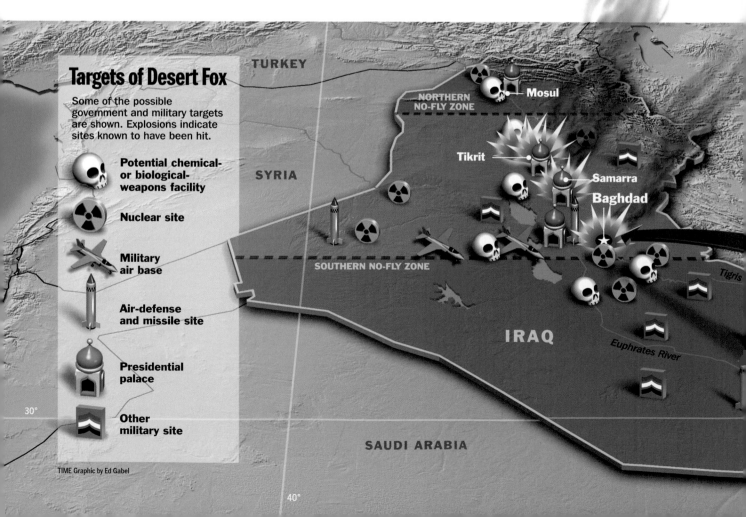

Targets of Desert Fox

Some of the possible government and military targets are shown. Explosions indicate sites known to have been hit.

- Potential chemical- or biological-weapons facility
- Nuclear site
- Military air base
- Air-defense and missile site
- Presidential palace
- Other military site

TURKEY

NORTHERN NO-FLY ZONE

Mosul

Tikrit

Samarra

Baghdad

SYRIA

SOUTHERN NO-FLY ZONE

Tigris

IRAQ

Euphrates River

SAUDI ARABIA

30°

40°

TIME Graphic by Ed Gabel

The U.S. and Britain attack Saddam's Iraq—on the eve of an impeachment vote

that war would come without warning if Saddam misbehaved again. Months of Iraqi duplicity had convinced him that UNSCOM wouldn't get compliance. So when he got advance word on the contents of Butler's report on Sunday, Dec. 13, Clinton, just beginning a Middle East trip, gave the Pentagon 72 hours to prepare an attack. Except for Britain, no Security Council members received so much as a phone call informing them of the pending action.

One thing could be said for the timing: just as Washington had hoped, the offensive stunned the Iraqis. But though Iraq's military infrastructure took a pummeling, it was difficult to assess the extent of the damage to Saddam's war machine. In the Administration's best-case scenario, the bombings would lead either to Saddam's downfall or to fuller inspections by UNSCOM—assuming a chastened Iraq would permit the teams to return. At the worst, the air war would end

UNSCOM inspections for good without having done much to debilitate Saddam's ability to manufacture his lethal weapons. Yet the strongman's fall from power—the Administration's ultimate goal—seemed as elusive as ever. Saddam showed his defiance in the last week of the year, firing missiles at U.S. and British planes enforcing the "no-fly" zones in northern and southern Iraq that were established in the wake of the Gulf War.

The events seemed to turn the world upside down. Iraq had weathered days of relentless assault, yet without UNSCOM's presence Saddam might have a freer hand for pursuing his destructive aims. Baghdad had defied the will of the international community for months, yet now the U.S. was battling it almost alone. The greatest irony of all: after the strike, Bill Clinton's destiny was far from certain, while America's sworn enemy, Saddam Hussein, kept a firm grip on Iraq. ■

Map labels

- Al Taji Airport
- Al Taji Missile Production Facility
- Communications Center
- Directorate of Military Intelligence
- Ministry of Information (where foreign press is stationed)
- Muthenna Airport
- Republican Guard Headquarters
- **Baghdad**
- Abu Ghurayb Military Barracks
- Iraqi Intelligence Headquarters
- Baath Party Headquarters
- Presidential Palace
- Rasheed Airport
- *Tigris River*
- *Caspian Sea*
- IRAN
- 0 5 mi.
- 0 5 km

- Basra
- *Persian Gulf*
- KUWAIT
- 50°

1ST NIGHT Eight warships, including a submarine, launched some 280 Tomahawk cruise missiles, and F-14, F-18 and EA-6B warplanes from the carrier U.S.S. *Enterprise* dropped bombs. The attack focused on 50 targets. Among those hit were a military-intelligence headquarters and a special Republican Guard barracks complex

2ND NIGHT B-52s launched nearly 100 cruise missiles. Other U.S. planes and British fighters flying out of Kuwait and Oman bombed additional targets, bringing the total to 89

3RD NIGHT Encountering little resistance, American and British fighters continued to pound their targets. By Friday, missiles and bombs had hit 18 Iraqi command centers, 11 weapons-production facilities and eight sites associated with the Republican Guards

Aftershocks

When militants destroy a pair of U.S. embassies in Africa, Uncle Sam targets the bombers' mastermind

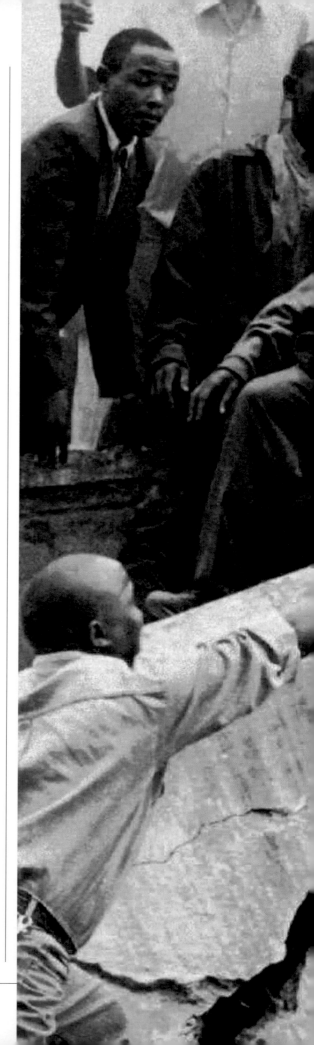

ONE MOMENT, MIDMORNING SHOPPERS WERE BUSTLING ALONG Nairobi's Haile Selassie Avenue at a downtown corner where a bronze eagle and a fluttering flag mark the five-story U.S. embassy. The next, the earth trembled as the thunderclap of a bomb unleashed a mighty shock wave. The bomb, delivered in a truck to the rear of the embassy, shattered every window within a quarter-mile into slivers, sucked out ceilings and furniture and people, pancaked a seven-story building next door into a mountain of rubble. More than five thousand innocent people were injured, and 213 died, including 12 Americans.

Nearly 450 miles away in Tanzania, at almost precisely the same moment on Aug. 7, a vehicle drove into the sunny grounds of the U.S. embassy in Dar es Salaam and exploded, wrecking the entrance, blowing off parts of the building's right side and setting cars ablaze. Eleven people were killed, and more than 70 others were hurt.

Two bombs, synchronized, with a single message: Don't forget the world's superpower still has enemies—secret, violent and determined. Who was behind the explosions, and how could the U.S. punish them? Both answers came quickly. The U.S. had a suspect from the start: Osama bin Laden, a multimillionaire Saudi businessman turned Islamist revolutionary [*for a profile of bin Laden, see* World Notes]. When the evidence against him piled up, quickly and conclusively in the eyes of the Administration, Bill Clinton decided to retaliate.

On Aug. 20, some 60 American Tomahawk cruise missiles fired from warships in the Arabian Sea struck the Jumiat-ul-Mujahedin guerrilla camp in a desolate, arid valley in Afghanistan, where the CIA said bin Laden maintained a major terrorist training camp. The missiles tore into three other training sites in the valley, along with the headquarters building and a support camp crammed with weapons and explosives. And at the same time in Sudan, about 20 more cruise missiles fired from U.S. ships in the Red Sea were laying waste to what Washington described as a chemical-weapons factory in Khartoum, also financed by bin Laden. Declared Clinton: "Today we have struck back."

▶ **"Today we have struck back," Bill Clinton declared after launching the cruise missiles**

Americans cheered the resolute response, though critics charged that the strike at terrorists—only three days after Clinton had admitted to lying about his affair with Monica Lewinsky—might have been timed to divert attention from the President's woes. Worse, in the following days, the White House had to dial back earlier claims that the chemical-plant target in Sudan had produced only chemical-weapons precursors and that bin Laden had financed its operation. But there was no question that bin Laden was emerging as the top terrorist of the '90s—and U.S. officials vowed they would stop him. ■

NIGHTMARE IN NAIROBI
Rescue workers carry a woman
from the building adjacent to the
U.S. embassy in Nairobi. The
bomb injured thousands of civilians

IN MEMORIAM: In an honor befitting their sacrifice, the bodies of Chestnut and Gibson lie in state in the building they died to protect

Murder in the Capitol

One of the glories of the U.S. Capitol building is that it has always opened its doors to the public; it is the people's house. But after a gunman killed two Capitol policemen and sprayed bullets through the building, Congress may be forced to institute tough new measures to ensure the building's security.

The sad story began on July 24, when Russell Weston Jr., 41, came through the Capitol doors and tried to bypass a set of metal detectors. Guard Jacob Chestnut, 58, an 18-year veteran of the Capitol Police who was looking forward to retiring in a few months, moved to stop him as he tried to barge through. Weston pulled out a revolver and shot Chestnut in the head, then ran down the hall toward the Crypt, the busy crossroads directly beneath the vast Capitol Rotunda. Tourists began

screaming, "He's got a gun!" and dropped to the floor, grabbing children, rolling behind columns, trying to get smaller. Weston, hit by a hail of fire laid down by other police at the entrance, slipped through a private door into majority whip Tom DeLay's office, where some 30 House staff members had gathered as the week ended. Special Agent John Gibson, 42, also an 18-year veteran, was there; he exchanged fire with Weston, and both men went down.

Officers Chestnut and Gibson died; their coffins were displayed in the Capitol Rotunda, and the two were honored at a memorial attended by President Clinton and leaders of Congress. Weston, who lived in Montana, was known to local police as a paranoid loner who believed the government was "after him." He survived and was later charged with the murder of two federal police officers, a death-penalty crime.

Hunting for a Bomber

What becomes a legend most? Mystery and elusiveness—and keeping several steps ahead of the

WANTED: Rudolph

law. When federal agents identified Eric Robert Rudolph as the man they believed responsible for the Jan. 29 bombing of an abortion clinic in Birmingham, Ala., which killed an off-duty police officer and severely wounded a nurse, they were confident they would arrest the itinerant carpenter within a matter of days. But like a latter-day, albeit sinister, Robin Hood eluding the Sheriff of Nottingham, Rudolph, 31, a former private in the 101st Airborne skilled at surviving in the wilderness, vanished into the mountainous woods of southwestern North Carolina. And despite being wanted for questioning in the Olympic bombing and two other Atlanta explosions, he became a local celebrity, an antihero evoking sympathy and ensconced in his very own Sherwood Forest.

On July 7, Rudolph visited George Nordmann, 71, owner of a health-food store in the small town of Andrews and an old friend. According to police, he borrowed food from Nordmann, then came back later and took a good deal of food and a truck, leaving $500, presumably as payment. The truck was found; Rudolph wasn't, even though the FBI doubled its task force of searchers and enlisted militia hero "Bo" Gritz to help in the hunt.

Ramblin' Man

Washington insiders often say that when troubles hit the President, the President hits the road. So when Bill Clinton took two major road trips in 1998—and several shorter excursions abroad—his critics charged it was to avoid the scandals besieging him. But Clinton's journey to Africa in March and his visit to China in June both turned out to be significant exercises in diplomacy.

The simple fact that Clinton visited Africa for so long—12 days, six countries—and with a huge entourage of businessmen, politicians and press in tow, was a telling new message. Sunning himself in the glowing welcomes he encountered everywhere, Clinton showed off his best self, friendly and empathetic; dressed in a dark suit among a gathering of Africa's

ON TOUR: Amid China's terra-cotta army

new leaders at Entebbe in Uganda, he conveyed the dignified persona of the world's unchallenged leader—or top CEO. If his talk of "partnership" at every stop was noticeably short on specifics, it was still a refreshing shift from the usual patronizing handouts.

Clinton's nine-day visit to China in June, reciprocating President Jiang Zemin's 1997 visit to the U.S., included a major victory for Clinton, when he and Jiang held a joint press conference that was broadcast live across the nation. Pushing Jiang over human rights, Tiananmen Square and Tibet, the President briefly liberated China's airwaves.

The Unabomber Cops a Plea

Agreeing to a plea bargain with federal prosecutors in January, the Unabomber, Theodore Kaczynski, accepted a sentence of life in prison without the possibility of appeal or release. Denied his belated request to defend himself in court, he abandoned his plan to argue that his 18-year bombing spree was justified. The bargain was sealed by evidence of an ameliorating factor that the former mathematician would never concede: after 20 hours of interviews, court-appointed psychiatrist Dr. Sally Johnson declared him a delusional paranoid schizophrenic. ∎

STARR-FREE ZONE: Clinton greets a crowd in Ghana

Founding Father

Historians have long debated whether Thomas Jefferson had a sexual relationship with one of his slaves, Sally Hemings. Now we may have an answer. Retired pathologist Eugene Foster collected blood samples from 14 men, black and white, who claim to be descended from Jefferson. The distinctive, largely unchanging Y (male) chromosomes of the third President's white descendants, Foster wrote in the science journal *Nature*, almost precisely match those of descendants of Hemings' third son Eston, born at Monticello in 1808. They do not match those of her first son, long thought to be Jefferson's, or those of his two nephews, often said to have sired her children. After Jefferson's

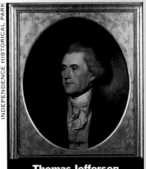

Thomas Jefferson

death in 1826, Hemings' sons Thomas, Madison and Eston all ended up as freedmen living near the town of Chillicothe, Ohio. The brothers were quite fair, being only an eighth black, and Jeffersonian in appearance: tall with reddish hair and gray eyes. But though Thomas and Madison lived as blacks, Eston's descendants have always regarded themselves as white.

One man's loss of control are no better off for anything

AUG. 17: The President prepares to admit to the "inappropriate relationship"

WE TREAT OUR VALUES, LIKE OUR CHILDREN, not equally but uniquely, and we don't like having to choose which one we would sacrifice to save another. Which matters more, honesty or privacy? Justice or mercy? The President or the presidency? What punishment is reserved for leaders who would force such choices upon us in the first place?

Bill Clinton did something ordinary: he had an affair and lied about it. Ken Starr did something extraordinary: he took the President's low-life behavior and called it a high crime. Clinton argued that privacy is so sacred that it included a right to lie so long as he did it very, very carefully. Starr argued that justice is so blind that once he saw a crime being committed, he had no choice but to pursue the bad guy through the Oval Office, down the hall to the private study, whatever the damage, no matter the cost. One man's loss of control inspired the other's, and we are no better off for anything either one of them did.

For rewriting the book on crime and punishment, for putting prices on values we didn't want to rank, for fighting past all reason a battle whose casualties will be counted for

inspired the other's, and we
that either one of them did

NOV. 19: Kenneth Starr is sworn in before the House Judiciary Committee

years to come, Bill Clinton and Kenneth Starr are TIME's 1998 Men of the Year.

Who has survived this odyssey without losing some part of himself? A public majority that listed declining morality as a top concern found itself defending a President who most of them believed had committed a crime. Republican lawmakers voted along party lines, over public protest, to impeach a popular President from the opposing party and in the process dissolved their authority in acid on the House floor. The press corps that viewed itself as the public's conscience became the object of its scorn. Hillary

Clinton, who for years had been vilified for leveraging the power of her marriage, was extolled for having handled with grace its public ruin and so finds herself loved for reasons she hates. Ken Starr, who was once viewed as too moderate to beat Oliver North in a Senate race, was recast as a zealot who twisted the law into a vendetta; he finds himself hated for reasons he can't understand.

Even the Justices of the Supreme Court were rendered unanimously ridiculous by the seemingly endless scandal, having blithely ruled that a sitting President could be made to stand trial in a civil suit without its

ROBERT BOREA—AP/WIDE WORLD

That conviction may explain the choices Starr made; it does not excuse them. By pressing his case, he forced us to define morality down. We don't approve of adultery. We abhor perjury. But we also don't like political plots and traps that treat the law as an extension of politics by other means, that leave us wondering whether we damage the Constitution more by making the President pay or by letting him go.

We rely on prosecutors to exercise discretion. A novice at the job, Starr saw no virtue in restraint, without realizing how his zeal in pursuit of the President would alarm the jury that was called to judge them both. If nothing else, his legacy is plain: he will probably destroy the institution that created him. The independent-counsel statute, born of an impeachment drama 24 years ago, is likely to die in the throes of this one. We may well conclude that the government can't be trusted to investigate those in the government who can't be trusted.

impeding the conduct of his office. The favor was returned, in spades: the Chief Justice cleared his 1999 schedule in order to preside over the impeachment trial that the civil suit was never supposed to lead to.

Alone among the players, the one who remained unchanged and unchanging was Bill Clinton. Many had long ago concluded that he was a rogue and a cheat and impervious to pain; in 1998 he was himself, only more so. Even those who reviled his reflexes acknowledged his charm. Ken Starr marveled at how attractive the President was, like a hunter who wants to pet the lion before he shoots it.

The very first thing a new President does is put his hand on a Bible and promise to do what no other citizen can: defend the Constitution and the country—to the point of sending soldiers to die for them. He had better be better than the rest of us. Bill Clinton took the oath, but exaltation is not his style. He has polled us and tested us and talked to us until he's hoarse and spent, and we know so much about him, right down to his choice of underwear, that he made it hard for us to hold him to a higher standard. So instead his allies defended what was worst in him by appealing to what is best in us. How could we not be generous and forgive him? Has he done anything that many of us have not done ourselves? Are these not private matters? Any gentleman would, of course, lie about his mistress. Judge not … He's one of us.

Ken Starr held a different view of Clinton's conduct. Though he would never quite say so, he came to see the President as the elusive head of a vast criminal enterprise, who over the past four years of investigation would admit nothing, hold back evidence, block inquiry—all the while professing to cooperate in public while destroying his adversary's reputation in private. To the righteous defenders of law and order, Clinton's not one of us. He's one of them.

Starr handed his sword to the lawmakers in Congress, where the Republicans' superior numbers protected them from having to offer superior arguments. Like Starr, they thought that it was long past time for Clinton to be held accountable for his actions; like the voters, they have strong personal feelings about the President. Unfortunately for Clinton, the feelings on Capitol Hill can be poisonous. In a country where everyone assumes that all politicians lie, politicians themselves regard a certain kind of lying as a special kind of sin. A President who breaks his word makes it impossible to do business when the doors are closed and the hard trading begins. Time and again, Bill Clinton made solemn promises, about taxes he would support and concessions he would make and difficult positions he would defend, and once they let him have his way he stepped out and all but said, "Suckers!" and pushed them off the ledge.

So most of them had no appetite for mercy in this season. They feared that if their punishment stopped at censure, he would claim vindication, light a cigar and lose not a moment's sleep. When in the final days the last undecided Republicans said, privately and publicly, just admit that you lied and we'll let you go free, Clinton would not run the risk of believing them. The terrain is laid with traps; assassination is a sport; trust turned to chalk long ago.

When the bombs began to fall on Iraq, the questions immediately arose: Was Clinton doing this to stop Saddam, or was he doing it to save himself? The very charge became evidence against him. A man who cannot be trusted to do the right thing is not trusted even when he does.

This, then, is the legacy of a painful year. A faithless President and a fervent prosecutor, in a mortal embrace, lacking discretion, playing for keeps, both self-righteous, both condemned, Men of the Year. ■

THE STARR REPORT

The controversial independent counsel discusses sex, lies and audiotape

THE DATE IS SATURDAY, DEC. 12, AND THE HOUSE Judiciary Committee has just approved the fourth article of impeachment springing from independent counsel Kenneth Starr's investigation of President Bill Clinton. Starr acknowledges a small sense of vindication as he settles in for the second of three on-the-record interviews with TIME—his only wide-ranging discussions with any print publication in 1998. The impeachment articles represent "a vote of confidence in the legitimacy" of his work, he says, and he feels a great deal of relief that the matter is now "the responsibility of the elected branch of government" and that his role has become "decidedly secondary in nature."

To get to this place, he had to go slow. To nail a politi-

cian as elusive as Clinton, he had to be maniacal in pursuit of the facts. To turn a lowly sex scandal into high crimes and keep going when a majority of the public wanted him to hang it up, he had to be not just dogged but extremely confident—many would say far too confident—of his own fairness and judgment.

Starr believes his reputation died for Clinton's sins. White House attacks, he says, left him "transmogrified." He had been a Washington wise man, a respected former federal appeals judge (he still wears those robes in his mind) who always avoided conflict and fancied himself the soul of civility and old-school judicial restraint. But now a great many people saw him as the commissioner of the sex police, the instrument of a G.O.P. plot to overturn two national elections. "It's been thoroughly unpleasant, and especially difficult for my wife and children," he says.

Sometimes defensive, occasionally disarming, always proper and polite—"bullpuckey" is as close as he comes to a curse—in his interviews he offered a fresh account of his own decision-making process, one that TIME corroborated, to the extent possible, with other sources. And for the first time, he showed how well he understood why so many loathe him. It bothers him that they do. "The whole thing is terrible," Starr said at one point. "You can put that on the record. This whole thing is terrible, for all of us." He knows that where he finds a criminal conspiracy to obstruct justice, millions of others find nothing more than a frantic effort to conceal an affair. "But it would have been illegitimate," he says, his soft voice growing louder, "to try to think [about] how this would be perceived at a broad public level. It was left to us the unhappy task of ferreting out information in these arenas that are so very personal." In other words, the statute made me do it.

During his interviews with TIME, Starr's basic civility was always on display. His detractors tend to view this refined manner as gaudy camouflage for fanaticism. But Starr's elaborate politesse runs deep: it is both a key part of his self-image and a buffer against the world. He insisted that his prosecutors refer to Clinton as "the President" even as they gathered evidence to impeach him.

Most of the charges leveled against Starr—that he colluded with Linda Tripp and the lawyers for Paula Jones to entrap the President, that his agents mistreated Lewinsky in their long Jan. 16 session with her—turned out to have little basis in fact, according to an investigation by TIME. Starr's last known contact with the Jones team, for example, came years before he ever heard of Lewinsky; Tripp—who clearly did collude with Clinton haters—had been briefing the Jones lawyers about Lewinsky for two months before she made her approach to Starr.

Starr has also been accused of discouraging Lewinsky from contacting her lawyer and of pressing her to wear a wire to set up the President. But Starr insists there was never a plan to secretly tape Clinton. Instead, he says, it was Betty Currie who might have been taped. And many of the actions of his prosecutors that day were approved in advance by senior Justice Department officials—including the outlines of the effort to persuade Lewinsky not to call

her attorney, whom Starr and his men suspected was part of the obstruction conspiracy. Starr argues that his team's moves were monitored by a Justice Department official; that man, Administration sources told TIME, was Josh Hochberg, then deputy chief of the public-integrity unit. He took copious notes, asked questions but raised no red flags.

Justice Department sources confirm that Starr's office briefed the department in advance on many of its dealings with Lewinsky. At year's end both the Justice Department's Office of Professional Responsibility and the District of Columbia Bar Association were looking into the events of Jan. 16, but in a ruling unsealed in December, Judge Johnson cleared Starr's prosecutors of White House charges that they denied Lewinsky her right to counsel.

But perhaps the most convincing evidence of Starr's good intentions was the way he structured his office, seeking a consensual, deliberative style. Every afternoon at 5 o'clock when he was in Washington, Starr and his 30 lawyers and 10 investigators crowded around a long conference table to hear the daily report and discuss strategy. Starr did not run the meetings so he could absorb more of the discussion. For major decisions, he assigned a prosecutor to summarize facts and evaluate the pros and cons. And he insisted on hearing opinions from everyone at the table as he sought the majority view. He made the final calls, but sources say he invariably went with the majority vote.

But if the man is so dedicated to fair play and consensus, why did his inquiry seem so wild and obsessive? Starr dragged bit players before grand juries, interrogated a Clinton aide about his media contacts, issued a subpoena for bookstore records and made Secret Service agents testify about the man they protect.

OUTSIDER: Starr (in glasses) during his undergrad years

"The whole thing is terrible. You can put that on the record. This whole thing is terrible, for all of us." —Starr

Part of the answer was in the makeup and background of Starr's handpicked team. He had tough prosecutors and brilliant litigators recruited from around the country, but his Lewinsky team had few lawyers with strong criminal-defense backgrounds to provide balance or weigh in on the treatment of witnesses. Starr's ethics adviser, Watergate eminence Sam Dash, signed off on major decisions but not the nuts and bolts. He resigned in November, calling Starr too strong an advocate for impeachment. When the scandal broke, there was nobody with the sensibility to point out, for instance, that subpoenaing Lewinsky's mother might not play too well in the real world.

In some ways, Starr was remade by his prey. Four years of butting heads against the Clinton stonewall changed the man. He and his lieutenants apparently became convinced that they were dealing with a kind of ongoing criminal operation. The more Clinton stalled, the more Starr pushed. The more Starr pushed, the more Clinton stalled. And in the end, each drove the other to a kind of madness. Starr claims the experience didn't change him. But even many of his friends and allies say he became tougher, more aggressive, more willing to assume the worst about Clinton and his people.

Starr became less deferential, summoning Hillary Clinton to the grand jury in 1996 rather than questioning her at the White House. He relied on tough-guy prosecutors. He became so intense in his pursuit that in early 1997, he authorized his agents to question Arkansas state troopers about Clinton confidants, including alleged paramours from a decade before. Starr was so convinced of his righteousness that he became outraged when people had the temerity to question his motives. For the White House, it provided the first piece of evidence it used to portray the counsel as a sex-obsessed keyhole peeper.

When Linda Tripp showed up to spill the beans about Monica and Bill, another prosecutor—one who was more streetwise, one who hadn't been up against Clinton for so long—might have shown her the door. But Starr saw a conspiracy to obstruct justice unfolding before his very eyes. He hurried to the Justice Department seeking authorization to expand the scope of his investigation, but he failed to remind the officials that he'd had contact years before with lawyers for Paula Jones, a fact that could have led Janet Reno to send the case elsewhere.

When Starr sent his referral to Congress, it turned out to contain graphic sexual details with no direct bearing on the perjury question. The report struck many as biased, intended to inflame opinion. Starr's reputation was sealed. He says he wanted to leave out those X-rated details, but a majority of his lawyers disagreed and, disastrously, he changed his mind. He stashed the naughtiest bits into the footnotes—as if that made a difference. He says he didn't know Congress would release everything and that he never anticipated being cast as Puritan pornographer. "I don't think my crystal ball was working especially well," he sighs. "It so frequently doesn't work well."

Starr also conceded for the first time that the report should have quoted Lewinsky directly, instead of paraphrasing her, when she said, "No one ever asked me to lie." He told TIME, "It really cannot fairly be said we were trying to hide that, but it did give [the other side] a nice debating point." When asked whether he would have found room to quote Lewinsky directly had she admitted that she was asked to lie, he said, "That's a good question. I think that's probably a fair question."

Starr decided not to participate in—or even observe—grand jury testimony or interviews, and that may have been another mistake. The idea flowed from his conception of himself as a judicious figure remaining above the fray. But his critics believe the decision allowed the investigation to be hijacked by aggressive deputies. "Starr's Cowboys," as they became known, were accused of bullying witnesses; Starr argues that his system kept them in line.

Time and time again, Starr's firm confidence in his own moral rectitude blinded him to, at the very least, the appearance of bias and conflict of interest. In 1994 Starr chose to continue his full-time law practice (even defending tobacco interests) while investigating Clinton. In 1997, when he decided to quit the probe and take a position at Pepperdine University, he knew the institution was funded in part by the Clinton-bashing billionaire Richard Mellon Scaife, who for years had been paying for right-wing fishing trips into Clinton's past. But again Starr didn't see the conflict. In fact, he saw Scaife as one of his *own* harshest critics because Scaife's minions had attacked a Starr report concluding that Vincent Foster killed himself. But his professed p.r. ineptitude appeared to be both a defense—the errors were about surfaces, he insisted, not substance—and a form of vanity, as if he operated on a higher plane and couldn't be blamed for losing a war of perceptions with Clinton.

In trying to explain his actions, Kenneth Starr has invoked such figures as Joe Friday, Atticus Finch, the Lone Ranger, George Washington and Christ in the garden at Gethsemane on the night before the Crucifixion ("Let this cup passeth from me"). The roster suggests that the independent counsel needed to place himself in the company of heroes and saviors. "I can't be the judge in my own case," he said, and maybe that's true. But like Bill Clinton, he still dreams of being found not guilty. ∎

FAMILY VALUES: With daughter Carolyn and wife Alice

Friends say Starr's experiences made him tougher and more aggressive; he admits he has been "transmogrified"

PAUL SAKUMA—AP/WIDE WORLD

THE BETTER HALF

The scandal that tarnished Bill Clinton proved his wife was truly America's First Lady

O NE MONDAY IN JANUARY, 1998, THE LONGEST YEAR of her life, Hillary Rodham Clinton was making her usual rounds. At the Harriet Tubman school in Harlem, third-graders told her they were studying the four values: honesty, caring, respect and responsibility. "Those are really important values," Mrs. Clinton said. "Boy, that's a big word—responsibility—isn't it?" She went on to visit a literacy program before heading to a 50th anniversary gala for UNICEF. She was talking about the things she had always cared about, normally to rooms full of earnest activists and an indifferent camera or two. This time CNN carried her live, and the UNICEF ballroom was packed with reporters, all wanting to see if she was falling apart, since her marriage looked as if it had. "Well, it's nice to see," she told an aide as they drove away in the limousine, "that the press now cares about children's issues."

It would not be the last time she would put that rude spotlight to use. All through the year, as she pursued the private rescue of a marriage and the public rescue of a presidency, she was the one person who seemed to see the

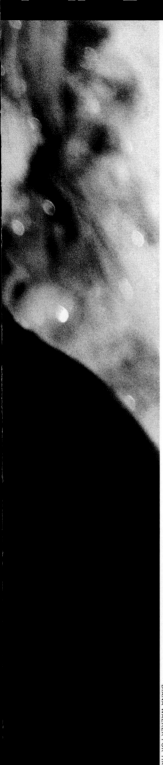

larger story and shaped its telling. When talk of resignation spread, she was the one who said, Let this unfold. When everyone thought the story was about Bill Clinton, she said it was about Kenneth Starr. When her husband's confession finally confronted her and us with the truth of his lies, she led the way, from denial through fury to a grudging acceptance. The code was always clear: if she can stand by him, she who had been so directly wronged, so should we. And in the fall, when the Republicans promised an election that would give Clinton his comeuppance, she went out and gave the Democratic faithful, many of whom she had let down in the past, something to cling to, straight on to victory in November.

At year's end Hillary Clinton found herself in places she had never been: embraced and admired by more Americans than at any other time in her public life, freed to work on her own causes—and cast as the "single most degraded wife in the history of the world," as Maureen Dowd lethally put it in the New York *Times*. Public pity, for the First Lady, was an enormous price to pay for popularity. Frustrated feminists and cutting commentators noted that her apotheosis came not in the *Congressional Record* but on the cover of *Vogue*—and not for what she had achieved but for what she had suffered. The role was not trailblazing but utterly traditional, born of a mythology of humiliation shared by Princess Diana and Kathie Lee Gifford.

Even beatification, if it comes on these terms, is a kind of punishment for a woman who swept into Washington wanting to put her stamp on social policy and bring government back into fashion. Instead she handed the G.O.P. control of Congress with her health-care plan and had her place in history established as the first First Lady ever to be forced to testify before a grand jury.

But with those defeats, Hillary also began to accept what Dolley Madison and Lady Bird Johnson had taken for granted, and what Eleanor Roosevelt must have told her when the two communed. As her former chief of staff Maggie Williams put it, "One of the things she's learned about being First Lady is, it's not just about doing, it's about being a symbol." Whatever judgments voters were asked to make about the flaws they would tolerate in a reckless politician whose leadership they valued, she mirrored in

her own decisions about a faithless husband whom she loved. She was his salesman, but also our surrogate.

When the scandal broke, she took control in the White House while Clinton crumpled. Right up until Hillary appeared on the *Today* show six days into the ordeal, the round-the-clock commentary had been entirely about the scandal: what Clinton had done, whether he could survive—with virtually no one defending him. Then she sat down on camera and challenged the press to pay attention to a different story: "this vast right-wing conspiracy that has been conspiring against my husband since the day he announced for President." She shone the light on Starr—his agenda, his henchmen, his ideological gene pool—and suggested that this was the real story, the real danger, rather than anything her husband might have done.

From the commentariat, at least, her "right-wing conspiracy" theory was mocked as the last resort of a woman in denial about the cad she had married. But that perception would change: by the end of the year, a majority of the public had come to agree with her about Starr, their fear of unaccountable government agents more intense than their distaste for even a lecherous, lying President.

In the fall, Hillary became the Democrats' national standard-bearer. The election could hardly have looked more dire for them. The President was useless to them as a campaigner; he was a prisoner of the briefing room and the fund raisers. She was the one politician in the country who would not be interrupted with questions about the scandal. In the miraculous month of October, while her husband worked for peace in the Middle East, the markets rebounded and John Glenn lifted off, Hillary barnstormed the country. Voters heard her on their car radios when they left for work in the morning and on their answering machines when they came home. The last week of the campaign saw her hitting nine states, with two stops each in Florida and New York. Her appearance in Iowa fueled the surge that made Tom Vilsack the first Democrat to be elected Governor there in 30 years. Said his media consultant David Axelrod: "Our voters had a lot more energy than theirs, and she was the major factor in that."

On Election Night, as the President downloaded results in chief of staff John Podesta's office, a television commentator caught Clinton's attention by noting that Hillary had won the day for the Democrats. "That's right," Clinton declared to the crowd around him. The First Lady's morning-after assessment: "We could have done better."

In mid-December she visited New York City. It was a bit of a coronation, packed with events nourishing her ego and her image and her agenda. Hillary gamely crooned a funny, off-key duet with Rosie O'Donnell. She lighted the Rockefeller Center Christmas tree with Garth Brooks under a full moon, and lingered later than anyone expected at a movie premiere. The day before the House vote to impeach her husband, Hillary spoke out on the scandal for the first time since January. She called for reconciliation. She counted blessings. She invoked the needs of those less fortunate. It was a Christmas card, to us and to him, preprinted but a keepsake nonetheless. Hillary had brought her husband and the country this far, and there was little chance she would let go now. ■

▶ In 1998 world leaders
and Chinese laborers found
similar employment:
treading water. Japan
slumped, Russia was
rudderless, and peace in
the Mideast moved inch by
grudging inch. Bucking the
status quo, Germans ousted
Kohl, Indonesians toppled
Suharto, and the Irish voted
to give peace a chance

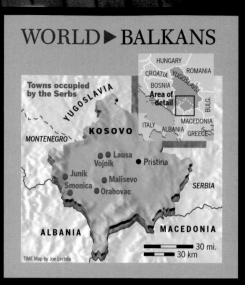

Towns occupied
by the Serbs

YUGOSLAVIA

MONTENEGRO

KOSOVO

● Lausa
Vojnik
Junik ● Malisevo ● Pristina
Smonica
● Orahovac

SERBIA

ALBANIA   MACEDONIA

30 mi.
30 km

TIME Map by Joe Lertola

HUNGARY
CROATIA ROMANIA
BOSNIA YUGOSLAVIA
**Area of
detail**
ITALY MACEDONIA BULG.
ALBANIA
GREECE

Once again "ethnic
cleansing" stalks
the Balkans as
Slobodan Milosevic's
Serbs strike back at
rebellious Kosovo

New Mourning

FTER THE DAYTON PEACE ACCORD OF 1995, MANY
hoped they had heard the last of conflict in the
Balkans. But ethnic warfare had not disappeared
from the crumbling remains of Yugoslavia; it had
simply moved south. The rebellious Yugoslav province of
Kosovo in 1998 looked dangerously like Bosnia several
years before: Serb soldiers marauding through isolated villages, firing wildly; corpses of women and children laid out
for identification by relatives; belligerent young ethnic
Albanian rebels waving Kalashnikovs at random road-
blocks. Even the sound track was familiar: keening
women grieved over coffins while NATO ministers earnest-
ly debated how to stop the killing.

Kosovo, about half the size of New Jersey, is internationally recognized as a territorial part of Serb-ruled
Yugoslavia. It is land the Serbs—led by strongman Slobodan Milosevic—hold dear as their sacred ancestral home.
But the province's 2 million inhabitants are not Serbs:
rather, they are 90% ethnic Albanians, known as Kosovars,
who have long felt stifled under the domination of Belgrade. Their patience has been running out since 1989,
when Milosevic revoked their autonomy; two years later he
launched a violent crackdown.

In 1998 tempers on both sides exploded as the Kosovars demanded full independence and Milosevic acted
to bring the rebels to heel. In March the Yugoslav army

A TIME TO DIE
Kosovar women grieve over the body of an ethnic Albanian killed in an anti-Serb protest in March

launched an offensive against the guerrillas known as the Kosovo Liberation Army. By July 50,000 Serb forces and several thousand K.L.A. fighters were skirmishing all over the province, targeting civilians in one another's villages. By September Milosevic was waging a campaign of general terror, as 26,000 Yugoslav soldiers and security police pillaged more than 400 ethnic-Albanian hamlets to root our guerrilla strongholds. By this time as many as 280,000 ethnic Albanians had been driven from their homes.

Concerned that escalation of the conflict could draw in Albania, Macedonia and even Greece, U.S. Secretary of State Madeleine Albright pushed for NATO action, and members finally agreed. When U.S. diplomat Richard

Holbrooke arrived in Belgrade on Oct. 5—as NATO began to tune up a massive strike against the Serb forces in Kosovo—Milosevic had the gall to challenge Holbrooke with a jest. "Are you Americans crazy enough to bomb us over our security police?" he asked. "Yeah," Holbrooke quietly replied. "We are." Holbrooke won a deal that called for a Serb pullback and 2,000 NATO "verifiers" to ensure compliance. As winter snows settled on the Balkans, Milosevic was keeping mum, and a fragile truce was holding in Kosovo. ∎

▶ **Milosevic to Holbrooke: "Are you crazy enough to bomb us over ... security police?"**

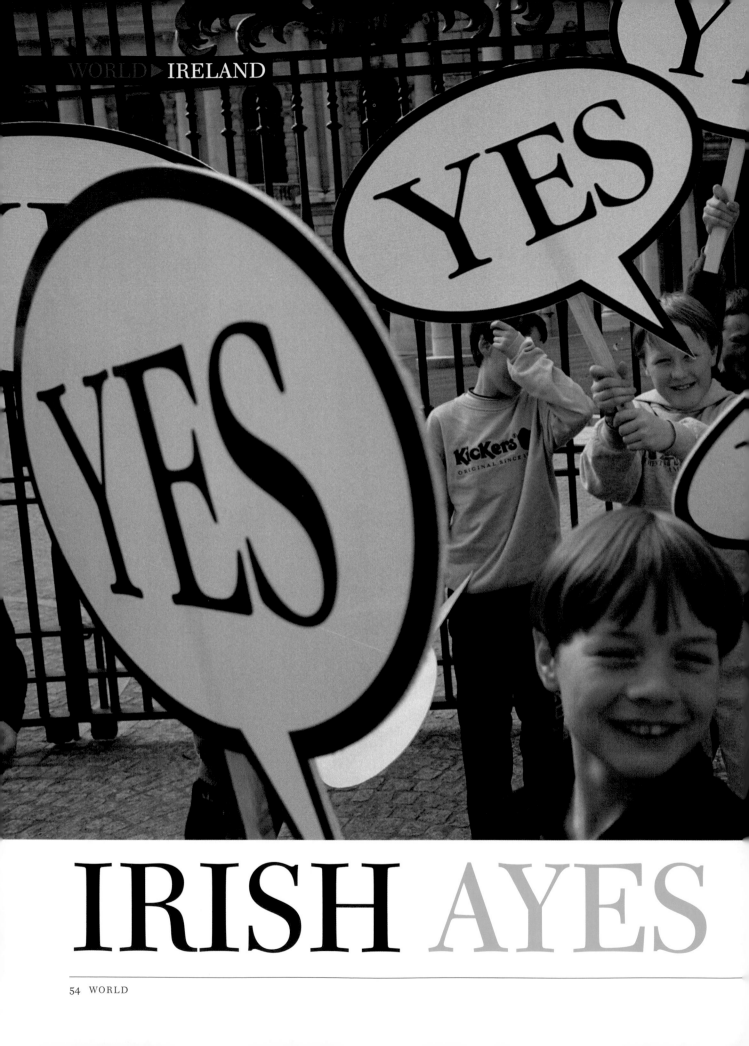

IRISH AYES

IRELAND IS A DECEPTIVELY BEAUTIFUL PLACE, soft and green, north and south. Its people, north and south, are deceptively kind, civil and wise. Deceptive, because vicious hatred and ugly violence have raged there for centuries, until suffering has seemed the price of living in such a lovely land. But on April 10—Good Friday—some of the awful weight of Irish history was lifted. The governments of Britain and Ireland and the key political leaders of the warring factions in Northern Ireland—with major assistance from Bill Clinton and a U.S. mediator, former Senator George Mitchell—agreed to replace terrorism with democracy and to let the people of the North decide their own ultimate fate.

The agreement was hammered out over 22 months of bargaining and concluded in a marathon 32-hour session captained by British Prime Minister Tony Blair (whose country has caused much of Ireland's torment). It permitted those who want a united Ireland to work for that goal through politics rather than violence, and permitted those who want to keep Northern Ireland part of Britain to retain that status until its citizens decide otherwise.

The agreement intricately balanced victories and defeats for both sides in the sectarian conflict. Protestant Unionists agreed to share power with Catholic parties in a new Northern Ireland assembly and to work together with Dublin in new cross-border government bodies. And Catholic republican parties—including Sinn Fein, the political wing of the Irish Republican Army, which has long fought for a united Ireland—agreed that the political status of the province would be changed only by a majority vote of its people.

▶ An I.R.A. bomb killed 28 in the town of Omagh— but failed to stop the peace train

In a May 22 referendum, Irish voters rousingly endorsed the deal, with 71% of voters in Northern Ireland and 94% in the Republic approving it. On Aug. 15 a car bomb planted by a renegade Republican group calling itself the Real I.R.A. ripped through a crowded shopping street in the small Northern Ireland town of Omagh, killing 28. Sinn Fein leader Gerry Adams declared, "I have condemned [the Omagh bombing] without equivocation"—a dramatic departure from usual form, and a sign that Ireland's time of Troubles may finally be over. ∎

After 30 years of the Troubles—a reign of terror by Catholic and Protestant extremists—Ireland says yes to peace in a Good Friday political accord and a rousing popular vote of approval

No Safe Harbor

Peggy's Cove was born of a shipwreck. Legend has it that the tiny hamlet on the coast of Nova Scotia was named for a woman pulled back from death at sea by a local sailor. The only survivor of a doomed ship, she was nursed back to health by her rescuer. They fell in love and married. Such romances and heartening miracles are woven into the visions of the village. At St. John's Anglican Church, two paintings frame the altar: in one, a fisherman clinging to a tattered sail searches for a lighthouse amid a storm; in the other, Christ walks on the waters of Peggy's Cove. Thus when a plane—not a ship—went down off the cove on Sept. 2, the seamen of the area felt the old instincts of rescue stir in their veins. What they found, however, was neither romantic nor miraculous.

Fishing boats, navy ships, even a passenger liner combed the waters off the Canadian coast. Visibility was poor, and in hindsight it was for the best. "We picked up women's purses—all blown to pieces, as if you put them in a meat grinder," said Eugene Young, who usually fishes the waters for pollock, hake and cod in September. "There was no hope." Despite cove legend, not one of the 229 people aboard Swissair Flight 111 emerged alive from the sea.

The airplane, an MD-11 jumbo jet built by McDonnell Douglas in 1991, left New York City's John F. Kennedy International Airport en route to Geneva, Switzerland, at 8:18 p.m. E.T. At 9:14, the Swiss pilot, Urs Zimmermann, radioed, "We have smoke in the cockpit" to a control tower in New Brunswick, Canada. He headed for Halifax, 70 miles away. At 9:24 he said: "We have to land immediately!" Six minutes later, the plane disappeared from the radar screen.

What caused the crash? In late October Canadian investigators said they had dredged up overheated electrical wires from the plane's sophisticated in-seat entertainment center, which featured a video screen that popped out of the armrest and could be used to play video games (including slot machines), select music and watch movies. The complex devices require a web of wires from each seat to powerful central computers, which generate a lot of heat. Investigators also learned that these wires had been connected to the same electrical pathway that powers vital aircraft functions, rather than the one that feeds nonessential devices, which pilots can deactivate if smoke fills the cabin.

Ironically, U.S. regulations kept passengers on Swissair 111, which took off from American soil, from playing the video slot machines. Still, 70 minutes after takeoff, their luck ran out. ∎

Salvage crews dredge up wires that implicate an in-seat video game system

DEATH AT SEA
Fighting darkness and
tides, rescuers recover a
body near Peggy's Cove

The Haunted Kingdom

Russia faces the past and buries its royal family, but under the feeble hand of Boris Yeltsin, both its ruble—and its future—are devalued

W HEN THE SOVIET UNION WAS DISINTEGRATING late in the autumn of 1991, a band of disillusioned demonstrators gathered in Red Square. Bobbing along in their midst, under the shelter of the Kremlin's looming brick walls, was a placard that read 70 YEARS ON THE ROAD TO NOWHERE. The accusation was an angry and poignant truth. As 1992 began, Russia was reborn under the old tricolor flag and set a new course toward not just reform but total transformation. But by 1998, with the economy in shreds and the government paralyzed, that hopeful path may have run into a dead end. For Russians, the 1990s had been seven more years on a road that once again led nowhere.

The year had brought an attempt at resolution with the past, as Boris Yeltsin attended a ceremony in which the remains of Czar Nicholas II and his family, murdered by Bolsheviks, were buried with honor. But no vision emerged of a viable Russian future—certainly not from the ailing President Yeltsin, and not from any of the three different men who served under him as Prime Minister in 1998.

What was happening in Russia was a disaster, a frightening one that threatened the world with prolonged instability at best and with the rise of an increasingly isolated and hostile state—armed with about 22,000 nuclear warheads—at worst. The Western countries have pumped tens of billions of dollars into the Russian economy to support reforms that were not carried through, and were now unlikely to give more. Russia was on its own.

The nation's troubles began at the top, with Yeltsin, who appeared to be turning into Leonid Brezhnev right before our eyes. The President was ever more frail and shambling, his eyes glazed and his speech slurred. He

LASKI DIFFUSION—GAMMA LIAISON

BONES OF CONTENTION
Guards protect the remains of Russia's royal family. Though DNA tests proved them authentic, the church refused to recognize them

ruled like a Czar—from on high, without attention to detail, and by decree. But like Brezhnev, Yeltsin had no intention of stepping down, and the people around him would do anything to keep him in power, lest they lose their own. Under his increasingly feeble hand, Russians lived through an *annus horribilis.* A chronological review:

MARCH: THE FIRST PURGE At 8:15 a.m. on Monday, March 23, Yeltsin and his motorcade (including the ever present rolling hospital, nicknamed "the catafalque") swept

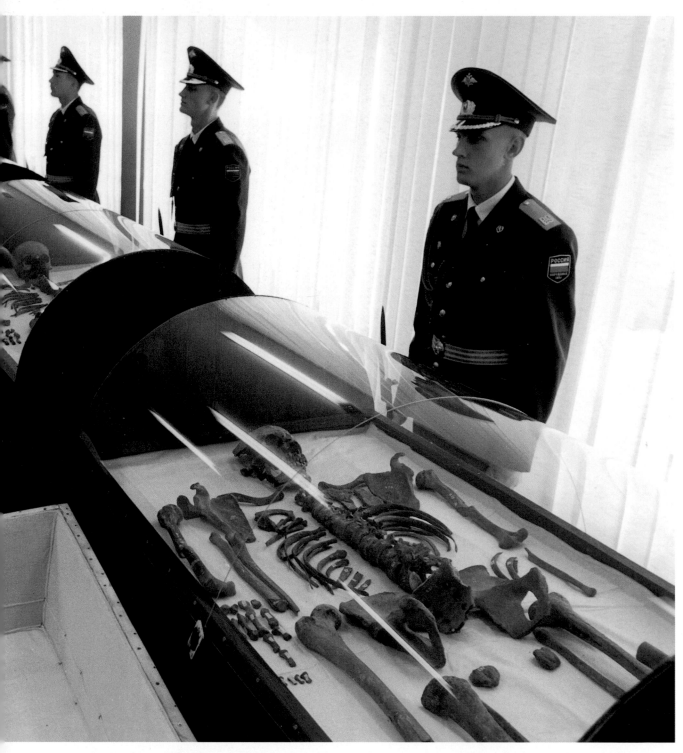

into the Kremlin. When Prime Minister Viktor Chernomyrdin arrived a bit later, Yeltsin called him into the presidential office, presented him with a medal for service to the state and fired him. Normally, this would have been a full day's work for Yeltsin, but he didn't stop to rest. He next fired his incessantly controversial Deputy Prime Minister Anatoli Chubais, the inflicter of Western-style economic reforms. Then he ousted the rest of the Cabinet. Yeltsin had become suspicious of Chernomyrdin, the most loyal and humble of

ministers since 1992, and that sealed his departure. But the Prime Minister had hinted he was interested in succeeding Yeltsin, and that was intolerable to the President.

On Friday Yeltsin named his new Prime Minister, Sergei Kiriyenko, 35, a petroleum expert who had held the post of Minister of Fuel and Energy in the old Cabinet. Kiriyenko's ally, Boris Nemtsov—a Yeltsin favorite—became First Deputy Prime Minister. Western observers hoped the combination of Kiriyenko and Nemtsov might

YELTSIN: More and more, he resembles Leonid Brezhnev

CHERNOMYRDIN: Rejected twice by the Duma in September

provide a small boost for reform, the lagging pace of which Yeltsin insisted was the main reason for the mass firing.

MAY: THE ASIAN FLU The collapse of the Asian financial markets, which rumbled around the world, hit Russia in late May, shaking the already wobbly economy and its twitchy investors. Even before the market bubble collapsed in Thailand, South Korea and Indonesia, Yeltsin's government was living dangerously, juggling $150 billion in foreign debt, running huge budget deficits and resorting to a kind of pyramid scheme in which it was selling new

tiful confines of St. Petersburg's Peter and Paul Fortress. It was intended to be an act of national repentance for eight decades of death and division, but that goal had been thwarted when the head of the Russian Orthodox Church, Alexi II, expressed doubts about the authenticity of the bones, despite positive DNA tests. (The Patriarch has been accused by former dissidents of collaboration with the Soviet-era KGB.) As a result, even though Yeltsin made a surprise appearance at the service, few people seemed touched by the event. The muted response to the funeral, in

Yeltsin is followed everywhere by a rolling hospital; Russians call

treasury bills to pay interest on those it had sold earlier. Now foreign investors, burned by losses in Asia, were taking their money and heading for the exits. Trying desperately to hold on to them and avoid devaluing the ruble, the central bank upped its interest rate to 150%, and Russia's cash flow all but dried up.

Yeltsin and his several governments have never learned how to collect the billions in taxes that corporations and individuals dodge. Other billions are not collected because of sweetheart deals Yeltsin made with Russian oligarchs when he needed their political support. As the crisis deepened, the President vowed the ruble would not be devalued and issued a fusillade of decrees on how to get tough with tax dodgers. The International Monetary Fund concluded, or pretended to conclude, that Yeltsin's decrees sounded good enough for it to hand over a delayed installment of $670 million, part of a $10 billion loan package.

JULY: REQUIEM FOR THE CZAR The funeral of Czar Nicholas II, his wife Alexandra, three of their children and four faithful retainers was held within the austerely beau-

political circles and on the street, suggested that Russians have not yet found a way of coming to terms with their past.

AUGUST: THE MELTDOWN As Russia's financial crisis continued through the summer, the President's mental and physical power seemed to be fading along with the value of the ruble. On Friday, Aug. 14, he seemed unaware that his chief ministers were preparing to devalue the nation's currency just as he was assuring Russians it would not happen. So, three days after Yeltsin had vowed yet again that he would not devalue the ruble—he ended up devaluing the ruble. The decision had been anticipated, even after the IMF in mid-July had put together a separate $22.6 billion bailout package. The deal didn't reassure investors, however, who continued to pull their money, in dollars, out of Russia.

In many countries, the pitch of chaos Russia reached by late August would have produced panic, fury, demonstrations, even riots. The street value of the ruble halved. Banks tottered and closed, and the Moscow stock market all but evaporated. But in Russia, home of the stolid and the depoliticized, the streets were calm and there was no sign of unrest. Ordinary people seemed not merely restrained but numb. On Aug. 23, Yeltsin dismissed Kiriyenko, Prime Minister for all of six months—and named Chernomyrdin, the man Kiriyenko had replaced, to once again take up the reins of government. But the communist-dominated Duma rejected Yeltsin's retread nominee twice.

Into this seething mess stepped Bill Clinton, who was escaping his own seething mess in Washington, the White House sex scandal. Refusing to cancel a summit meeting, the embattled Clinton arrived in Moscow in early September. The meeting of the two leaders made quite a picture: Clinton looked weary and spent, his head sunk in his hands, his lips tight in a glum line as reporters badgered him about Monica Lewinsky. Yeltsin sat next to him, befuddled and disoriented. Clinton's visit only served to expose Russia to the world's view as a country with no functioning government and no plan for recovery.

SEPTEMBER: PRIMAKOV ASCENDS After Clinton departed, Yeltsin reluctantly concluded that he would never persuade the Duma to accept Chernomyrdin as Prime Minister. His new choice: Foreign Minister Yevgeni Primakov, who was backed by Communist Party leader Gennadi Zyuganov as well as Grigori Yavlinksy, who heads the liberal-reform Yabloko Party. The Duma overwhelmingly confirmed Primakov. His appointment solved the political stalemate at the top but did nothing to cure Russia's economic crisis. By late November, two months after his appointment, Primakov had yet to produce a plan to stabilize

it "the catafalque"

the economy. And while the politicians fidgeted, the ruble lost half its value in a month. In November, Galina Starovoitova, a leading voice for democracy, was assassinated, while Yeltsin was admitted to a hospital with "pneumonia." On December 7 the feeble President roused himself, went to Moscow, fired four assistants, then returned to his sickbed.

Under Boris Yeltsin, Russia acquired the trappings of a civilized state: an office of the President, a federal parliament, private banks. But they only looked authentic. The presidency resembled the throne of the Czar, upon which the entire welfare of the nation rested. The year ended with the erratic Yeltsin physically and politically out of touch, having lost control of his Cabinet, the parliament and the people. How long would Yeltsin's Russia survive? How long would Yeltsin himself survive? In a land haunted by failed regimes, all roads seemed to lead nowhere. ∎

Russia's New Icon

A secretive figure may succeed Boris Yeltsin—but can he succeed in healing his nation's troubles?

YEVGENI PRIMAKOV WAS A COMPROMISE CANDIdate for Russia's premiership in September when it became clear that Boris Yeltsin's attempt to reappoint Viktor Chernomyrdin Prime Minister was leading the country deeper into crisis. Primakov, then Foreign Minister, was well known in the diplomatic community but was a fresh face to most Americans. Who is this man who is increasingly seen as the potential victor in the presidential election of 2000—or who may succeed Yeltsin earlier, should the ailing President not live out his term?

The new premier is a combination of opposites: ambition tempered with caution; forcefulness allied with compromise; a secretive, taciturn official persona paired with a reputation for gregariousness and wit in private. He was born in Kiev, Ukraine's capital, in 1929, and is said to never have known his father; he was brought up in the Georgian capital of Tbilisi, where his mother Anna was a gynecologist. He went to Moscow in the late 1940s to study Arabic, then became a journalist, first for the state radio corporation, later as Middle East correspondent for *Pravda*.

After *Pravda* Primakov became director of his alma mater, the Institute of Oriental Studies, and then, in 1985, of the country's premier think tank, where he soon became a key reformer for Mikhail Gorbachev. He also forged close ties with both Iraq's Saddam Hussein and Libya's Muammar Gaddafi. Some believe he also worked with the KGB. But his private life was marked by tragedy; his first wife and son both died unexpectedly. His current wife Irina is a doctor.

Primakov's opposition to U.S. policy in the Middle East, the Persian Gulf and the Balkans has made him the bane of U.S. officials. But a NATO official said, "Primakov is smart, and he's realistic." What he seems to lack is any clear vision for Russia. For the nation to survive, the secretive Primakov must step out of the shadows and begin to lead. ∎

WORKING OVERTIME: On the eighth day of the conference, Netanyahu and Clinton struggled to find common ground

Waging Peace, Inch by Inch

Nine tough days of diplomacy revive hope for the Mideast peace process

THE TERMS OF THE WYE RIVER MEMORANDUM, FOUGHT for and won over nine tumultuous days in October at a resort on Maryland's Wye River, 70 miles east of Washington, were modest. The agreement provided for the return of a parcel of sparsely inhabited land in the West Bank. It firmed up the details of the implementation of accords the P.L.O. and Israel had reached in 1993. But it left far tougher disputes unresolved, including the future of Jerusalem and the return of Palestinian refugees. According to the original timetable, all these issues must be settled by May 1999—when Palestinian leader Yasser Arafat has threatened to declare a Palestinian state.

Yet the agreement deserves to be called a breakthrough: it created new momentum toward a permanent peace, the first such movement in 19 months. It also opened the tantalizing possibility that Israel's Prime Minister, Benjamin ("Bibi") Netanyahu, had at last committed himself irretrievably to work toward a final settlement.

After a White House send-off, Netanyahu and Arafat settled in at Wye on Thursday, Oct. 15. The American camp was impressed by Arafat's apparent eagerness to find a deal. Netanyahu, by contrast, seemed unwilling to give an inch. Things got worse Monday morning, when the leaders of the two camps were greeted by horrific news from home: two grenades had been tossed into an Israeli bus station in Beersheba at rush hour, wounding 64 people. An activist from Hamas—Palestine's largest Islamic group, which has a strong militant wing—was caught at the scene. Arafat condemned the deed, but Netanyahu briefly declared the talks suspended.

The next day, Tuesday, brought progress: Bill Clinton, commuting to the conference by helicopter, got Arafat to accept Netanyahu's five security demands, but that afternoon Israel responded by putting forward a kitchen-sink collection of complaints. The next day, the Israelis threatened a walkout, which further soured the mood.

By Thursday the final agreement on the land-for-security swap was in hand. Now Clinton and his team took on the two most emotional issues of the conference. The Palestinians were demanding the return of their prisoners held in Israel; the Israelis were demanding the revision of the P.L.O. charter, which calls for their nation's destruction. A frustrated Clinton finally pulled out a trump card: a badly weakened King Hussein of Jordan, who was in the U.S. for treatment of non-Hodgkin's lymphoma. Gaunt and hairless, the King lectured the leaders. "You can't afford for this to fail," he said. "You owe this to your people, to your children, to future generations." His eloquence lifted their spirits—briefly. Then Clinton tried his own stagecraft: he stormed out of the room just after midnight, looking at no one. "That was a powerful moment," said one of Clinton's aides. "It pushed all the leaders back on their heels."

▶ King Hussein: "You owe this to your people, to your children, to [the] future"

And they got back to work. No one seemed to sleep. The Israelis agreed to a phased release of some Palestinian prisoners. The Palestinians agreed to rethink the language of their charter but noted that Arafat had failed once before to get the hard-liners on the Palestine National Council to consent. Clinton found a way out: he would fly to Gaza to speak to the council when it met. At dawn Friday, the three leaders shook on a deal.

But Netanyahu wasn't finished. The Prime Minister pulled Clinton aside and asked for clemency for Jonathan Pollard, the U.S. intelligence analyst convicted in 1985 of spying for Israel. Netanyahu said the release would mollify hard-liners in his Cabinet. Meanwhile, his aides told the press that Clinton had consented—which he hadn't. The

TERROR: After the meeting, bombers struck in Jerusalem

Americans were livid. Three hours later, having reaped the benefits of delay for domestic political consumption, Netanyahu declared himself ready to sign.

The leaders went back to Washington to sign the accord at the White House. When they returned to their nations, each faced yet another hurdle: selling the deal to their own people. After the vote was postponed several times, Netanyahu managed to secure the Knesset's approval. But Arafat returned to the worst anti–Palestinian Authority riots ever in the West Bank, the attempted slaughter of 40 schoolchildren on an Israeli bus (a Hamas plot that was foiled when an Israeli jeep intercepted the bomber) and another botched bombing of a Jerusalem market. When he responded by arresting more than 100 Hamas activists and placing Sheik Ahmed Yassin, the founder and spiritual leader of Hamas, under house arrest, he was heavily criticized by Islamic zealots. With hard-liners on both sides vowing never to accept peace, the path to a final settlement in May 1999 seemed more challenging than ever. ■

MAN OF THE HOUR: Back at the White House to sign the agreement, the participants salute Jordan's ailing King Hussein

NO NUKES! Most Indians rejoiced at the nuclear tests. Only a few, like these marchers in New Delhi, opposed them

Sprinting to Destruction?

The world trembles as virulent foes India and Pakistan test nuclear arms

THEY ARE, IN THE CLASSIC METAPHOR OF THE NUCLEAR age, like two scorpions in a bottle, eyeing each other warily, showing off their stingers, aware though not properly concerned that an attack by either would mean death to both. But in this scenario the scorpions are largely Hindu India and overwhelmingly Muslim Pakistan—and their stingers are 15-kiloton, Hiroshima-size bombs. Lofted by missiles on densely populated cities like Bombay and Karachi, such nuclear weapons could kill thousands of civilians and spread deadly fallout throughout the subcontinent. In 1998 that nightmare moved far closer to reality, as both nations successfully exploded test bombs and a nuclear arms race gripped the region.

India struck first. Though Prime Minister Atal Bihari Vajpayee and his Hindu nationalist Bharatiya Janata Party rule a coalition government, its 17 fractious parties shared one belief: it was time to declare India a full nuclear power. At 3:45 p.m. on May 11, three devices exploded in five seconds at India's nuclear test site in Pokhran: a normal fission bomb, a low-yield bomb for tactical battlefield use and something like a hydrogen bomb, which U.S. officials later insisted was a less powerful weapon.

After the Indian tests, other nuclear powers, like the U.S., Britain and China, launched intense diplomacy to dissuade Pakistan from retaliatory tests. The reply? At 3:30 p.m. on May 28, the earth at Pakistan's Chagai test site shook, then collapsed. Pakistani Prime Minister Nawaz Sharif grimly announced that five nuclear bombs had been exploded. U.S. intelligence officials suspected there had been fewer. Two days later, Pakistan conducted one more test to mirror India's back-to-back blasts.

The international community shuddered at the nuclear race. (And many Americans shuddered when they learned that the CIA had failed to predict the explosions.) As Bill Clinton darkly put it, the two countries were repeating "the worst mistakes of the 20th century." India and Pakistan have fought three wars in the past 50 years. But neither of them has in place any of the protective mechanisms—spy satellites, hot lines, missile treaties—that helped keep the United States and the Soviet Union from pushing the button that would initiate mutual assured destruction (MAD) in the cold war. As the scorpions of the subcontinent warily circled, a State Department official grimly commented, "[the] MAD [deterrent] requires a level of rationality that we may not have in this region." ■

▶ **Clinton accused the two nations of "repeating the worst mistakes of the 20th century."**

Jakarta's Year of Turmoil

Protesters oust aging ruler Suharto—but usher in a new era of instability

WITH ROCKS CRASHING THROUGH HIS WINDOWS, AN iron spike punching holes through his kitchen door and a mob outside baying, "Burn! Burn!," Philip Lo cowered for two hours with his family inside a locked bedroom in Jakarta in May. The ethnic-Chinese pastor's church and adjoining house were attacked during riots that left around 400 dead and hundreds of stores looted and gutted by fire. He and his family escaped injury, but their car was burned and the inside of the church was ransacked. Lo was targeted because the Chinese minority is perceived as more affluent than most other Indonesians. "If there are no reforms, the riots will get even worse," he said. "This is amok."

"Amok"—literally, "to go berserk" in the Malay tongue that is spoken across Indonesia—is what the outside world feared for Jakarta since it was hit by a currency crisis late in 1997 that the aging President Suharto, 76, seemed unable to control. Indonesia's 200 million people had seen per capita income drop from $1,200 to $300 almost overnight. Tinted-glass towers in the business district of what had been one of Asia's hottest cities for investors stood virtually empty. Meanwhile, poor households had no way of paying escalating prices for rice and cooking oil. Yet Suharto, in power for 32 years, balked at economic reforms that might damage the income of family members and friends.

The crisis came in May, when the fatal shooting of six students by police in Jakarta sparked riots and looting. Clouds of smoke hung over the city as the nation Suharto had patiently built up for three decades burned. After Parliament threatened to begin impeachment proceedings and the armed forces commander, General Wiranto, paid a private visit to Suharto's residence, the old man finally agreed to step down, and his longtime top aide, B.J. Habibie, 61, took over. [*For a profile of Habibie, see* World Notes.]

But Suharto's fall opened increasingly bitter divisions among the forces jockeying for a place in the new Indonesia: the armed forces, pro-democracy leaders, Muslim activists and students. In November, student marchers clashed with riot troops protecting a special session of the nation's highest constitutional body; 16 students were killed, and more than 200 were reported wounded. Could Habibie survive? Would he be forced to give way to martial law and a military junta led by General Wiranto? Or could power be assumed by a more progressive coalition of opposition figures? Indonesia's days of running amok appeared to be far from over. ∎

> ▶ **Who holds the reins of power: new boss B.J. Habibie—or the hard-line military?**

JOHN STANMEYER—SABA

COPS VS. KIDS: Well-armed security forces outnumber a lone protester in the May riots in Jakarta that toppled Suharto

APWIDE WORLD

Osama bin Laden

Public Enemy

Even as the dust settled in the terrorist attacks on two U.S. embassies in Africa, Osama bin Laden, a militant Muslim multimillionaire, was emerging as the mastermind behind them. Bin Laden's outspoken screeds against America and suspected collusion in many of the most spectacular terrorist assaults of the '90s have earned him the reputation of a virtual Dr. No who has connections to secret cells around the globe.

The Saudi-born Bin Laden first fought for Islam by supplying the Afghan Muslim *mujahedin* who fought the U.S.S.R. in the '80s. He condemns America's influence in the Middle East and wants U.S. forces out of his homeland. Bin Laden runs a network of Islamic charitable and educational organizations (as well as terrorist training camps) from a base outside Jalalabad, Afghanistan; he keeps in touch with the world via computers and satellite phones. In August U.S. officials said that prior to the embassy bombings a federal grand jury had already issued a sealed indictment accusing bin Laden of building a terrorist network that targets U.S. interests.

Britannia Waives the Rules

Why is Tony Blair smiling? Well, in 1998 Britain's Prime Minister may have been the most successful politician on the face of the earth. He completed his first year in office in May, and by nearly every measurement, things could not be better. He was more popular in 1998 than when he won his landslide victory in 1997. His Labour government was so far ahead of the opposition Tories in the national polls that Margaret Thatcher's party had almost disappeared as an effective political force. To cap it all off, Blair helped engineer a historic peace agreement in Northern Ireland, reasserted a British presence in Middle East politics and teamed up with Bill Clinton to stop Slobodan Milosevic's war on the Kosovars. The British economy was surging: the pound was up, unemployment was down.

Then there was Britain's boom in the arts: from movies like *The Full Monty* to

JON JONES—SYGMA

ROLLIN': Tony Blair's popularity surged

bands like Oasis and the Spice Girls, to designers like Stella McCartney, the buzz these days seems to come from what is cloyingly known as "Cool Britannia." Blair and his coterie of young advisers have relentlessly, even shamelessly, courted and promoted the hip as a way of proclaiming to the world that Britain is changing. And wait—did we forget to mention the Teletubbies?

Rushdie: Free at Last

Back in 1989, Iranian spiritual leader Ayatullah Khomeini issued a *fatwa*, a religious sentence of death, against novelist Salman Rushdie, saying his book *The Satanic Verses* slandered Islam. Since then the author had spent his life in hiding and under constant police protection. But on Sept. 25, Rushdie stood in front of a gaggle of microphones and cameras in London to say he expected "to resume the

PETER JORDAN—PRESS ASSOCIATION

STROLLIN': Rushdie

ordinary life of a writer at very high speed." The day before at the United Nations in New York, Iranian Foreign Minister Kamal Kharrazi had assured British Foreign Secretary Robin Cook that Iran "disassociates itself" from the reward being offered for the taking of Rushdie's life. The gambit was part of a charm campaign by Iran's moderate President Mohammed Khatami, who is eager to edge his nation back into respectable diplomatic circles—and to expand its access to the U.S. and Europe.

Rebellion in Albania

While the West was preoccupied with the Serbs' bloody rampage through Kosovo, another brush fire broke out across the border in Albania. The blaze was started by former Albanian President Sali Berisha, who has been stirring up trouble since his ouster by enraged citizens in 1997. After the assassination of Azem Hajdari, a close ally, on Sept. 12, Berisha rallied supporters under the banner of the Democratic Party in Tirana, the capital. Then he watched as the armed

ON TO TIRANA! Rebels loyal to Albania's former

Milestones

▶ **GERMANY:** After 16 years in power, Chancellor Helmut Kohl and his Christian Democrat Party were ousted by Gerhard Schröder and his Social Democratic Party.

▶ **JAPAN:** The ruling Liberal Democratic Party replaced Prime Minister Ryutaro Hashimoto with longtime party man Keizo Obuchi after a resounding election defeat.

▶ **CHILE:** In October former Chilean dictator Augusto Pinochet Ugarte, 82, was arrested in London on an extradition warrant issued by a Spanish court. Thousands died in his 17 years of iron-fisted military rule.

throng stormed Prime Minister Fatos Nano's office and other public buildings. Western pressure finally reined in Berisha, but Nano resigned in late September and was succeeded by Pandeli Majko, also of the ruling Socialist Party.

North Korea's New Weapon

Say this much for North Korea's quirky leader, Kim Jong Il: he knows how to get the world's attention. In September a powerful new missile lifted off from a secret base on North Korea's eastern coast and streaked toward Japan. Dumping its

President Sali Berisha commandeer heavy metal

first stage off the west coast of Japan, the rocket sped high over the country and plunked down into the Pacific Ocean. The message: North Korea may be broke and short of food, but the Stalinist state has a dangerous new toy. With a range of up to 1,240 miles, far greater than anything else in the North's arsenal, the Taepo Dong-1 can reach all of Japan—and the 41,000 U.S. troops stationed there. Worse, Pyongyang sells its missiles to Mideast clients like Libya and Iran.

The Lady of the Lake

Althorp is the ancestral estate of the Spencers, the aristocratic clan of the late Princess of Wales, who is buried on an island in its lake. Her brother Charles,

CULT: The crowds reflect Diana's magic

Earl Spencer, has now opened it to the public as a memorial. In "Dianaland," even the trees tell her story. The drive to the memorial is flanked by 36 young oaks, one for each year of Diana's life.

But numbers tell a bit of her brother's story too. With an estimated 152,000 tickets sold at $15.70 apiece in 1998, the earl will be bringing in nearly $2.4 million. Much of the world is aware of how expensive it is to be an earl and master of one of the realm's more historic properties. It is costly too to deal with a scandalous divorce. So Spencer declared he would tithe the proceeds to charity.

In other royal news, Prince Charles turned 50, to modified rapture. His great and good friend Camilla Parker-Bowles finally met Prince Harry—by chance—at Charles' London apartment; after the close encounter with the heir, she reportedly called swiftly for a vodka-and-tonic. ∎

SNAPSHOT

The New Boss

When Indonesia's aging ruler Suharto was finally pushed from office, he was succeeded by B.J. Habibie, 61, a man whose entire political career was based on his closeness to the corrupt, repudiated strongman. Suharto had been a father figure for his successor since the death of Habibie's real father, a close friend, in 1950.

With his shrill voice and constant gesticulating, Habibie comes across as an excitable, almost manic individual. A man of complex character, he is a devout Muslim who fasts on Monday and Thursday, even when he is traveling abroad. His religious supporters hope he will spread their dream of Islamic ascendancy for Indonesia. He is also a serious scientist who studied aeronautical engineering and worked for a German aircraft maker before Suharto called him home in 1974 to help prime Indonesia's industrial pump. Like his mentor, he has dabbled lucratively in private enterprise through his family— and reigns only with the military's say-so. While Jakartans marched for reform, Habibie's tune was: "Meet the new boss —same as the old boss."

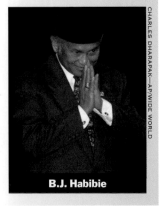

B.J. Habibie

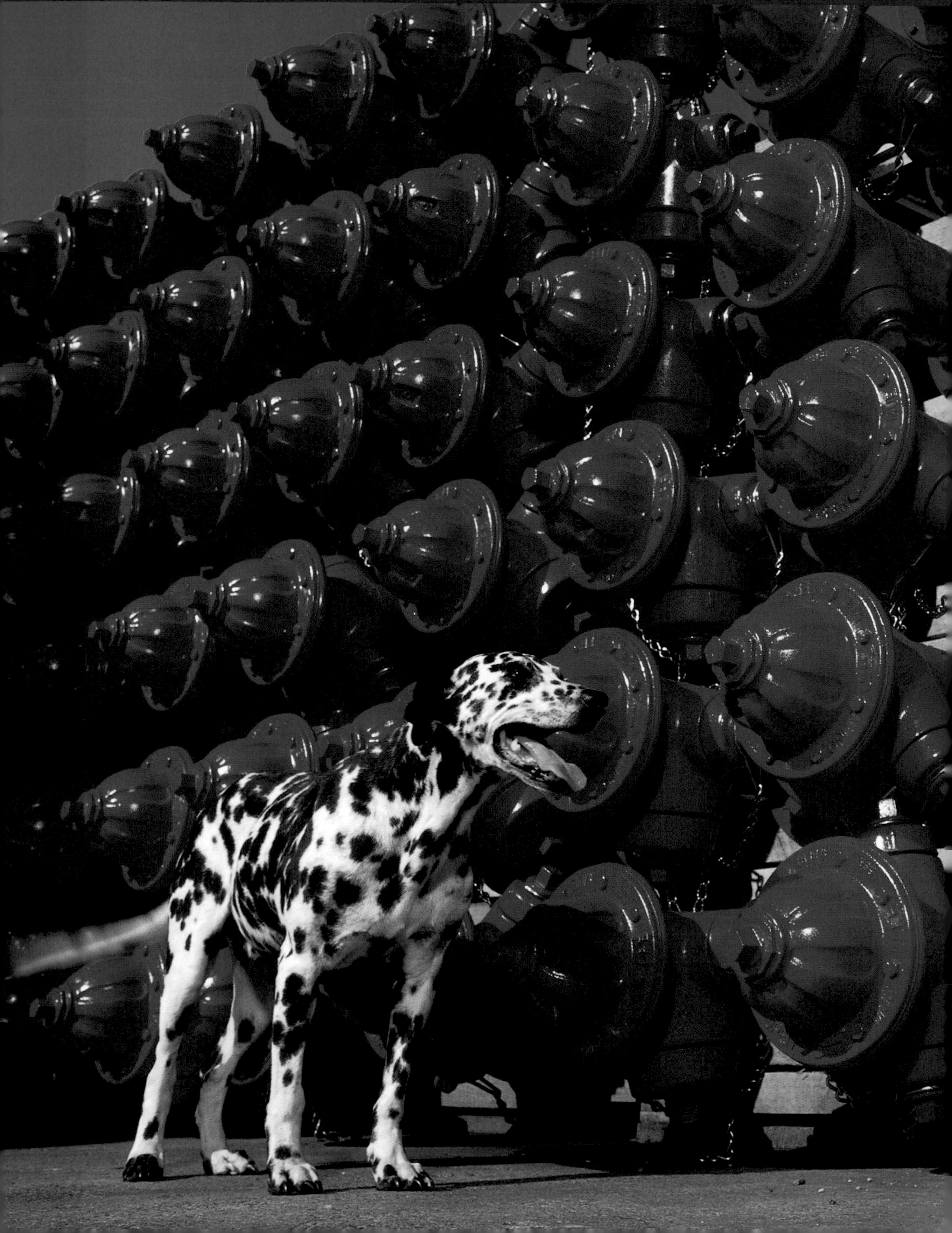

► **It's raining ampersands! A series of can-you-top-this mergers united some of the world's biggest companies: Mobil & Exxon, Bell Atlantic & GTE, Travelers & Citicorp. Asia's economies melted down, but U.S. traders kept the long-dreaded stock market bear at bay**

HYDRANT TOWN, U.S.A.
Albertville, Alabama, one of
America's "secret capitals"
of industry, makes half the
fire hydrants in the country

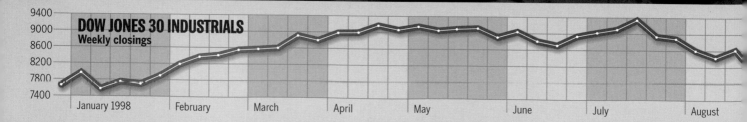

DOW JONES 30 INDUSTRIALS
Weekly closings

9400								
9000								
8600								
8200								
7800								
7400	January 1998	February	March	April	May	June	July	August

RICK MAIMAN—SYGMA; CHART BY JOE LERTOLA

Whew!

Markets around the world catch the "Asian flu," yet Wall Street's bull stumbles, only to rise again

WHAT A RIDE! AFTER A LONG BULL RUN THAT REPAID investors with returns of more than 20% a year for three years in a row, the stock market finally took a tumble in 1998. After eight fat years, investors awoke to a world where stocks go down as well as up, and where America's engagement in the global economy brings risks as well as rewards. For a few rough weeks in the late summer and fall, it looked as if the market might bottom out in what Wall Street calls, charmingly, a "correction." But by December the bulls were back in charge of the Street, leaving investors both shaken and stirred.

The roots of Wall Street's roller-coaster year extended directly back to the currency crisis that began in Thailand in July 1997, where a shaky economy cantilevered on unsecured loans finally collapsed, leaving the economy a shambles. The slump spread like a contagion to Malaysia, Hong Kong, China and Japan. The "Asian flu" invaded Russia and Latin America in the summer, hammering down local currencies and slashing demand for U.S. exports. Result: the stock market took back, in only seven weeks, almost a quarter of the $9 trillion that stocks had pumped into U.S. portfolios during the '90s. The Dow Jones industrial average suffered a grinding 1,798-point decline, hitting bottom on Aug. 31 at 7539, a loss of 19.3% from its July 17 peak at 9337.97.

The near panic over emerging markets was strongest among some of the hedge funds, the high-risk vehicles that often deliver high returns to wealthy investors. Famed investor George Soros lost $2 billion in Russia, and John Meriwether's Long Term Capital Management announced in August that it had lost $2.1 billion, half its asset value. In a controversial deal, the Federal Reserve Board led a $3.6 billion bailout of the staggering fund by a coalition of 14 banks and brokerages.

Pushing against these negative currents was the fundamental strength of the U.S. economy. The trend in wages and employment, which wield far more influence over consumer confidence than stock prices, was rising. Even as the market slumped, most other leading indicators—orders from U.S. factories, housing values, real wages—still pointed upward. And unemployment was holding at 4.5%, nearly a 28-year low.

> ▶ In a seven-week stretch, the U.S. stock market lost 25% of its $9 trillion gain in the 1990s

After looking at these figures, after absorbing the calming influence of three interest-rate cuts in seven weeks by the Alan Greenspan–led Federal Reserve Board and after taking heed of a wave of big merger announcements signaling that the U.S. economy was continuing its profit-generating restructuring process, investors decided to vote on the bull. Money poured back into the market, and on Nov. 23, the Dow Jones average plowed back into record territory, closing at 9374.27—a nearly 2,000-point rebound from its summer slide. The wild ride was over—for now. ∎

October	November	December

9400
9000
8600
8200
7800
7400

The Affluent Armada

A surge of middle-class vacationers has cruise-line companies riding high, so it's "Anchors aweigh!" for a new flotilla of extravagant floating resorts

NOT SINCE THE *TITANIC* SET SAIL HAS THE SEA SEEMED so alluring or the cruise industry looked so unsinkable as it did in 1998. With 5 million customers booking passage in 1997—a ten-fold increase from two decades ago—major carriers such as Carnival and Royal Caribbean have steamed to record sales and profits by turning a once snooty form of travel into a mass-market vacation. Flush with cash, cruise lines have ordered an astonishing $10 billion worth of floating pleasure palaces, some of which will be the largest passenger ships ever built.

▶ **For sale: condos on a luxury liner that will circle the globe. A steal for only $6.6 million!**

The new vessels, to be delivered through 2002, will increase the number of berths a whopping 50%. Among them: the $450 million *Grand Princess*, flagship of the Princess line, which will carry 2,600 passengers. At a record-breaking 109,353 tons (the *Titanic* displaced, temporarily, 46,328 tons), the *Grand Princess* will have 15 decks, three show lounges and the world's largest floating casino. The Walt Disney Co. is also taking to sea, launching a pair of $370 million ships that will each carry 1,760 passengers. Backed by a $130 million marketing budget, these floating Mouse traps will offer cruises as part of Disney World vacations.

Who will fill all those new berths? The cruise companies claim that the market is largely untapped: only 8% of North Americans have taken a cruise. That leaves room for bookings to grow a robust 9% to 10% a year. (To ensure that growth, however, the industry must counter one cloud on its horizon: the last few years have brought a number of sensational allegations of sexual assault and other crimes on cruise ships, along with charges of company cover-ups.)

The prospect of all those new prows bounding over the main has already caused a couple of smaller companies to run up the white flag. The five-ship Celebrity Cruise Lines, 51% of which was owned by London's Chandris Group, sold out to Royal Caribbean (sales: $1.9 billion) for $1.3 billion. Cunard, whose five vessels include the legendary liner *Queen Elizabeth 2*, was acquired for $500 million by a group headed by Carnival ($2.4 billion). The buyout expanded Carnival's fleet to 42 ships and seven separate lines. Not to be outdone, Royal Caribbean is spending more than $2.8 billion to add seven new liners to its 16-ship fleet by 2002.

The recent consolidation has created a two-tier industry: in the first tier, the three dominant lines; in the second, everybody else. The Big Three—Carnival, Royal Caribbean and Princess—hold a 73% share of the North American market. The combatants are locked in perhaps the world's costliest game of "Can You Top This?" in which the bragging rights to the world's largest passenger ship change from week to week. Carnival's *Destiny*, the current titleholder at 101,353 tons, is about to be overtaken by the *Grand Princess*. Both ships will be too wide to fit through the Panama Canal. Both will also be overshadowed next year when Royal Caribbean's 136,000-ton flagship hits the water, with berths for 3,840 passengers and 1,181 crew members. By comparison, an aircraft carrier weighs in at

CAN YOU TOP THIS?

The ships dazzle with lavish spaces. Far right: the atrium on Carnival's *Elation* combines shopping and dining. Right, the theater on the Royal Caribbean's *Enchantment of the Seas*, awash in excess

ANDY NEWMAN—CCL

about 100,000 tons and carries a crew of more than 5,000. The superliners offer everything from towering atriums to nightclubs to conference centers, gymnasiums and rock-climbing walls designed to keep passengers from ever having to contemplate the ocean. In their quest for synthetic perfection, the cruise lines have even created their own ports of call. At Coco Cay, Royal Caribbean's 140-acre island, aquamarine waters lap at the dazzling white sand beach, while snorkelers explore a 16th century sailing ship and a small plane that the company submerged to give divers a sense of adventure. Such elaborate ploys lure young travelers: the average age of Royal Caribbean customers has dropped to the low 40s from the 60s and 70s not so many years ago.

Just over the horizon: Knut Kloster Jr., the former chairman of the Norwegian Cruise and Royal Viking lines, plans to launch a ship that will be a permanent home for its passengers. The globe-trotting vessel, called *World of ResidenSea*, will have 286 condominiums, some of which will sell for as much as $6.6 million. And for those who can't get enough *Titanic*, a U.S.-Swiss partnership plans to build a $500 million replica that will take its maiden voyage on the 90th anniversary of the *Titanic's*, in 2002. Two thousand passengers may enjoy the same kind of Gilded Age service as the original—and with enough lifeboats for everyone. ∎

FANTASYLAND AT SEA: The first Disney ship, *Magic*, launched late, but its bookings were strong

TRAVELING ON
Citicorp's John Reed
and Travelers' Sanford
Weill, right

THE MATCH GAME

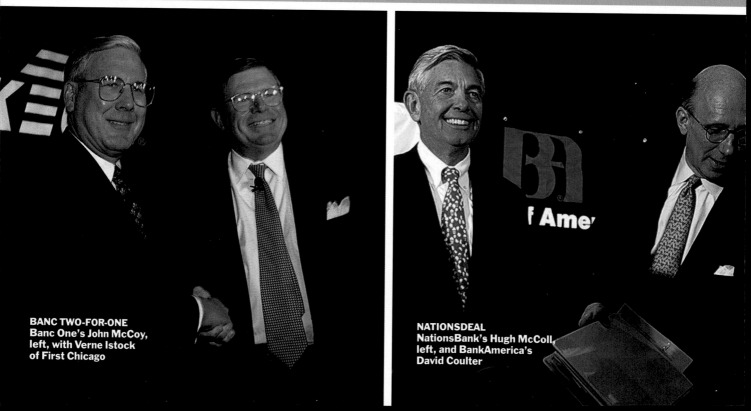

BANC TWO-FOR-ONE
Banc One's John McCoy,
left, with Verne Istock
of First Chicago

NATIONSDEAL
NationsBank's Hugh McColl,
left, and BankAmerica's
David Coulter

ONE WAY OR ANOTHER, THE UNPRECEDENTED MERGER wave sweeping across America has touched your life. The local bank is long gone. You've been reunited with the same dreadful HMO you thought you had ditched a few years back. Your mutual-fund statement has a new logo. Off-putting. Irritating. Confusing. Or, if you've been merged out of a job, debilitating.

But before we hang all the dealmakers, consider the flip side. In any business, size can bring good things—clout, easier access to capital, lower costs—that allow a company to keep prices down, provide better service, win business and keep profits up. That's the favored recipe for large-scale corporate survival in the global, capitalist '90s and a prime driver of the record $919 billion in mergers in 1997.

In 1998 the deals got even bigger. Corporate marriages realigned entire industries, from airlines to banking to oil. One result will be more lost jobs as well as other dislocations and inconveniences for employees. But a clear benefit of the merger trend is that it goes hand in hand with companies' unrelenting focus on keeping costs and prices down. From computers to cars to commissions on stock trades to the rate on your mortgage, the 1990s have been a buyer's market. In no small part that disinflationary environment derives from the robust activity of dealmakers in mixing and matching to get the most out of every asset.

Still, the onslaught of big deals—in a year when Microsoft found itself in a federal antitrust suit—raised concerns about companies' generally getting too big and powerful.

AIRLINES

	NORTHWEST	CONTINENTAL
CEO	John Dashburg	Gordon Bethune
1997 Revenues	$10.2 billion	$7.2 billion
The deal	An "alliance." The two will operate with no name change; Northwest will control a majority share of Continental voting stock	
Big idea	Merging route neworks to capture passengers who would otherwise have changed to another airline while making a connection	

BIGGER BANKS Only a week after the Travelers Group–Citicorp deal, the banking industry was rocked by its two biggest deals ever. Noted fiduciary raptor Hugh McColl Jr. announced a plan to merge his Charlotte, N.C.–based NationsBank with California-based BankAmerica to create a golden Godzilla with deposits of $346 billion. Through more than 50 acquisitions, McColl, a fiery former Marine, has turned NationsBank into the third largest U.S. lender, with branches in 16 states and $316 billion in assets. On the same day, Banc One chairman John B. McCoy announced plans to merge his $116 billion bank with the much merged $115 billion First Chicago NBD Corp. The pace of bank mergers is likely to accelerate as McColl and his rivals battle for market share.

From the car you drive to the gas you put in its tank to the bank $ where you get the cash to pay for it—the big mergers of 1998 are shaking up your life

The endgame of relentless merger activity, after all, is a few companies in each industry owning their markets and having unfettered opportunity to do and charge whatever they like. The good news: the history of megamergers is that they tend not to work as planned. Big firms can't react to small opportunities, so new businesses pop up to fill the void. Some inevitably grow enough to challenge the giants. So, for better or for worse, here is a review of some of the year's largest corporate nuptials:

BIGGER FINANCIAL GROUPS In April financial-services giants Travelers Group and Citicorp agreed to a stock swap worth some $76 billion. The deal created the world's biggest company, to be called Citigroup, with $700 billion in assets and a market value of nearly $160 billion. It joined under one name some 100 million customers in 100 countries, 162,600 employees and 3,200 offices. The new company promised to offer every conceivable financial service for individuals and corporations. Under one umbrella you could get money to buy a house; trade stocks, bonds or foreign exchange; insure your life or find export financing. Heck, you could even open a checking account.

BIGGER AUTOMAKERS After a rapid courtship, replete with the secret rendezvous (London, Frankfurt) and code name (Operation Gamma) that lovers and business executives are wont to employ, Juergen Schrempp, 53, chairman of doughty Daimler-Benz, pledged his troth to Chrysler chief Robert Eaton, 58. The result was announced in May: the largest industrial mar-

FINANCIAL SERVICES

	TRAVELERS	CITICORP
CEO	Sanford Weill	John Reed
1997 Revenues	$37.6 billion	$34.7 billion
New name	Citigroup	
The deal	A merger, cemented by a $76 billion stock swap	
Big idea	Create a Procter & Gamble of financial services and insurance, waging warfare in a hot new global industry—"bancassurance"	

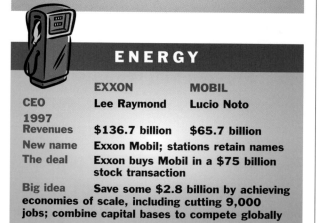

BANKS

	NATIONSBANK	BANKAMERICA
CEO	Hugh McColl Jr.	David A. Coulter
1997 Revenues	$21.6 billion	$23.6 billion
New name	BankAmerica	
The deal	Stock swap valued at $60 billion	
Big idea	Bigger is better: McColl wants to be the nation's banker; he's spread like kudzu from North Carolina across the country but was missing a West Coast base. Now he's got one	

AUTOMOBILES

	CHRYSLER	DAIMLER-BENZ
CEO	Robert Eaton	Juergen Schrempp
1997 Revenues	$58.6 billion	$73.4 billion
New name	DaimlerChrysler	
The deal	$38.3 billion stock swap	
Big idea	Cut costs and share talent. Chrysler can help Mercedes get into the luxury-minivan market in Europe; Mercedes can help Chrysler get into the luxury-sedan market in the U.S.	

TELECOMS

	AT&T	TCI
CEO	C.M. Armstrong	John Malone
1997 Revenues	$51.3 billion	$7.6 billion
New name	AT&T	
The deal	AT&T acquires TCI in $37.3 billion stock swap	
Big idea	AT&T can use TCI's extensive cable network to offer new digital technologies to consumers—and to enter local telephone markets	

ENERGY

	EXXON	MOBIL
CEO	Lee Raymond	Lucio Noto
1997 Revenues	$136.7 billion	$65.7 billion
New name	Exxon Mobil; stations retain names	
The deal	Exxon buys Mobil in a $75 billion stock transaction	
Big idea	Save some $2.8 billion by achieving economies of scale, including cutting 9,000 jobs; combine capital bases to compete globally	

riage in history, taking what had been the world's No. 6 car company, Chrysler, and stuffing it right in the trunk of erstwhile No. 15 Daimler-Benz. In one stroke, the two had created the planet's fifth biggest auto concern, valued at $40 billion. It will generate $130 billion in sales and employ more than 400,000 people. The merger marked the triumph of the global economy and the end of car companies as national symbols of industrial might.

BIGGER AIRLINES After steadily losing altitude, not to mention money—$13 billion between 1990 and 1994—the airline industry posted record profits in 1997. In the pilot's seat: mammoth carriers like American and United, which stitched together quilts of global partnerships that threatened smaller carriers. That encouraged an alliance between Northwest and Continental, announced on Jan. 26. In the unorthodox agreement, Northwest will buy 14% of Continental's common shares—but 51% of the company's voting shares—effectively creating a domestic and international network to compete with the megacarriers. The two partners said they would merge their route networks and frequent-flyer programs but keep separate corporate identities and management teams.

BIGGER TELECOM COMPANIES When C. Michael Armstrong became chairman and chief executive of AT&T in 1997, he inherited what looked to be one of America's last business dinosaurs. Balky Baby Bells were frustrating Ma Bell's costly drive into the $110 billion local-service market; meanwhile, the largest U.S. telephone company (1997 revenues: $51.3 billion) was stuck on the sidelines, while upstarts such as WorldCom and MCI were teaming to deliver everything from long-distance service to high-speed Internet access. So in June, Armstrong scooped up TCI, the second largest U.S. cable operator after Time Warner, led by deal-happy visionary John Malone.

The two men see a convergence of TV, telephone and computer services that will allow customers to access all three separately or at once, simply by aiming and clicking a handheld device at a TV set. But the real sweet spot of the TCI deal for Armstrong is that it may allow AT&T to outflank the Baby Bells and provide local-calling services.

One man determined not to be outflanked: Ivan Seidenberg, 51, the hard-charging CEO of Bell Atlantic. Once a technician who spliced phone wires, he now excels at splicing companies—witness his 1996 merger with NYNEX. In July he proposed his most spectacular linkup yet: a plan to merge $70 billion Bell Atlantic (which serves roughly 40 million customers in 13 states) with GTE, a $52 billion company with some 21 million widely scattered customers.

BIGGER OIL COMPANIES The match-game year was topped off late on December 1 with—what else?—the biggest merger in history. Exxon (the nation's largest energy company) announced it would acquire Mobil (the nation's second largest energy company) in a deal valued at $75 billion. The merger united two former components of John D. Rockefeller's Standard Oil trust, which was busted apart in 1911 by the Department of Justice in one of America's first great antitrust suits. The century was ending where it started, with the big guys getting bigger. Who says history doesn't have a sense of humor? ■

BOWIE: Once again, he's a trend setter

Own a Piece of the Rock

Pop star David Bowie performed for a sellout crowd in 1997 on Wall Street and ended up pocketing $55 million; in 1998 dozens of impressed entertainers sought to play the same venue. The show is a financial maneuver that, if bankers get their way, will explode in popularity in the next year or two. By issuing bonds that pledge future royalties on assets like record sales and publishing fees, celebrities can get their money up front. The investors collect the royalties as interest and principal payments over, typically, 10 to 20 years. David Pullman, the banker behind the "Bowie bonds," closed three more celebrity-bond deals in July.

Meet the Beetles—Again

From its groovy arched roof and fenders to its funky blue speedometer to its built-in bud vase on the dash, Volkswagen's new Beetle—introduced in

SO DAMN CUTE:
Good vibes—starting
at $15,200

January—is a motorized monument to Flower Power nostalgia. The only thing missing is a Day-Glo paint job and a roach clip in the ashtray. VW brought the Beetle into the '90s by adding an array of modern amenities such as an adjustable steering column, a six-speaker stereo system, an air filter for the passengers and air bags front and side. The price tag—starting at $15,200—was also up-to-date. VW needed a boost: in 1997 it sold only a third of the metal it had moved in its mid-1960s heyday. By December, an impressive 48,326 Bugs had been sold.

Say It Ain't So, Isaac!

Since his winning debut collection in 1988, Isaac Mizrahi had been considered the heir to the American sportswear throne shared by Calvin Klein, Donna Karan and Ralph Lauren. His wit and

MIZRAHI: Far from a model businessman

verbal agility earned him a reputation as the Oscar Wilde of Seventh Avenue. But as it turns out, a wry spirit and big personality are not enough to move $1,400 mink-trimmed skirts off store racks. In the fall Mizrahi startled the rag trade when he announced he was shutting down his business. The final blow came when Chanel Inc., which had bankrolled the designer since 1992, decided to dissolve its partnership with him after three years of financial losses. Next stop: an acting career. ■

SNAPSHOT

Tina Brown

Talk of the Town

Tina Brown stopped the media world dead in its tracks in July when she announced that she would quit as editor of the *New Yorker,* one of the most prestigious jobs in magazines, to lead a promising but also somewhat vague-sounding new media enterprise. While many disparaged the 44-year-old Briton's trend-fixated *New Yorker,* she is indisputably a great buzz generator, author of the notion that a magazine must be talked about and not just read.

Bankrolling the project was Harvey Weinstein, co-chairman of Miramax Films, whose gift for salesmanship has helped generate 110 Academy Award nominations and 30 Oscars for his company's generally ambitious movies (*The Piano, Pulp Fiction, Good Will Hunting*). The other partner was *Vogue* publisher Ron Galotti, once Brown's colleague as publisher of *Vanity Fair.* Their goal: synergy, baby! They aim to create television shows, books and a new general-interest magazine (possible title: *Talk*) that will foster ideas for films that they hope to produce.

▶ **What a year! Apple went back to the future with its nifty new iMac, Microsoft went to court with trust-busting feds, online commerce went on a roll and Netscape went to AOL for keeps. To top it off, while profits kept bulking up, the gizmos behind them kept slimming down**

MACHINE OF THE YEAR
Apple's snazzy new iMac turned heads, turned the company around—and won TIME DIGITAL's nod as the year's best hardware

John Wilkes for TIME

Stalking the Giant:

The Justice Department launches an antitrust suit against America's largest

The U.S. v. Microsoft

software company, headed by America's wealthiest entrepreneur, Bill Gates

RELYING ON NUANCED READINGS OF COMPLEX STATUTES as well as analogies to dusty cases about oil refineries and railroad gauges, antitrust is one of the most labyrinthine fields of the law. But the Justice Department simplified matters on Oct. 19, the first day of its sweeping antitrust suit against Microsoft: it dispensed with the case law and put Bill Gates front and center. Disembodied, larger than life, the company's chief executive officer hovered on a 10-ft.-tall video monitor over Judge Thomas Penfield Jackson's courtroom as government lawyer David Boies argued in his opening statement that the fidgety, spectral man-in-the-monitor was coolly dissembling about his plans to dominate the world technology market.

U.S. v. Microsoft was supposed to be an epic ideological showdown, perhaps the greatest since the government ordered the breakup of John D. Rockefeller's Standard Oil trust in 1911. The Department of Justice's antitrust chief, Joel Klein, would argue the liberal view that government must intervene when a monopolist abuses its position of dominance in the market. Microsoft would make the libertarian case that markets work best when they work freely.

Yet as the trial developed, the real battle seemed to be between two contrasting views of Gates. Is he the brilliant innovator who has brought the wonders of the information age to millions of satisfied customers? Or is he the rapacious capitalist leveraging his software monopoly to crush competitors? How the courts viewed the world's richest man (his net worth in 1998 moved upwards of $50 billion) rather than what antitrust ideology they adopted, would probably determine the outcome of what could be a landmark case.

The focus of the suit was two dueling World Wide Web browsers: Microsoft's surging Explorer vs. Netscape's increasingly vulnerable Navigator, whose market share had slipped from a near monopoly to around 55%—and continued to fall. The Justice filing was a long, closely reasoned and fairly persuasive argument that Microsoft engaged in corporate monopolist no-nos—intimidation, exclusionary dealmaking, old-fashioned dumping and so on—in its zeal to supplant Navigator.

In Klein's version, the story went something like this: in mid-1995, with Navigator on fire and Microsoft's fledg-

> The trial presented two contrasting versions of Gates. Is he a brilliant innovator who pioneered the digital revolution, or a rapacious capitalist leveraging his monopoly to overwhelm all rivals?

ling browser effort looking like toast, Microsoft executives visited Netscape's lovely office park in Mountain View, Calif., and, like conquistadores carving up the New World, offered to split this emerging market down what they tried to define as the middle. (Microsoft disputed Justice's account of the meeting.) We'll build the browsers for the upcoming Windows 95, Justice claimed Microsoft suggested; you supply them for Windows 3.1 and everything else. Well, clearly once Win 95 got rolling, there wasn't going to be much of an "everything else" left to supply; Netscape declined to settle for Gates' table scraps.

At which point, Klein claimed, Microsoft proceeded to do everything it could think of to sweep its rival into the dustbin of Internet history. The strategy involved offering allied companies something they couldn't get anywhere other than bundled with Windows and extracting total fealty to Explorer in return.

Computer makers had to feature Explorer on their PC desktops on pain of losing their Windows licenses. Internet-service providers and websites clamoring for tasty placement on Windows' opening screens got it—as long as they marketed their services with the Explorer browser alone. The result, said Klein: Netscape was unfairly excluded from competing on the PC platform, and computer makers were unable to offer their customers software titles and desktop designs other than those Microsoft had expressly approved. And consumers were deprived of choice.

In his opening statement, Boies tried to give the court a glimpse of the darker Gates. At Boies' signal, Gates appeared on the courtroom video monitors flatly denying the government's crucial charge that Microsoft tried to buy off Netscape. "Somebody asked if it made sense investing in Netscape, and I said it didn't make any sense," Gates maintained, in a clip from his August 1998 deposition. But a moment later, the video monitors were displaying a seemingly contradictory 1995 e-mail, in which Gates had written of Netscape, "We could give them money as part of the deal, buy a piece of them or something."

Microsoft's spin team peddled the view that Boies' opening statement was based on "snippets that were not in any reliable context." But court watchers were already

TALKING HEAD: Justice's lawyers contrasted Gates' videotaped testimony with conflicting e-mail from the Microsoft boss

Netscape's Marc Andreessen on a meeting with Gates: "It was like a visit from Don Corleone. I expected to find a bloody computer monitor in my bed the next day."

arguing whether Gates' statements were actually perjurious or merely Clintonesque. Could the U.S. government really be suggesting that Gates is evil incarnate? On Day 2 of the trial, lead Microsoft lawyer John Warden accused Boies of trying to "demonize Bill Gates" and of casting Microsoft as "the great Satan."

The first and only witness during the first week was Netscape CEO James Barksdale. Recalling the key 1995 encounter with Microsoft, he said, "I have never been in a meeting in my 33-year business career in which a competitor had so blatantly implied that we should either stop competing with it or the competitor would kill us." Barksdale quoted his partner, Marc Andreessen, on the meeting: "It was like a visit from Don Corleone. I expected to find a bloody computer monitor in my bed the next morning."

Justice Department lawyers had good tactical reasons for keeping Gates' own words and deeds at the heart of their case. Justice began its antitrust campaign against Microsoft with a straightforward claim that the company was guilty of improperly "bundling" its Internet Explorer browser into its popular Windows software. Judge Jackson

bought the argument, but this view was shot down in June by the D.C. Circuit Court of Appeals—a reversal that Microsoft eagerly embraced as decisive.

Justice decided on a more wide-ranging argument: that there is a pervasive pattern of Microsoft's using its monopoly on PC operating software—the ubiquitous Windows system—to coerce other companies to do its bidding. Microsoft, Justice argued, engaged in a pattern of "predatory acts" involving other key technology players, including America Online and Compaq, in its crusade to crush Netscape.

In the case of America Online, the government said, Microsoft refused to put AOL's icon on the Windows desktop unless AOL dumped Netscape in favor of Internet Explorer. In the case of

KLEIN: DOJ's top trustbuster

Compaq, the government said, Microsoft threatened to terminate the company's license for Windows after it dropped Explorer in favor of Navigator.

In the third week of the trial, Boies showed two hours of Gates' videotaped deposition. The excerpts, culled from about 20 hours in all, made Gates look like the worst CEO in America—detached, unfocused, ignorant of basic business terminology, even goofy in his personal tics. Was this the face that launched a thousand chips? The man whose intelligence and drive are the stuff of legend? It just didn't compute. If Boies was aiming to cast doubt on Gates' credibility, he seemed to have hit the mark.

But late in November a shocker altered the tenor of the case and heartened Microsoft: AOL, the giant online portal, said it would acquire Netscape. Shortly afterwards, South Carolina—one of the 20 states backing the government's antitrust suit—switched sides; the state's attorney general, Charlie Condon, said the proposed merger proved that Microsoft does not monopolize the online world.

Still, as executives from Intel, Apple and other high-tech leaders continued to parade into the court with tales of being bullied, bloodied and browbeaten by Microsoft, even onetime skeptics among the experts following the case were starting to ask, What if the government actually wins this thing? The Justice Department had not tipped its hand about what remedy it might seek. But several ideas had emerged about how the giant could be tamed. In one scenario, Judge Jackson would personally monitor Microsoft's behavior in the future, much as Judge Harold Greene oversaw AT&T for more than a decade after the breakup of the phone company. In another, the court could supervise the sharing of Microsoft's most basic codes and thereby ensure a level playing field for all programmers who want to write for Windows.

In a third scenario, the court could force Microsoft to add a "commercially reasonable" charge when it bundles features like Internet Explorer with Windows. If consumers had to pay extra for items like Explorer—and less when it was absent—rival companies would have a more competitive market for their own applications software.

The most extreme remedy would be to bust up Microsoft, just as AT&T was forced to spin off its regional divisions as Baby Bells, and Standard Oil was chopped into Mobil, Exxon and other companies. Microsoft could be split in two: one company to make operating systems like Windows, another to make applications like Word, the word-processing program. Alternatively, the court might decide to split the company into a handful of "Baby Bills" that would compete against one another with equal access to Windows—none would have monopoly power.

In that case, Microsoft might simply decide to pack up and leave the country. One of the more intriguing scenarios being discussed in high-tech circles was that if the courts did get tough, Microsoft could always move its Redmond, Wash., headquarters 100 miles north to Canada., which has less stringent antitrust laws than the U.S. Or Gates could buy a Caribbean island and take Microsoft offshore. On the Isle of Gates, every computer would run Windows, and there would be no such thing as antitrust law. ∎

Steve's on the Case

Online giant AOL buys Netscape—and takes on Microsoft

Steve Case had plenty to be thankful for at Thanksgiving. The CEO of America Online sat down to turkey with his family just two days after announcing a deal to devour Netscape Communications nearly whole (he carved off a piece for his friend Scott McNealy, CEO of Sun Microsystems). In exchange for $4.2 billion, roughly 10% of its high-flying (if arguably inflated) stock, AOL took charge of Netscape. The company whose trailblazing browser jump-started the World Wide Web back in 1994 was supposed to become the fastest hot

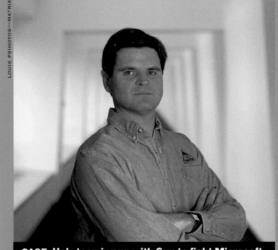

CASE: He's teaming up with Sun to fight Microsoft

rod on the Infobahn. Instead, Bill Gates side-swiped it into a ditch and left America Online to strip the wreck for parts: a browser, a website and a treasure chest of software.

Sun chief McNealy has been flacking his "The network is the computer" vision for years, arguing that his Web-focused Java language is the platform on which to build a new generation of cheap, single-purpose network appliances, from TV set-top boxes to cell phones, that could finally break Microsoft's stranglehold on the digital universe.

By marrying Netscape and taking Sun as a mistress, Case gets a battalion of geek Netscape programmers and Sun's 7,000-strong sales force to sell the e-commerce software they are building. With this deal, the epic confrontation between Netscape and Microsoft is officially over, but an epic confrontation between AOL, Sun and Microsoft has begun. ∎

Mouse Marketing

Yahoo! Jerry Yang and David Filo click with an Internet portal that's (get ready) downright disintermediationary

JERRY YANG MAKES A HALFHEARTED EFFORT TO TIDY UP his cubicle for a visitor. "I know we're not normal," he says with a boyish grin. It's not much of an office by mogul standards: just a nondescript desk, a couple of cheap plastic milk crates bulging with papers, an old futon. Magazines are piled in a corner, and a window offers a distinctly declassé view of the parking lot.

Of course, by the standards of David Filo, 32, Yahoo's other co-founder, 29-year-old Jerry's digs are West Coast

Donald Trump. Filo's office is not exactly your father's executive suite. You could think of it as a Goodwill collection truck of a workspace, with dirty socks and T shirts jumbled in with books, software and other debris. But there's something even more mind-bending to be found on his desk. His office computer is a poky clone that runs on an outdated Pentium 120 chip. The chief technologist of the Internet's No. 1 website doesn't use a top-of-the-line machine? Filo shrugs: "Upgrading is a pain."

Could this be the face of 21st century capitalism? You'd better believe it. Two years ago, conventional wisdom still derided the World Wide Web as an amusing toy with little practical application. No more. With striking speed, the business that Yahoo (or, as the company formally calls itself, Yahoo!) pioneered has been growing into nothing less than a new economic order, a Net Economy! whose exclamation point came in July, when Yahoo stock, climbing all year,

what Bill Gates called it as far back as 1990. Then cyber-commerce was an unimaginably seductive vision. Now it has become a lucrative reality for a select few pioneers. Compare.Net, for instance, has grown from four employees to nearly 40 in less than two years, and its revenue growth is a stunning 25%—every month.

But the real promise of all this change is that it will enrich all of us, not just a bunch of kids in Silicon Valley. With online price comparisons, automatic grocery shopping and the ability to get whatever we want whenever we want

Why does the chief technology officer of Yahoo use a clunky computer that is years out of date? Billionaire David Filo just shrugs: "Upgrading is a pain."

split 2-for-1. And it kept surging, closing 1998 at 237, making billionaires of two young men who 30 years ago would just be starting their climb up the organization ladder.

The Net industry that Yang and Filo are building doesn't exist merely in the 115 million Web-page views that Yahoo serves up to hungry surfers every day. It exists in the thousands—even tens of thousands—of sites that together with Yahoo are remaking the face of global commerce. Looking for that hard-to-find anthropology book? Amazon.com is a good bet. Yearn to order groceries and have them delivered without leaving home? Peapod.com can help, and it even lets you specify how ripe you like your bananas. How about if you want to know the difference between two brands of stereo receivers? Try Compare.Net, which offers a free online buyer's guide that allows users to compare features on more than 10,000 products.

And that's the pitch for this new electronic world: faster, cheaper, better. "Information at your fingertips" is

it, 21st century Americans will face a radical reshaping of the consumer culture we've been building since the 1950s. Think, for a second, about the revolution that shopping malls created in the 1970s and '80s. They defined not only how we bought stuff but also how we spent our time. The malls themselves became essential parts of a new suburban design, where castles of consumption shaped town layouts in the same way the Colosseum shaped Rome.

At its heart, cybercommerce isn't just about building businesses either. It is also, explains Jerry Yang, about building an entire new culture of independence, convenience and speed. "The new economy," says Joe Carter, managing partner at Andersen Consulting, "could rapidly overtake the existing economy as we know it."

Not convinced? Talk to the folks at 230-year-old Encyclopaedia Britannica, which two years ago dismissed its entire home sales force in North America after the arrival of the Internet at $8.50 a month made the idea of owning

TIME DIAGRAM BY JOE LERTOLA

WHO
Profile of online shoppers in the U.S.

Median age	33
Average household income	$59,000
Single	59%
Married	41%
Children under 18 at home	34%
College degree	57%
Professional	30%

Source: Jupiter Communications

HOW MANY
Estimated number of online shoppers in millions

'95	'96	'97	'98	'99	'00	'01	'02
3	6	10	16	23	33	45	61

Source: Jupiter Communications

HOW MUCH
Estimated total online shopping revenues in billions

'96	'97	'98	'99	'00	'01	'02
$.7	$2	$6	$11	$17	$27	$41

Source: Jupiter Communications

PAPER, PLASTIC—OR MODEM? Beyond the hype, the statistics on e-commerce prove it is booming

BOOKIN'!

While the big guys slumbered, an online bookseller soared

T o get a snapshot of the e-economy, 1998, you could do worse than Jeff Bezos, the founder of bookseller Amazon.com. As his stock price rises and falls with typical volatility, he stalks through his shuttered Seattle office, on a phone call, staring at his wristwatch, pacing, talking, thinking, plotting, scheming, then glancing at his watch again. Like the Net economy, Bezos is all about motion.

His conversion to the Web came in 1995, when he read a report that projected annual Web growth at 2,300%. First he checked that he'd read the figure correctly. Then he quit his job as a hedge-fund manager in New York City, packed his bags and drove out to Seattle. Or rather, his wife drove; Bezos was busy tapping out a business plan on his laptop.

The idea behind the company is devilishly simple: type in a book's title, the author's name or even just a general subject, and the site will present you with a list of every matching book in its database. Choose your title, type in your address and credit-card number, and service reps at Amazon.com's Seattle warehouse will find your book and mail it to you, usually within one or two days, and often at a hefty discount. Three years after its launch, the company has 4.5 million worldwide customers, and its sales through the first three quarters of 1998 were more than $350 million.

None of this, you can imagine, made bookstore chains very happy. But they held back on the Net. For years the buzz in the book industry was all about building new megastores, where shoppers could sip mochaccinos and chew over big ideas while they sat on comfortable couches. But in the two years that Barnes & Noble and Borders were focusing on what kinds of vanilla-sugar cubes to put in their coffee bars, Bezos was building an empire.

Now B&N under president Leonard Riggio is playing catch-up, forging close ties with the gigantic online service America Online and challengng Amazon.com over its use of the tag line "Earth's Biggest Bookstore." In November B&N announced it would spend $600 million to acquire Ingram Book Group, a book distributor that is Amazon.com's biggest supplier. The battle of the e-booksellers was shaping up as one for the ... well, you know. ∎

PAUL SOUDERS—GAMMA LIAISON

BEZOS: Zero to $350+ million in three years

a $1,250, 32-volume set of books seem less appealing. Kids, everyone knew, were just as happy to get their information online. In fact, they preferred it.

The geeks have usurped an old financial term, disintermediation, and given it a new meaning to describe what happened to Britannica. To them it means the removal of middlemen, the intermediaries who smooth the operation of any economy—folks like travel agents, stockbrokers, car dealers and traveling salesmen. These people have been the grease of a consumer economy, the folks who help you do things more efficiently. But the Net is creating a new, self-service economy. Gates calls it "frictionless capitalism."

It's working. Dell, which sells $5 million worth of computers a day on its website, claims that the efficiencies of Web-based sales give it a 6% profit advantage over its competitors. Eddie Bauer, the outdoor-clothing retailer, has an online operation that has been profitable since 1997 and is growing 300% to 500% a year.

Customers have begun to think differently as well. Charles Hintz, a retired psychiatrist from Des Moines, Iowa, has found a kind of salvation in the Net's limitless ease and bounty. Hintz, a 68-year-old quadriplegic, was paralyzed in a fall 12 years ago, but for the past three years he has been doing the birthday and holiday shopping for his large family on the computer, which he operates by poking the keyboard with a stick he holds in his mouth. He buys clothes from Lands' End online, CDs from CDnow and books from Amazon.com. "It makes me feel independent," he explains.

The lure of megasites like Yahoo is that in an environment like the Net there are very few locations that attract a mass audience of the sort that advertisers can get through, say, the Super Bowl. As a result, search and commerce sites like Yahoo and chief rival Excite have become gateways (the Net buzz word is portals) to the rest of the electronic universe. And owning a portal is a lot like owning a toll bridge. Yahoo charges about 4¢ for every ad it serves up on its pages every day. And those prices will rise as Yahoo develops technology that lets it more closely match advertisers with consumers who are looking, finding and buying.

That notion of personalized content and advertising has been a kind of Internet holy grail for years. Now, finally, the Web is delivering. Today it's possible to get everything from custom newspapers to electronic newsletters that alert you to sales of items you've always craved. Futurists used to call these services *The Daily Me*, a play on the idea of daily newspapers. But customized websites are delivering something more like *The Instant Me*: real-time collections of information you want, whenever you want it. That leaves only one question: How to pay for all this online bounty? We hope you've bought some Yahoo stock. ∎

In Electronics, Small Wonders

The Next Big Thing in consumer electronics isn't big at all. It's laptop computers that are skinnier than a *Vogue* model—or even *Vogue*. It's cell phones that fit back pockets better than a wallet, and stereo speakers as flat as matzo. The cutting edge continues to get sharper. The prosperous TV set—whose middle-age spread has resisted slimming despite 50 years of technological breakthroughs—has finally gone on a diet. Local computer stores, not to be out-thinned, are at long last selling decent-size monitors that don't take up half your den or break your back when you try to get them there. Why now? It's a combination of technology (we can make it thinner) and consumer taste (we want it thinner). Developers have labored for years to mass-produce slender, affordable replacements for TV sets and monitors. In 1995 these were prototypes; now they're products. In the fall Philips Electronics introduced its 42-in. FlatTV, a 4½-in.-thick slab of state-of-the-art plasma-display technology some 4 ft. across and 2½ ft. tall. Other flat screens use liquid crystals or, thanks to Cambridge Display Technologies, special plastics that may soon make TV wristwatches not only a reality— but a reality you can afford.

PAUL GUBA FOR TIME

ANOREXIC? ViewSonic's VP0150 computer monitor is only 3 in. thick

Love That Linus!

Pale, fleshy groupies surround him on all sides, adoration in their eyes. Some are overwhelmed, speechless in his presence. Some ask for his autograph; some just want to thank him for all that he's done for them. Some call him a god and want to be among his disciples, helping spread the word. No, he's not the Dalai Lama or Mark

OLIVIER LAUDE FOR TIME

Linus Torvalds

McGwire. This god is a geek who wears socks with his sandals. His name is Linus Torvalds. He's 28 years old, and his religion is called Linux, after an operating system based on the Unix format that he wrote for kicks in 1991, while studying at the University of Helsinki, and then loosed— for free—upon the world.

In the seven years since, Torvalds' little program became the center of gravity of a large, even fanatical movement. Programmers love Linux (rhymes with cynics) because it is small, fast and free—and lets them participate in building a library of underground software. Silicon Valley loves Linux because it offers an alternative to Sun, Apple and, especially, Microsoft. In 1998 Intel, Netscape and some of the Valley's richest venture capitalists invested in Linux operations.

TAKA FOR TIME

3COM'S PALM III: It commands 41% of the handheld market

A Chip off the Old Palm

Computer wars used to center on the desktop. Now the battleground not only fits in the palm of your hand, it *is* the palm of your hand. When Palm Computing first introduced its tiny Pilot in 1996, the gizmo hit the jackpot. At $299, the device was cheap (for a computer), elegant—and as easy to use as a calendar. In March Palm introduced a third-generation device, the Palm III ($369), into a marketplace crowded with competitors. Among them: Microsoft, which launched a new version of its condensed Windows CE operating system for devices it called Palm PCs. Palm's angry parent company, 3Com, sued Microsoft in Europe for trademark infringement.

Apple to Earth: We're Back!

Apple's snazzy new iMac computer was an instant hit with the public. But was it good enough to save the company? The stakes were that high for Apple, and no one knew better than Apple co-founder Steve Jobs, who ousted CEO Gil Amelio to take charge of the firm in July. "This [machine] is Apple's future," said Jobs. That Apple even had a future was debatable in 1997. Its market share had plummeted to around 3%, even die-hard Mac fans were defecting to Windows, and employee attrition was heading toward 33%. But Apple roared back, ending its fiscal year in September with a profit of $106 million in the last quarter; in 1997 the company lost $161 million in that quarter. ■

MARK RICHARDS—CONTACT FOR TIME

JOBS: At Apple's core

LICENSE TO KILL?
This truck was used in the murder by dragging of James Byrd Jr., a black resident of Jasper County, East Texas

Americans had much to celebrate in 1998: both crime rates and teen pregnancies were down. But now and then sparks of bigotry flared: a black man was dragged to death in Texas; a gay man was murdered in Wyoming ... and in the schools, kids kept killing kids

94 ★ TEXAS
02585274U

454

How can we stop—or even fathom—an epidemic of schoolkids killing schoolkids?

ROSES AND LILIES DROOPED FROM THE CHAIN-LINK fence outside Thurston High School, and a makeshift plywood cross jutted from the ground nearby. Beneath it, a hand-printed sign read WILL WE EVER LEARN? But as the timber town of Springfield, Ore. (pop. 51,000), grieved in May, the lessons were far from obvious.

Add Springfield to the atlas of American juvenile violence. The map is dotted with names now searingly familiar: Pearl, Miss., where Luke Woodham, 16, killed his mother and fatally shot two classmates with a rifle in October 1997; West Paducah, Ky., where Michael Carneal, 14, killed three girls with a .22 semiautomatic Ruger in December 1997; Jonesboro, Ark., where Drew Golden, 11, and Mitchell Johnson, 13, ambushed their schoolmates, killing five with handguns and rifles in March 1998.

And now Springfield, where, at the Lane County courthouse, Kipland Phillip Kinkel, 15, the son of two schoolteachers, sat slumped in his chair, his face blank. The day before, police said, Kinkel had carried a semiautomatic rifle and two pistols into his high school cafeteria, then discharged 51 rounds of ammunition, fatally injuring two students and wounding 18 others. When deputies drove to his family home, they found his parents shot to death. After his arrest, a handcuffed Kinkel managed to get at a knife taped to his leg and lunge at an officer. He was finally subdued with pepper spray.

In this lush valley 110 miles south of Portland, all the grownups could talk about was what nurturing parents Faith and Bill Kinkel had been. All the kids could talk about was how "Kip" Kinkel liked to torture animals, collect guns, build small pipe bombs and joke about killing people.

There were startling similarities with the previous cases: Woodham in Pearl tortured animals too and, like Kinkel, went through a "Goth" phase, dressing in black and voicing grim imaginings; Kinkel had a fascination with guns to match that of the Jonesboro boys, Golden and Johnson; like Carneal in West Paducah, he seemed possessed of a death wish. When he was finally in custody, Kinkel pleaded with his captors, "Just shoot me."

▶ **The warning signs: a love of guns, torturing animals, violent talk, a death wish**

Once again the deadly drama featured a troubled youth and a community in which obtaining guns is easy. Once again a high school became the stage, with classmates the unwitting cast. Once again there was a chilling disconnect, with adolescents shrugging off threats of violence as idle chatter and harried school administrators ignoring the warning signs. Once again, Americans wondered why kids were killing kids. Once again, they found no easy answers. ∎

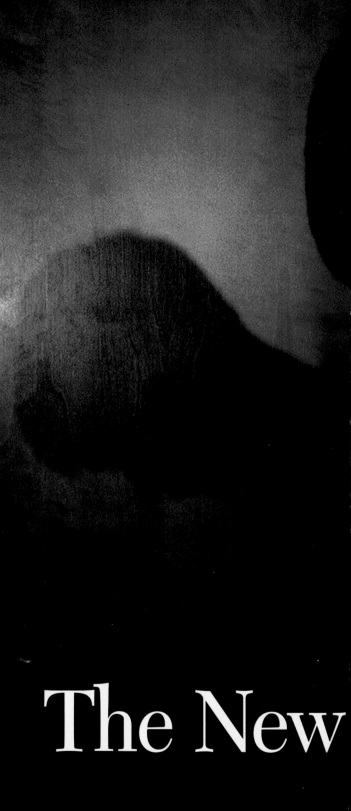

The New

Face of Murder?

KIP KINKEL IN CUSTODY
Oregon police charged the
15-year-old with four killings

The Pope and the Prophet

A historic journey pairs two aging legends in an assault on Cuba's status quo

DEEP INSIDE HAVANA'S *PALACIO DE LA REVOLUCION* IS the spare, book-lined office from which Cuba is ruled. It lies down a corridor lined with columns of rough native marble and ferns from the Sierra Maestra, recalling the mountain redoubt where the revolution was born almost 40 years ago. Few are allowed to penetrate to the heart of the last socialist bastion in the western hemisphere, one of a handful of communist regimes struggling to ride out the 20th century. Here is where an aging Fidel Castro secretly pulls the strings guiding his country—and where he still pursues with unswerving dedication the same sacred mission he pledged himself to decades ago: the preservation of the revolution.

It was in this office that Castro, faced with the crushing failure of his Marxist economy after the collapse of his country's patron, the Soviet Union, decided to pursue an idea that had intrigued him for some time: a visit by Pope John Paul II to Cuba.

The Pope too has his inner sanctum, a tiny private chapel off his sparsely decorated bedroom. It is adorned with a large bronze crucifix and a small icon of the "Black Madonna" of

GET MY POINT? Fidel Castro gesticulates as he welcomes the Pope to Cuba just after the pontiff's landing at the Havana airport in January

Czestochowa, symbol of Polish nationalism. Each morning and evening he privately speaks to God there, as he shapes the mission he too has pursued with relentless single-mindedness for 20 years: Go forth and spread the word.

His is a highly public reign, not limited to words and gestures. Whether preaching from the throne of St. Peter or from some makeshift altar in one of the 116 countries he has visited, John Paul II can have a powerful, concrete impact not only on the conduct of millions of Catholics but also on the unfolding of world events. (Ask Mikhail Gorbachev.) In his moral vigor, he too is a revolutionary force. And for reasons of his own, he accepted Castro's invitation.

Millions around the globe watched with fascination as these two giants of the 20th century collided in January on Castro's little island, and the world according to Marx touched hands with the word of God. A 100-year-old ideology that proposed a collective paradise of social justice and economic equality on earth confronted a 2,000-year-old belief in the eternal power of devotion to the divine and reverence for human dignity.

The men themselves are fitting adversaries. Both are absolute rulers of their realms. Both are traditionalists and conservatives within their faiths, standing firm against revisionist thinking from within. Each is charismatic, charming, larger than life. Even their biographies are curiously alike: Catholic schooling, top students, athletes.

Both are also in that sad twilight of their life when the body begins to betray even an indomitable spirit. Castro's 71 years are etched on his face. Rumors circulate of strokes, Alzheimer's and other infirmities. The Pope, 77, looks even worse. The bounding stride of his early pontificate has been reduced to a shuffle. He takes care to hide the shaking left hand that signals the onset of Parkinson's disease, but he cannot disguise the frozen features and slurred words that at times betray the illness. Yet those close to him say the Pope retains all the mental drive of his early days, and his continuing magnetism is undeniable.

Americans may be forgiven if they don't recall the exact details of the trip: the Pope's journey took place just as the breaking news of the White House sex scandal dominated U.S. media. Here is what they missed: John Paul II traveled the length of the island to conduct four outdoor Masses, attracting a mix of Catholic believers eager for a papal blessing and party faithful curious to see a real, live Pope. Some of the images were startling: a giant turquoise-and-pink Jesus Christ butted up against a black mural of Che Guevara; Fidel Castro's hand gently guiding Pope John Paul II's shuffling steps.

The Pope chided Cuba's lapsed family values harder than its lack of human rights. He came down hard on abortion, divorce, premarital sex—all common practices in Cuba. He openly criticized both the U.S. economic embargo and communist ideology, but in equally muted terms. Cubans often seemed more respectful of the Pope than moved by his words. The Vatican said Castro agreed to "consider" freeing some political prisoners as the Pope asked, but there is little sign yet of tangible concessions to requests for more priests, parochial schools or media access. What impact the Pope has on this aging revolution will be measured mainly in human hearts, where any real challenge to the Cuban system will have to begin. ■

CHRISTOPHER MORRIS—BLACK STAR FOR TIME

Danger! Reporters at Wrok!

A swarm of errors, fabrications and plain old lies give journalism a black eye

RETRACTED STORIES. INVENTED STORIES. PLAGIARIZED stories. All too often, that was the story of American journalism in 1998, as a plague of errors tarnished the nation's newspapers, magazines and TV channels—even while the public squirmed as the opposing sides in the White House sex scandal conducted what TIME called a "war of leaks." Among the unfortunate incidents:

INVENTED STORIES Stephen Glass's editors at the *New Republic* regarded him as a rare talent, able to land the juicy, fly-on-the-wall anecdotes that make for memorable stories. They weren't alone. Glass, 25, was hot, juggling assignments from *Rolling Stone, George, Harper's* and the

to be thinly disguised versions of material in George Carlin's best-selling 1997 book, *Brain Droppings.* Barnicle claimed he'd never read it. But when Boston's WCVB-TV, where he was a contributor, produced a tape of a June 22 segment in which Barnicle held up the book and said it had "a yuk on every page," the paper asked for his resignation. Barnicle refused, and the *Globe* fired him weeks later.

RETRACTED STORIES On June 7 CNN debuted a new program in collaboration with TIME called *TIME NewsStand,* with a story alleging that sarin nerve gas was used by U.S. forces in Laos in a secret operation known as Tailwind, and that U.S. defectors were intentionally killed. TIME ran a

Boston *Globe* columnist Patricia Smith was fired for inventing quotes

Brill's Content slammed both Ken Starr and the press in its first issue

Smith's fellow *Globe* columnist Barnicle was fired for lifting gags

New York *Times* Magazine. But apparently many of his stories were pure fiction. Glass made up not just quotations but people, corporations—even a "National Memorabilia Convention" where vendors hawked an inflatable Monica Lewinsky doll that recited *Leaves of Grass.*

Glass appeared to be a serial fabulist, who concocted story after story and slipped them all past his editors and fact checkers, often buttressing his claims with forged notes and other bogus documents. But when a reporter at the online magazine *Forbes Digital Tool* tried to verify a Glass story on a 15-year-old computer hacker, it turned out that the entire story was fake. The *New Republic* fired him and retracted several of his stories. Editors at other magazines subsequently retracted other stories he had written.

PLAGIARIZED STORIES In June the Boston *Globe* fired popular columnist Patricia Smith for making up 48 different characters in her columns. Only two months later the newspaper fired a second columnist: 25-year veteran Mike Barnicle, a beloved, tough-guy metro writer. A reader had noticed that many of the gags in an Aug. 2 column seemed

companion story in that week's issue, "Did the U.S. Drop Nerve Gas?" under the bylines of CNN producer April Oliver and famed correspondent Peter Arnett.

When the stories provoked strong denials, CNN launched an investigation, overseen by the eminent attorney Floyd Abrams, which found that the allegations were not supported by the evidence. Moreover, Arnett said he had minimal involvement in writing the article, despite his byline credit. Oliver, CNN's producer on the segment, continued to stand by the story, but she was dismissed by the network. TIME managing editor Walter Isaacson wrote a detailed account of the botched story, concluding: "Like CNN, we retract the story and apologize."

Small wonder that perhaps the most anticipated magazine launch of 1998 was *Brill's Content,* under the direction of Stephen Brill, creator of *American Lawyer* magazine and the Court TV cable channel. Brill claimed the magazine would seek to raise the standard of U.S. journalism by aggressively reporting on its virtues and vices. If 1998 was any indication, he wouldn't lack for material. ■

Black. Gay. And Lynched For a Label

Matthew Shepard and James Byrd Jr. came face to face with prejudice— and the brutality of the bigots who murdered them shocked the nation

MARK R. SHUGHART—SYGMA

RON JAPP—BEAUMONT ENTERPRISE-SYGMA

THE VICTIMS: Shepard, left, was killed because he was gay; Byrd, right, died because he was black

Matthew Shepard
1976-1998

Peace

WHEN PEOPLE SAY THE MURDERS OF JAMES BYRD JR. and Matthew Shepard were lynchings, they mean that both men were killed to make a point. When Byrd was 49 years old and Shepard only 21, the world's arguments reached them with deadly force and printed their worst conclusions across them. So Byrd was dragged behind a truck until he was torn limb from limb. And Shepard was beaten, then stretched along a Wyoming fence to die. Both murders were more than ruthless criminal deeds: they were signposts. "When push comes to shove," the signs said, "this is what we have in mind for blacks. This is what we have in mind for gays."

Byrd's body was found on the morning of June 7, in Jasper County, East Texas, torn apart as if some wild animal had set upon it. His torso was at the side of a country road. His head and an arm were just over a mile away, ripped from his body as it hit a concrete drainage culvert. Police marked a piece of flesh here, his dentures there, his keys somewhere else—75 red circles denoting body parts and belongings along a two-mile stretch of asphalt. Fingerprints were the only key to Byrd's identity. The night before, the African-American man, on the way home from a fam-

ily reunion, had apparently hitched a ride on a truck with three white men: John King, Shawn Berry and Lawrence Brewer. Prosecuters said they drove him to a wooded area, where he was beaten, chained by his ankles to the pickup and dragged down the road for at least two miles. His body fell to pieces. Among the remnants, someone had dropped a cigarette lighter with the Ku Klux Klan insignia.

Jasper, which is 55% white and 45% black, thinks of itself as part of the "New South," where racial equality is embodied in a black mayor and a white sheriff, both of whom came swiftly forward to declare the attack an isolated hate crime. "We have no Aryan Nation or K.K.K. in Jasper County," said Sheriff Billy Rowles. Jasper mayor R.C. Horn agreed: "This town has been about loving each other." Residents of Jasper (pop. 7,500) loudly decried the murder; so did the suspects' relatives. Even the Imperial Wizard from the nearby town of Vidor sent condolences, saying the Klan had nothing to gain from the "senseless tragedy."

But some citizens were not persuaded by the protestations of harmony. The remarks by Sheriff Rowles were greeted with hoots. In Jasper people still wonder about the suicide a few years back of a popular black high school

REMEMBERING: After his murder, Shepard was mourned in candlelight vigils around the country, like this one in Denver

gay. If people asked and he felt comfortable with them, he'd say, "I'm gay." There was no flaunting it. After all, he was a freshman at the University of Wyoming in the Cowboy State, where real men are supposed to love football and all-night parties. Shepard, barely 5-ft. 2-in. tall and 105 lbs., preferred political debate and languages (German and Arabic) to more stereotypical masculine pursuits.

Shepard was comfortable enough to join his school's gay organization. Perhaps he was too comfortable. On Oct. 6, at the Fireside Lounge, a campus watering hole where he was a regular, Shepard struck up a conversation with two tall, muscular men, Russell Henderson, 21, and Aaron McKinney, 22, both high school dropouts. In fact, Shepard was comfortable enough to get into a pickup truck with them at about midnight. According to Laramie police, the pair had apparently led him to believe that they too were gay. But when the three had gone barely half a mile on Grand Avenue, Laramie's main street, the car abruptly pulled over and McKinney said, "Guess what? We're not gay. You're going to get jacked. It's Gay Awareness Week."

Taking turns, they allegedly began pounding Shepard on the head with a .357 Magnum revolver. The pair then drove about a mile east of town and, on Snowy Mountain View Road, they dragged Shepard out of the car. "They tied him to a post," said police commander Dave O'Malley, and as he begged for his life, they "beat him and beat him." The back of his head bashed to the brain stem, his face cut, his limbs scorched with burn marks, Shepard hung spread-eagled on a rough-hewn deer fence through a night of near freezing temperatures, unconscious and losing more and more blood. On the evening of the next day, 18 hours after he was abandoned, two bicyclists saw him. At first, they thought they were looking at a scarecrow. He was taken, barely alive, to a hospital where he died.

Shepard's brutal murder came at a time when the U.S. is buzzing with a dissonant debate over sexual orientation. What seems like an irresistible force of cultural change is meeting an immovable object of political resistance. There may be more openly gay men and women in America now than in any other country at any other time in history. As a consequence, even the anti-gay right has had to shift the tone of its message as more and more straight Americans become acquainted with friends and family who are homosexual.

It says something about how difficult it is to demonize gay people these days when Senate majority leader Trent Lott is reduced to comparing them merely to kleptomaniacs, as he did in the summer, or when Christian groups run ad campaigns insisting gays can be cured. While that language may try to throw the debate back more than 20 years, before psychologists concluded that homosexuality is not a mental illness, it acknowledges that pure contempt is tricky when you are talking about people's children or friends. But as Matthew Shepard learned, there are still places in America where being gay is not only contemptible, it is grounds for murder. ∎

▶ **One assailant sneered: "Guess what? We're not gay. You're going to get jacked."**

football player who dated a white girl. People ask, though without evidence, Did he really hang himself, or was he lynched? And just two weeks before Byrd's murder, a white youth was beaten up by black teens.

Jasper, a refuge for Confederate deserters after the Civil War, was fertile ground for the Klan. Nowadays the pedigree of prejudice often leads through prison. Berry and King served time on the same burglary charge. It was in prison that they met the third suspect, Brewer, 31. King was involved in a racial disturbance between Anglo and Hispanic prisoners in 1995. The Houston *Chronicle* reported that he sent letters from prison proclaiming race hatred and allegiance to the Aryan Brotherhood, a white-supremacist gang founded in California's San Quentin State Prison in the 1960s.

But hatred does not need an organization to destroy. "Ninety to 95% of hate crimes are not committed by hate groups," says Brian Levin, director of the Center on Hate and Extremism in Pomona, N.J. That was the case with the murder of Shepard in October. Shepard was not openly

The Joy of NOT Cooking!

American moms are out bringing home the bacon—so who's fixing dinner?

YOU'RE DRIVING FROM THE OFFICE, THE FUEL TANK IS nearing empty, and so is your refrigerator at home. For Americans ravenous of appetite but starved of time, a quick turn into the Chevron station off Interstate 680 in San Ramon, Calif., is the answer. That's right: Chevron, purveyor of premium gasoline, is serving fresh panini, three-cheese pesto and double espressos along with its usual selection of octanes.

Chevron cooked up its Foodini's Fresh Meal Market early in 1998. It's the latest player in the $100 billion bake-off known, charmingly enough, as home-meal replacement (HMR). You know it better as the store-bought, ready-to-eat food that is supposed to taste as if Mom made it. Foodini's is part of the evolving, highly moveable feast that has become dinner, catering to a country that wants its food fast but restaurant-quality fresh. "I work, my husband works, my daughter dances and plays soccer, and my son plays baseball," says Jan

Tulk, an attorney, during her fourth trip to Foodini's. "I'd say I end up cooking about half the time. The rest of the week it's usually fast food. This [pizza, clam chowder, salad] is a lot healthier." Although just a gourmet-pizza toss from the gas pump, Foodini's has a decidedly upscale ambiance: light jazz, vodka-blush pasta sauce and not a microwave burrito in sight.

According to the marketing firm NPD Group in Chicago, of the $691 billion that Americans forked over for food in 1996, 46% was for dishes bought outside the home. And half of that went to takeout. Result: even as the corner gas station is turning into Lutèce-for-Less, the traditional gro-

> ▶ **Your gas station is Lutèce-for-Less; your supermarket is morphing into a take-home pantry**

cery store is morphing into a catering hall–delivery service. And the kitchen seems increasingly a place to pursue cooking as a hobby, not a daily grind. In 1987, 43% of all meals included at least one item made from scratch; in 1997, that dropped to 38%.

Credit Boston Market (formerly Boston Chicken) with fomenting the HMR decade. The company, which first featured rotisserie chicken, transformed the notion of fast food by serving the kind of fare one would expect to come piping-hot out of the kitchen oven but instead comes straight out of a ready-to-eat or ready-to-heat package. The 1,159-store nationwide franchise hatched a host of imitators that have added chickens roasting on spits and homey side dishes to their menus. Though its management stumbled badly as it tried to manage the chain's booming growth, Boston Market fundamentally changed the restaurant industry. Now more than half the meals ordered in a sit-down restaurant get up and go home to be eaten.

EatZi's in Dallas, an unconventional hybrid of supermarket and restaurant, may offer a glimpse into the future of cuisine. Started by Phil Romano, the founder of the Fuddruckers restaurant chain, EatZi's serves more than 400 items like poached raspberry salmon (at $4.99 a portion) or grilled tenderloin ($19.99 per lb.) prepared by 35 on-site chefs and bakers daily. Shoppers can sniff 100 different kinds of cheeses or put together their own six-packs of microbrews to the lilting strains of Italian opera. "Women come in and say, 'Thank you. I never have to cook again,'" says Romano. "And men come in and say, 'Thank you. I never have to marry again.'" Bon appétit! ■

ERIC WHITE FOR TIME

Road Warriors

Ah! America, 1998: incomes were up, crime was down, inflation was low. Maybe so—but on the country's highways, it was a battle zone, and the buzz words of the year were road rage, as drivers tailgated, braked swiftly, bumped each other—and fought about it. Such incidents were up 51% in the first half of the decade, according to a report from the AAA Foundation for Traffic Safety. One reason for the decline of freeway civility: courses in traditional driver's education, once a near universal part of the curriculum in America's secondary schools, have declined drastically, often as a result of budget cuts. Today perhaps only 50%, even 30%, of newly licensed

drivers have completed a driver's ed course. What to do? Buckle up.

Drug of the Year

WILLIAM CAMPBELL FOR TIME

Crank. That's what its abusers—who are often white rural residents of Middle America—call it. The man-made stimulant was invented 80 years ago in Japan and issued to soldiers in World War II. It is known to scientists as methamphetamine, to aging '60s hippies as speed, and is now sometimes passed out to antsy third-graders with attention-deficit disorder.

But in its crumbly, powdered street form, crank is known to police as the year's most alarming trend in drug abuse. Smoked, snorted or injected, crank can render even casual users clinically psychotic. Worse, its production requires little overhead, so it is often produced in makeshift home labs. Too cheap, too available and too addictive, the stuff is a cop's nightmare: a do-it-yourself guerrilla narcotic spread by paranoid insomniacs running on overdrive. Ever wonder why they call it crank?

Guerrillas for the Planet

On a Monday morning late in October someone set Vail Mountain ablaze. Seven fires spread along a mile-long ridge overlooking the tony Colorado ski village, demolishing a restaurant and impairing several lifts. No one was hurt, but the damage totaled $12 million. A group called the Earth Liberation Front later said

MARK MOBLEY

VAIL: Arson destroys a restaurant

it had sponsored what was probably history's costliest ecoterrorist strike "on behalf of the lynx," a spike-eared wildcat all but gone from the state. The month before, when Earth First activists challenged Pacific Lumber Co. loggers at work in California's Humboldt County, protester David Chain, 24, of Austin, Texas, was killed in the fracas. No charges were filed. ■

SNAPSHOT

The Good Doctor

After centuries of bad p.r., Death has a media strategy, and its chief spin doctor is named Kevorkian. His latest stunt: the televised killing of Thomas

Youk, 52, shown on *60 Minutes* in November. "Dr. Death" has an unerring sense of what excites journalists—and incites prosecutors. Three days after the show aired, he got what he had wished for: a first-degree murder charge. Though he has

been acquitted three times of helping patients end their life, this time he crossed a significant line by administering the lethal injection himself. He thus moved the debate over the right to die from doctor-assisted suicide to mercy killing.

STEVE LISS FOR TIME

Dr. Jack Kevorkian

PILING ON
New York's potent Yankees celebrate their four-game World Series sweep over San Diego's plucky Padres

▶ The wide world of sports?
For once the cliché rang
true, as fans flocked to
France for the World Cup
and Japan for the Winter
Games. Back in the U.S.A.,
pro basketball fouled out,
while the New York
Yankees and two amiable
sluggers put baseball
back on top of the heap

Photo credit (vertical): RUSTY KENNEDY—AP/WIDE WORLD

CHAMPS: A "home team"—from Toms River, N.J.—beat a tough squad from Japan to win the world Little League title

Grand Old PARTY

Going ... going ... gone! Baseball slams a season for the record books

AMERICANS LOVE TO CALL BASEBALL "THE NATIONAL pastime," and we're suckers for the magical phrase "field of dreams." The problem is, in recent years we haven't loved the game itself as much as we've loved the *idea* of it. Compared to the jazzy pace of basketball, football and hockey—not to mention snowboarding, skateboarding and skydiving—the national pastime has seemed to hail, well, from a past time.

But baseball not only lived up to its billing in 1998; it showed people how to live. While America's leaders disgusted most folks and the economy frightened them, a wholesome epic was unfolding on the diamond. Sluggers Mark McGwire and Sammy Sosa congenially ribbed each other into amassing 136 home runs, while Cal Ripken ended his fantastically mundane consecutive-game streak by silently slipping away because it was time to let someone new have a turn. The New York Yankees played hard, worked together and won a lot of ball games. Heck, even a bunch of kids from Toms River, N.J., managed to wrest the world Little League championship away from the dreaded Asian nines. Americans got everything we wished for from baseball in 1998—and here's hoping next year we won't need baseball as badly as we did in 1998.

Let's start with the big guys. Because, when it comes to baseball, the suicide squeeze is cool, and the double steal is all right, but a guy who can smack the bejesus out of a ball—that's the guy for us. Like most great things American, the home run deconstructs strategy with a beautiful act of aggression. So the St. Louis Cardinals' Mark McGwire, 250 lbs. of muscle in a game full of the unfit, doesn't shock us when he sends the ball more than

500 ft. The crowd expects it, the crowd gets it, the crowd goes home happy. Americans delight in the obvious. Give us a 6-ft. 5-in. guy named McGwire, and we're going to nickname him "Big Mac." We are not a complicated people.

Even more than Babe Ruth, Big Mac symbolized stark simplicity. He is a redhead of the kind we haven't seen in centuries—not a pasty Thomas Jefferson or a cutesy Ron Howard, but a scary Redbeard. In his red Cardinal uniform, with red Oakley sunglasses and his bright-red goatee, McGwire is more frightening than Carrot Top. He also happens to be Oprahfied in all the right ways. He missed the opportunity to hit 50 homers in his rookie season in order to be present at his son's birth. In 1997, when Big Mac declared he'd be giving $1 million a year to child-abuse charities, he wept: he's got that gentle giant thing down. He cried at *Driving Miss Daisy*. You want to hug this guy. Or at least get your arms as far around him as they'll go.

Whereas Ruth drank staggering amounts, McGwire lifts weights and spends his free time with his son—though late in the season he owned up to taking androstenedione, a muscle-building performance enhancer that is outlawed in some professional sports but is legal in baseball.

Hard on McGwire's heels was the Chicago Cubs' Sosa, long regarded as an amiable if somewhat erratic outfielder. But at 29, in his 10th major league season, the native of the Dominican Republic dueled Big Mac homer for

TOP YANKEE NEEDS HANKY: Visibly moved, Yankee boss George Steinbrenner puts a squeeze play on Manager Torre

1961) with every game. On Sept. 7, McGwire hit his record-tying 61st home run of the season, and the next night he hit No. 62. By season's end, McGwire had cracked a total of 70 dingers, and Sosa had weighed in with 66.

Big Mac's got that gentle-giant thing down. He cried at *Driving Miss Daisy*. You want to hug this guy—or at least get your arms around him as far as they'll go.

homer. His playful nature kept fans beaming: after McGwire admitted to taking androstenedione, Sosa made sure the media caught him pulling Flintstones vitamins from his locker. In September, Big Mac and Sosa drew closer to the Babe's 60 homers (set in 1927) and Roger Maris' 61 (set in

HAPPY WARRIORS: Even when dueling for the top spot in the record books, McGwire and Sosa found time to kid around

Meanwhile, in the New York Yankees, 1998 may have offered us baseball's greatest team ever—even though it was difficult to remember the starting lineup—and none of the players were the best in their position in the American League. Tino Martinez wasn't even the best Martinez (Pedro, Boston). Or the second best (that would be Edgar, Seattle). Superstars Ken Griffey, Barry Bonds and Roger Clemens played in other towns. The secret of the Yankees' magic? Manager Joe Torre awkwardly called them "a great team team." They were. With every single player contributing, the Yankees won by playing "small ball": by massaging the first run over the plate, and then another and another. They nibbled their way to massive leads, 50 come-from-behind wins and a league-record 114 victories in the regular season, with a .714 winning percentage.

Darryl Strawberry, the one-time troublemaker, was stricken with colon cancer in the middle of the play-offs. So the Yanks stitched his number on their caps, even ex-teammate Jim Leyritz, who played for the opposing, over-matched San Diego Padres in the Series. Ace pitcher Orlando Hernandez had paddled on a raft to escape Cuba and pitch for the Yankees: after the Series win, his family was permitted to leave Havana for a ticker-tape parade in New York City. Even diamond fan Fidel Castro was a softy for this team. That's one other thing about the national pastime: on this field of dreams, ya gotta have heart. Baseball in 1998 had miles and miles and miles of it. ■

BASKETBALL

"DA BULLS" DO IT AGAIN:
As the clock runs out, the Jazz slump—
and Jordan, 23, and the Bulls go vertical

S THE BUZZER SOUNDED, MICHAEL JORDAN AND his fellow Chicago Bulls took to the air in a moment of exaltation. The Bulls had just defeated the Utah Jazz, 87-86, finishing off the talented squad led by veteran star Karl Malone in six games and taking the National Basketball Association championship for the third year in a row. It was another scalp on the Bulls' belt—a sixth N.B.A. championship in eight years—and it cemented the team's stature as one of the greatest dynasties in professional history.

But this exhilarating moment at the end of the 1997-98 season was to be the last N.B.A. celebration of the year. By fall an ugly labor dispute between the league's franchise owners and players had sidetracked the opening of the 1998-99 season. On Nov. 3, when the games were scheduled to begin, the amphitheaters of professional basketball were empty, and the only sounds the pro game was generating were the angry voices of owners, players and the players' agents calling fouls against one another. Pro basketball, whose popularity had soared in the past two decades—eclipsing not only major league baseball but pro football as well—was deep in the process of shooting itself in its very expensive sneakers.

The message: basketball's wealthy owners and players seemed to care more about money and control than about the fans. The players, already the highest-paid pro ath-

The Last Hurrah?

The Chicago Bulls repeat as champs, but the N.B.A.'s players and owners look like chumps

letes, with an average annual salary of $2.6 million, were demanding that they retain the ability to earn unlimited pay as free agents. The owners were insisting on a firm salary cap for each team, to reduce the share of revenue that is allotted to players; in 1997 that sum was 57% of $1.7 billion. To that purpose, the owners proposed phasing out the so-called Larry Bird exception, which lets each team break its salary cap ($26.9 million a franchise last season) to retain its popular veteran free agents. The players vigorously opposed the notion. Jump ball!

The lockout came as the N.B.A. was struggling to rebound from the 1997 arrests of five players on marijuana charges and from the ugly spectacle of Golden State guard Latrell Sprewell's assaulting his coach. The league was also facing the prospect of life without Jordan, who made pro basketball a global franchise. Although the 35-year-old Chicago star had threatened to retire, he took an active role in the labor spat. Worse, the sport was turning off its fans at a time when sports pages throughout the land were hailing baseball's 1998 year as the best season ever. The buzzer that ended the Bulls-Jazz championship series may just have sounded the knell for the N.B.A.'s glory days. ∎

▶ **With an ugly labor dispute, the N.B.A. shoots itself right in its flashy sneakers**

WINTER CARNIVAL

Tiny Tara! Smokin' snowboards! The Olympic circus parades into Japan

THE OLYMPICS, TO INVOKE ONE OF 1998'S FAVORITE analogies, are much like the *Titanic*, both the movie and the ship. In other words, it's a grand, old-fashioned blockbuster that stirs you in some primal, half-forgotten place, however vigilant your defenses, throwing up simple human images of panic and delight and loss; and a huge, showy, zillion-dollar model of the family of man that, for all its state-of-the-art grandeur and planning, cannot outswerve a block of ice. It shouldn't work, but it does; things should work, but they don't. As the surprise U.S. silver medalist in the doubles luge, Chris Thorpe, said of his surprise bronze-medalist teammates, "They don't have great lines; they don't have great form. They just fly."

If medals were awarded for staging an Olympics, Nagano would doubtless receive a silver, the color of its snowfall: almost everything Japanese was delicate and accommodating except the weather, which turned skiers on their heads when it wasn't doing the same to schedules. In the end, however, true grit prevailed: the fastest man on skis, Hermann Maier ("Other Name: Das Monster," his official bio explains), confirmed his extraterrestrial status by getting up from a horrific crash and picking up two golds in four days. Even little Denmark claimed its first Winter Games medal ever, in curling—quite a feat for a nation that doesn't have a functioning curling rink.

For Japan, the Games were a happy windfall, as the host nation rode on the cheers of its faithful fans to win more golds in 16 days than it had won in 70 years of Winter Games. Ski jumper Kazuyoshi Funaki assured his heartthrob status by flying away with three medals; more movingly, Masahiko Harada, who had let glory elude him in his

> ▶ **"[U.S. lugers] don't have great lines; they don't have great form. They just fly."**

final jump in two consecutive Olympics, redeemed himself by somehow pulling off the longest jumps in Olympic history in two events in a row. Roar after roar ran through the crowd, larger than in all the other arenas combined, and the grand swelling of emotion in a people not usually demonstrative touched even foreign hearts.

Americans were less happy with the proceedings. The millionaire-filled hockey "Dream Team" won just one of its four games, and some of its members trashed parts of the Olympic Village before departing Nagano. It generally fell to women to lift America's spirits: Nikki Stone, told she could never ski again after a back injury two years ago, claimed a gold in freestyle aerials; and Chris Witty won a bronze and a silver in speed skating.

Picabo Street, the supercharged performance artist from the Idaho hamlet of Triumph, streaked through the super-G course in 1:18:02. A few months before, Street had been a spectator, having torn a ligament in her knee; in only her fourth race back, just 11 days before, she had knocked

herself out while whizzing through a course at 75 m.p.h. Now she stood at the bottom of the course and delivered an irrepressible commentary as the rest of the 43 skiers came down, some within a whisper of her time. Only the woman in the shocking-orange tiger helmet, with the diamond stud glinting in her right ear, would say, "I knew it was only a matter of time before the spirits would come through." Street won the race by one-hundredth of a second.

Picabo had style to burn, but she wasn't on skates—and once again, women's figure skating was the most eagerly anticipated event of the Games. Michelle Kwan, just 17, had come to Nagano for a coronation. But by finding a balance between technical perfection and blossoming artistry, a tiny confection of a girl—15-year-old Tara Lipinski—showed the world that she would be queen.

First, though, Lipinski had to survive the short program, a 2-min. 40-sec. contest in which one misstep, one deviation from the eight required elements, can mean instant elimination. American Nicole Bobek, 20, was out in under a minute: she hit the ice during her first triple Lutz and never recovered, taking with her the talk of a red-white-and-blue sweep; she finished 17th. Other nations offered up their best—Russian siren Maria Butyrskaya, China's comeback kid

Let the Dames Begin!

From hockey to ice skating to the ski slopes, the women of winter stole the show in Nagano

▶ **STARS, STRIPES AND GOLD**
Karyn Bye, above, celebrates as the U.S. team beats a tough Canadian squad to take the first Olympic gold in women's hockey. Right, the post-victory scrum

AL BELLO—ALLSPORT FOR TIME

Chen Lu and French wonder woman Surya Bonaly—but one competitor, Elena Sokolova, voiced what everyone knew: "It's really between Tara and Michelle."

At a loss to articulate the mechanics of her whirlwind style, Lipinski once said, "I just rotate." In a fairy-tale blue-and-yellow frock, she flew to the *Anastasia* sound track, whipping through her triple flip, exploding into a grin that dwarfed her 80-lb. frame and skating circles around everyone but Kwan. Then the veteran showed that having soul as well as legs counts. Kwan displayed a smooth legato line as she flowed, left leg extended, straight toward the panel of judges. When she emerged from that, the audience and judges swooned, and Kwan had gold in her sights. Eight of nine judges placed her first.

Going into the final 4-min. free skate, the message was clear: just rotating wouldn't be enough. Could Lipinski rise to Kwan's level of artistry? In the last group of six skaters, Kwan drew the first position, often considered a disadvantage because judges tend to be reluctant to give the highest marks right away in case later competitors perform better. William Alwyn's *Lyra Angelica*, the score that inspired her radiant performance at the U.S. nationals a month before, failed to work the same magic. Perfection is never easy to repeat, especially in a sport decided by a whisper-thin blade and the mood of nine judges. The fluidity and the grace were there, but Kwan never really left the ice, skating without her usual speed. She wept uncontrollably after her final pose, sobbing "Oh, my God, oh, my God," as she found a measure of release. But her earlier restraint and a minor glitch on the triple flip left the throne in question.

Lipinski didn't give the judges time to think. In her signature triple-loop, triple-loop combination, she launched herself off the back edge of her skate, shot through three revolutions in less than a second, landed on the same outside edge, and then she did it all over again. No one could touch those pyrotechnics, and her interpretation of the sound track from the movie *The Rainbow* scored marks as high as 5.9. When the music stopped, she ran across the ice and pumped her fists in the air. When six judges placed her first, she squealed and leaped into the air. Her medal matched her gold-painted nails.

► **PICABO STREET**
Only months after tearing a ligament, the indomitable Street came roaring back to win the super-G event

▶ **TARA LIPINSKI**
The 15-year-old stayed loose at the competition, playing video games and making friends, while nemesis Kwan remained aloof and isolated

▲ **MICHELLE KWAN**
The celebrated stylist, 17, was expected to take the gold but never regained the elegance that had carried her to victory in the U.S. championships

SHAUN BOTTERILL—ALLSPORT FOR TIME

For many American fans, the most rousing moment of the Games came when the U.S. women's hockey team beat four-time world champion Canada, 3-1, to take an emotional gold in the first-ever Olympic final for the event. The two games between the fierce enemies introduced fans to a style of fluency and electrifying intensity that put many an NHL game to shame. Though body checking is not allowed in women's hockey, it would have been hard to tell that to any of the bodies flying across the ice, as Maple Leafs clashed with Stars and Stripes.

"We have an intense dislike and an intense rivalry," said Canadian coach Shannon Miller. But even when the American women beat her team for the second time in three days, Miller looked up and "had a feeling of joy going through my body. Because … an Olympic gold medal was being hung around the neck of a female hockey player."

All the new sports, in fact, left their mark: snowboarders tried to turn the Olympics into their own private party, as expected, but the group's free-wheeling lifestyle clashed with Olympic gravity. (*see box below*). As a skyful of freezing rain pelted spectators, riders and the media, the halfpipe (snowboarding's freestyle discipline) managed to go off without incident, as riders hurled themselves into the air before judges and the entire world. "Sticking" (landing) such "sick" (impressive) maneuvers as caballerials (backward 360° rotations), McTwists (inverted 540° spins) and the Haakon flip (a 540° spin with a flip), snowboarders showed everyone that rebels can be athletes.

Above all, the joy of these Games was to be found in the unity the athletes felt. Before they began, a Japanese organizer rallied his troops by exclaiming, "We should regard even a slice of meat and a piece of tomato as representative of Japan." In fact, though, the Winter Games opened out into a new postnational order in which an athlete named Kyoko skated for the U.S. and a Dusty tended goal for Japan. Speed skater Gianni Romme said there was nothing special about his country's program: "We are Dutch, but we could be Norwegian or German."

Next to him, Bart Veldkamp, who had broken the Dutch monopoly in speed skating only by switching nationality to compete as a Belgian, said, "I was born in Holland; I skate for Belgium. But if you are looking at the moon and ask, 'Where do you come from?' I come from Earth." Good words for the lumbering *Titanic* of sporting events as it heads Down Under—for the Summer Games in Australia in the year 2000. ∎

Snowboarding? No Left Turn Unstoned

The Olympic Committee huffs and puffs over suspected snowboarder puffing

THE INTERNATIONAL OLYMPIC COMMITTEE HOPED TO create a buzz and draw in a generation of sports fans used to pierced noses when it added snowboarding as a full-medal sport to the Nagano Games. A buzz, indeed. Three days after Canadian Ross Re-bagliati took snowboarding's first-ever gold medal in the giant slalom, the I.O.C. asked him to give it back. The 26-year-old from British Columbia had tested positive for marijuana, and after a 3-to-2 vote, the I.O.C.'s executive board recommended he be stripped of his prize. Rebagliati admitted he had smoked in the past but claimed the test only registered that he had ingested secondhand smoke at a farewell party before the Games.

Then came the next twist. A day later, the Court of Arbitration for Sport ruled that because there was no formal agreement between the I.O.C. and snowboarding's governing body to ban marijuana outright, the I.O.C. could not strip Rebagliati of his medal. After the final ruling, Rebagliati stayed cool, fishing out the medal he had kept in his pocket during the three-day fracas. He refused to condemn drugs outright. "I am definitely going to change my life-style. But I will not change my friends." He added, "I may have to wear a gas mask from now on." ∎

HOLD THE GOLD: Canada's Rebagliati won gold, almost lost it, then got it back again

SHAUN BOTTERILL—ALLSPORT FOR TIME

Gold Medal Winners

TARA LIPINSKI

PICABO STREET

JONNY MOSELEY

Nagano

1998

BOBSLED		
Two-man	Canada, Italy (tie)	
Four-man	Germany	
ICE HOCKEY		
Women's	U.S.A.	
Men's	Czech Republic	
LUGE		
Women's Singles	Silke Kraushaar, Germany	
Men's Singles	Georg Hackl, Germany	
Men's Doubles	Stefan Krausse and	
	Jan Behrendt, Germany	
FIGURE SKATING		
Women's	Tara Lipinski, U.S.A.	
Men's	Ilya Kulik, Russia	
Pairs	Oksana Kazakova and	
	Artur Dmitriev, Russia	
Ice Dancing	Pasha Grishuk and	
	Yevgeny Platov, Russia	
SKI JUMPING		
90K	Jani Soininen, Finland	
120K	Kazuyoshi Funaki, Japan	
Team 120K	Japan	

SPEED SKATING	**Women**	**Men**
500-m	Catriona LeMay Doan, Canada	Hiroyasu Shimizu, Japan
1,000-m	Marianne Timmer, Netherlands	Ids Postma, Netherlands
1,500-m	Marianne Timmer, Netherlands	Adne Sondral, Norway
3,000-m	Gunda Niemann-Stirnemann, Germany	
5,000-m	Claudia Pechstein, Germany	Gianni Romme, Italy
10,000-m		Gianni Romme, Italy
SHORT TRACK SPEED SKATING		
500-m	Annie Perreault, Canada	Takafumi Nishitani, Japan
1,000-m	Chun Lee Kyung, South Korea	Kim Dong Sung, South Korea
SKIING		
Downhill	Katja Seizinger, Germany	Jean-Luc Cretier, France
Combined	Katja Seizinger, Germany	Mario Reiter, Austria
Giant Slalom	Deborah Compagnoni, Italy	Hermann Maier, Austria
Slalom	Hilde Gerg, Germany	Hans-Petter Buraas, Norway
Super G	Picabo Street, U.S.A.	Hermann Maier, Austria
SNOWBOARDING		
Halfpipe	Nicola Thost, Germany	Gian Simmen, Switzerland
Giant Slalom	Karine Ruby, France	Ross Rebagliati, Canada
FREESTYLE SKIING		
Moguls	Tae Satoya, Japan	Jonny Moseley, U.S.A.
Aerials	Nikki Stone, U.S.A	Eric Bergoust, U.S.A..

SNAPSHOT

Mark O'Meara tops Tiger

Masterly Mark

**What a year! What a guy!
No, we're not talking
about what's-his-name—
the kid in red—we're
talking about the guy who
looks like his caddy. We're
talking about the great
Mark O'Meara, 41,
winner of the 1998
Masters Tournament, the
1998 British Open and
the 1998 World Match
Play Championship—just
to mention a few. While
1997's phenom, Tiger
Woods (O.K., we knew his
name all along) was trying
to get a grip on his putting
game, his good friend and
next-door neighbor,
O'Meara, was soaring.**

**At Augusta, O'Meara
won the green jacket with
three birdies in the final
four holes, the last on
a 20-ft. putt. At Royal
Birkdale, he birdied four
of the final eight holes of
regulation, then won the
British crown in a four-
hole playoff. At Britain's
Wentworth Club, the man
who calls himself a "nice
player, not a great one,"
took the World Match
Play Championship after
administering a one-on-
one tutorial to … yep, the
kid who lives next door.**

Liberty! Equality! Go-o-o-al!

As France played host to soccer's World
Cup, the biggest event in the globe's
most popular sport, the whole world was
watching—with the exception of one out-
of-synch nation that we won't name.
Britain's Prince Harry jumped from his
seat in Lens when England scored against
Romania; the Pope is known to favor goal-
keepers, having been one in his youth in
Poland; the Three Tenors happily sang a
World Cup concert (it got them good
tickets!). In China, President Clinton's visit
was overshadowed by more important
news; in Thailand, eight men escaped
from prison while guards were absorbed
watching the Germany-Croatia game.

For the French hosts, the possibility
of *triomphe* began to hit home after their
team won the semifinal against Croatia—
the Cinderella of the tournament in its
first appearance in the finals. After that
game, 300,000 people took to the streets
of Paris waving flags, faces painted blue-
white-and-red. Nothing like it had been
seen since the Liberation. And when the
French beat the defending champions,
Brazil, who boasted the game's most
celebrated player, Ronaldo, in the final
game, well—*Vive la France!* Uncle Sam
was not so fortunate: the Americans lost
to both Iran and Yugoslavia and finished
dead last among the finals' 32 teams.

A Good Drive Spoiled

And they say there's no controversy in
the game of golf. For months throughout 1998, querulous guys on golf talk
shows were—in all seriousness—uttering
such statements as "Yeah, but without

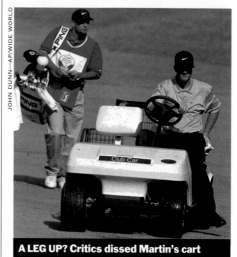

A LEG UP? Critics dissed Martin's cart

walking between holes, where's the ath-
leticism in the sport?" That scary question
was posed by the plight of golf pro Casey
Martin, 25, who suffers from a blood
disorder in his right leg so severe that
excessive walking might cause lasting harm.
So in 1997, after the Professional Golf
Association refused to allow him to use a
golf cart, Martin sued under the Americans

JOY: What better place to celebrate triumph?

TOM HAUCK—ALLSPORT

SKATEBOARDER HAWKE
Alternative sports are luring
both viewers and advertisers

with Disabilities Act. An injunction allowed Martin to drive a cart in the year's first Nike Tour tournament, in Lakeland, Fla. To the horror of the guardians of the ancient game's honor, Martin won. Some players, including old college teammate Tiger Woods, protested that the cart gave Martin an unfair advantage. Take a hike, guys.

Fakie, Phat and Where It's At

Tony Hawke has lived the dream of the modern American athlete, turning pro straight out of high school, scoring a luxurious home in San Diego and becoming no-worries wealthy through the sport he loves. He has appeared in commercials for Mountain Dew, AT&T, Gatorade and the milk industry, taking his place beside the white-mustached Pete Sampras and Cal Ripken Jr. But Hawke isn't a tennis or baseball player. He's a professional skateboarder who spends his time in swimming pools. Empty swimming pools. Preferably lefthanded, kidney-shaped pools with lips of grindable concrete coping, perfect for landing nollie backside 180s, pulling fakie 540 kick-flip indies or even busting his phat 720 front-side airs.

If you don't understand that skateboard speak, then you're probably outside the 12-to-34 age demographic that advertisers and programmers covet—and that alternative-sports stars like Hawke can deliver. He's one of a new band of athletes who are helping drive the fast-growing world of nontraditional sports such as surfing, skateboarding, snowboarding, mountain biking, rock climbing, NASCAR racing and even bass fishing to ever increasing TV exposure and ad dollars. Even as TV ratings for baseball, basketball, football and hockey have declined, the fees that the leagues charge the networks for broadcast rights have skyrocketed. The 1998 World Series, despite the presence of a historic Yankee team, was the lowest-rated World Series in history. *Monday Night Football* audiences were down 10% in 1998 compared with 1997.

While pro athletes with big salaries and bad attitudes were wearing out their welcome with fans, participation rates were booming for pursuits like snowboarding (up 33% in 1997 over 1996), skateboarding (up 22%) and fly fishing (up 6%). Baseball was down 10%. "Extreme athletes take their sports more seriously. Mainstream athletes make so much money, it's just a job for them," says Jonathon Meir, 14, of Incline Village, Nev. His friend Tyler McPherron, 14, adds that he associates football with "a bunch of old guys sitting on the couch and drinking beer." Phat observation, Tyler. ∎

Pit Boss

When Jeff Gordon won the Coca-Cola 600 in May, he celebrated with a liter of Pepsi, his new soft-drink sponsor. It was only fair. He won the Pepsi 400 while representing Coke. The two cola giants went wheel to wheel to roll up the endorsement of stock-car racing's golden boy, one measure of his crossover status as a national icon. The Winston Cup is the National Association for Stock Car Auto Racing's award for best driver of the year; in 1998 Gordon grabbed it for the third time in the past four years. The California-born, Indiana-honed speed merchant was the hottest athlete in an even hotter sport.

The chisel-chinned Gordon, 26, is by far the brightest of NASCAR's top stars. He appears with Letterman and Leno, shows up at trendy Oscar parties and on PEOPLE magazine's list of the 50 most beautiful people. As he shifts into a broader marketplace, Gordon is drafting NASCAR in his wake: attendance at the 32 Winston Cup races was up 66% since 1990.

RIC FELD—AP/WIDE WORLD

JEFF GORDON: He's driving NASCAR from a regional to a national attraction

▶In science, 1998 brought mixed tidings. The good news: John Glenn took a ride on a rocket and confirmed that space was A-OK for seniors. The bad news: extreme weather roiled the globe, with Hurricane Mitch leaving thousands of people dead across Central America

SOLAR POWER
NASA's Transition Region and
Coronal Explorer spacecraft
(TRACE), launched on April 1,
provides detailed images of
plasma (hot gas) eruptions

5 ... 4 ... 3 ... 2 ... 1 ... Blast-off! John Glenn's return to space is A-O.K.

BACK TO THE
FUTURE

THE FIRST TIME JOHN GLENN FLEW INTO SPACE, HE MADE A POINT OF MENTIONING CHEWING GUM to his wife. Whenever the former combat pilot was preparing for an especially hazardous mission, he and Annie always talked about gum, and Feb. 20, 1962, was no exception. That morning Glenn was perched atop a steaming Atlas missile while Annie waited at home in Arlington, Va., following his doings on a bank of television sets. At just past 8:35, the phone rang. On the line—through a roar of static—Annie could hear John, patched directly from his spaceship to his home. "Well," Glenn said, "I'm going down to the corner store and buy some chewing gum." "Well," Annie said bravely, as she knew she was supposed to, "don't take too long." An hour later, the spacecraft carrying her husband left the ground. Five hours after that, it splashed down in the Atlantic; when it did, the world turned over.

In 1998 Glenn flew off to buy one more pack of gum. This time it was not the silvery pencil of an Atlas booster carrying the 77-year-old Senator into space but the great technological temple of a space shuttle. This time he wasn't flying alone; he was one member of a seven-person multinational crew. And this time, he said, he was flying not for glory but for something as simple as geriatric science. Whatever Glenn modestly claimed, however, the public was having none of it. When he lifted off on Oct. 29, climbing aloft on a column of hellfire that made his puny Atlas look like a sparkler, the nation paid heed in a way it hadn't in decades. Some 2,500 journalists crowded into Cape Canaveral, Fla.—seven

times the number that turned out for Glenn's first flight. Nearly 250,000 spectators darkened the roads and waterways around the cape. Even the surviving Mercury astronauts—a plumpish Wally Schirra, a leathery Scott Carpenter, a frail Gordon Cooper—were there, showing the colors the way they always did when a member of their élite fraternity was setting out on a mission that would kill him or not, but in either event would provide him with that transcendent thrill he got nowhere else.

"I don't see how anybody can say it's an ordinary happening," said Margaret French, 78, a North Carolina resident who traveled to Florida just to watch the

launch. "It's not." Yet extraordinary as the day might have been for the people watching it unfold, for the man at the center of things it was surprisingly familiar stuff. The seven crew members of the shuttle *Discovery* were awakened in their quarters at 8:30 on this Thursday morning and sat down to the traditional NASA breakfast of steak and eggs, along with lighter options like fruit, cereal and bagels—fussy fare unheard of in the meat-and-potatoes Mercury days. The suit-up, all-smiles walkout and ride to the pad that followed were unchanged from the way things were done so many years before.

It was only when the crew members were climbing into their seats that the John Glenn of 1998 started to seem truly different from the John Glenn of 1962. Though Glenn had been the solo commander and only crew of his first ship, for this mission he wasn't even in the cockpit: he was flying belowdecks, between payload commander Stephen Robinson and Dr. Chiaki Mukai, the first Japanese woman in space. "I'm a payload specialist," Glenn said before he left. "There are seven of us flying, and my name is not at the top."

The lift-off was different as well. The last time Glenn flew, the Atlas rocket that carried him aloft gave him a very gentle ride—at least at first. With a thrust that barely exceeded its weight, the booster struggled off the pad so slowly that a passenger couldn't be sure he was moving at all. It wasn't until later that the Atlas built up the crushing 8 Gs that made it such a hard horse to ride. The shuttle, by contrast, leaps straight from the gate. When its engines light, hold-down clamps keep it in place until it has built up sufficient thrust. Explosive bolts then blow the clamps away, and the shuttle springs upward, going in an instant from 1 to 1.6 Gs—not much for a centrifuge-hardened pilot like Glenn, but a jolt nonetheless.

After two brief delays in the countdown, the engines were lighted at 2:19 p.m. E.T. The ship needed just 8½ min. to sprint into space. "Zero-G, and I feel fine," Glenn called from orbit, echoing his words 36 years earlier. "Let the record show," said mission commander Curtis Brown Jr., "John has a smile on his face, and it goes from one ear to the other one."

At ground level, not everyone was so happy. Just after *Discovery's* engines fired, launch controllers noticed a small rectangular object drop from the bottom of the ship, carom off an engine bell and vanish into the exhaust flames. It was a heat-resistant tile protecting a

JOHN GLENN THEN: 1962

THE ASTRONAUT
Height	5 ft. 10 in.
Hair color	red
Age	40
Salary	$12,000
Daily workout	2-mile run

THE SPACECRAFT
Name	*Friendship 7*
Crew size	1
Crew area	36 cu. ft.
Windows	1
Computers	0
Toggle switches	56
Lift-off thrust	360,000 lbs.
Weight	4,256 lbs.

THE MISSION
Name	Mercury 6
Launch date	Feb. 20, 1962
Duration	4 hr. 55 min. 23 sec.
Orbital velocity	17,544 m.p.h.
Maximum Gs	7.7
Time per orbit	88 min. 29 sec.
Distance flown	75,679 miles
Landing site	Atlantic Ocean, 800 miles southeast of Bermuda
Recovery	Navy destroyer picked up capsule after splashdown

THE AUDIENCE
Most Americans watched Walter Cronkite announce the flight on CBS, or tuned in the other two broadcast networks

THE PRESIDENT
Glenn met with John F. Kennedy in Washington after the flight

RALPH MORSE—LIFE

Jay Leno: " Does Senator Glenn keep telling you about the good

WORKOUT: Glenn exercises, while mission commander Brown works on an experiment

man Walter Cronkite, who covered Glenn's first flight, came out of retirement to cover this one. There's a reason Jay Leno of NBC's *Tonight Show* was thrilled to air a live interview with the astronauts—even if they turned out to be faster with a gag. There's a reason the people of Perth, Australia, who turned on their lights so Glenn could see them from orbit in 1962, turned them on again. NASA's missions have long been as much about the sheer, what-the-hell outrageousness of flying in space as about science. John Glenn knew that 36 years ago; after the nation's reaction to this particular trip for chewing gum, he almost certainly knew it again. ∎

compartment where the shuttle's drag chute is stored. The snafu was not a serious concern, and didn't faze the crew. During the eight days and 22 hours the mission ran, they kept on the go, releasing and retrieving a sun-sensing satellite, testing components for the Hubble Space Telescope and conducting experiments in an onboard laboratory.

Some of them were experiments Glenn alone could take part in. Since the changes the body goes through in zero-G are so similar to the ones it goes through as it ages, studying a weightless senior citizen should shed light on both processes. During the mission, Glenn was more experimental subject than experimenter, as his blood was drawn, his sleep cycles measured, his balance and heart function gauged. "We've always flown astronauts between the ages of 30 and 60," said NASA boss Daniel Goldin. "John Glenn represents a sample beyond our experience domain."

Critics, however, dismissed Glenn's mission as everything from a victory lap for an aging national hero to a political payoff from a President who was grateful for Glenn's support during Senate campaign-finance hearings. Others questioned how NASA could claim to be making much progress in space exploration when the greatest accomplishment it could point to 36 years after sending Glenn into orbit was sending Glenn back into orbit.

But Glenn's return to space resonated far beyond politics and science. There's a reason news-

JOHN GLENN NOW: 1998

THE ASTRONAUT
Height	5 ft. 10 in.
Hair color	White
Age	77
Salary	$136,673
Daily workout	2-mile fast walk

THE SPACECRAFT
Name	*Discovery*
Crew size	7
Crew area	2,325 cu. ft.
Windows	10
Computers	5
Toggle switches	856
Lift-off thrust	7,000,000 lbs.
Weight	153,819 lbs.

THE MISSION
Name	STS-95
Launch date	Oct. 29, 1998
Duration	8 days 22 hr.
Orbital velocity	17,500 m.p.h.
Maximum Gs	3
Time per orbit	90 min.
Distance flown	3,600,000 miles
Landing site	Kennedy Space Center, Fla.
Recovery	None necessary

THE AUDIENCE
Walter Cronkite announced the flight for CNN, but Americans had a wide range of media to choose from: they watched on five networks, assorted cable channels—and via the Internet

THE PRESIDENT
Bill and Hillary Rodham Clinton watched the launch live in Florida

SHELLY KATZ—GAMMA LIAISON

old days?"   Commander Curt Brown: "Only when he's awake."

Far Out!

Critics say the new International Space Station is overbudget and overhyped. Fans say: Get over it!

THE FINAL PRODUCT

When—and if—the International Space Station is completed in 2006, it will be longer than a football field, tip the scales at 460 tons and contain about as much living space as four three-bedroom houses

O N NOV. 20, THE FIRST PIECE OF THE 16-NATION, NASA-led International Space Station was launched from the Baikonur space center in Kazakhstan, marking the start of an eight-year construction project that ranks as the greatest peacetime engineering job in history. Was the program one of the first great monuments of the 21st century—or was it a white elephant, a warmed-over dream, a bankrupt idea first launched from a bankrupt land?

The notion of putting a permanent manned U.S. platform in orbit was first proposed by Ronald Reagan in his State of the Union address in January 1984. For all the station's great size, Reagan envisioned it as a fat-free piece of engineering: a lean $8 billion dream machine. What Reagan could imagine and what engineers could build were two different things, however. To spread out the expense, NASA invited international partners to join in. Still, when its first component launched, the station was three or five or 12 times over budget, depending on who was counting the fiscal beans. While everything from rubles to yen to pounds was supposedly bankrolling the work, American dollars were really keeping it going. The project was also years behind schedule, and will probably slip even further before the 360-ft.-long, 460-ton station is finally completed.

> ▶ **Reagan saw a fat-free piece of engineering: a lean $8 billion dream machine**

Worst of all, once the ISS gets into orbit, there are very real concerns about whether it will have anything useful to do. NASA says the station will explore results-oriented research, particularly in the areas of protein-crystal growth and materials manufacturing. But the value of this sort of study is disputed. Protein crystals, which grow more uniformly in zero-G and can help scientists develop drugs, are fragile and can be deformed by a mere bump—something that can happen a lot when weightless astronauts are onboard. Materials manufacturing is also subject to human error. A cheaper solution would be to conduct those studies aboard unmanned spacecraft.

Even so, when the first launch was quickly followed by a second, from the Kennedy Space Center on Dec. 4, and as space-walking U.S. astronauts linked electrical wires from Russia's Zarya module to power up America's United module, the old magic of man-in-space asserted itself, and it was difficult to be entirely cynical about the colossal project. Reservations, anyone? ∎

SERVICE MODULE:
Provides propulsion and
living quarters. Set to
launch in July 1999

ZARYA: Propulsion and
power module, built in
Russia with American
funds. Launched Nov. 20

UNITY: Six-porthole
docking pod. Launched
Dec. 4

**CANADIAN
MANIPULATOR ARM:**
Upgraded version of
shuttle arm

**JAPANESE
LABORATORY:** Includes
manipulator arm and
outdoor "porch" for
exposure experiments

SOYUZ SPACECRAFT:
Serves as return vehicle
for three astronauts

U.S. LABORATORIES:
Include a centrifuge for
materials studies

ESCAPE VEHICLE: Can
accommodate up to
seven crewmembers in
the event of emergency

**U.S. HABITATION
MODULE:** Contains
galley, toilet, shower,
sleep station and
infirmary

**EUROPEAN
LABORATORY:** Built by
the European Space
Agency, a consortium of
14 countries

NASA

Mitch's Legacy:

Mother Nature's deadliest kin?
Hurricane Mitch and El Niño

NO MAN'S LAND
One survivor and one victim
of a mudslide in Nicaragua

FOR MUCH OF 1998 THE WORLD'S CLIMATE WAS DRIVEN by El Niño. The cyclic Pacific Ocean phenomenon led to forest fires and killing smog in Southeast Asia, torrential rains in California and Mexico, deadly heat waves from Texas to India. Yet the year's worst weather tragedy was not born in the Pacific but in the Gulf of Mexico. In November, Hurricane Mitch smashed south across the Gulf, hooking through Mexico, Guatemala, Honduras and Nicaragua. The mighty storm devastated an ill-prepared Central America, leaving at least 10,000 dead and 2 million homeless.

In Honduras, Mitch spawned the worst floods in 200 years. The waters may have killed more than 5,000 people and left 11,000 missing. Even as the heavy rains washed out roads and bridges and left people stranded in trees, on rooftops and small islands of high ground, they created mudslides that smothered entire villages. In all, the storm caused a staggering $3 billion in damage. Central America's development, already lagging far behind the rest of the world, may be set back by decades.

Around the globe, 1998 was a year of wild extremes of weather that all too often proved deadly. A brief summary:

HURRICANES To the relief of residents of America's Atlantic coast, Hurricane Bonnie fizzled out in early September. But weeks later, Hurricane Georges roared across the Caribbean, killing more than 300 people and leaving a trail of destruction from Haiti and the Dominican Republic to the Florida Keys.

FIRE In Indonesia, uncontrollable fires cut a 7,700-sq.-mi. swath of devastation and created a killing smog across the region.

HEAT Global warming? Believers and unbelievers could agree on one point: the weather in 1998 was too darn hot. In August alone, the worst hot spell in 50 years killed some 3,000 people in India. In Texas 120 deaths were blamed on a grueling heat wave.

▶ **Chain of grief: Hurricane Mitch's torrential rains led to floods, which led to mudslides**

FLOOD The worst floods in four decades along China's Yangtze River killed some 2,000 people and left 14 million homeless.

ICE A January storm hit southern Canada, glazing everything in sight with thick layers of ice and knocking out power to 4 million people in one of the worst natural disasters in Canadian history.

TSUNAMIS On Papua New Guinea, a series of three giant ocean waves—the first as high as 30 ft.—crashed ashore, washing away several villages and leaving some 1,500 dead. Scientists blamed the tsunamis on an earthquake that hit the ocean floor some 12 miles offshore. The majority of the victims were children. ∎

A Trail of Tears

The Thing with Feathers

New finds paint startling pictures of dinosaurs—complete with plumage

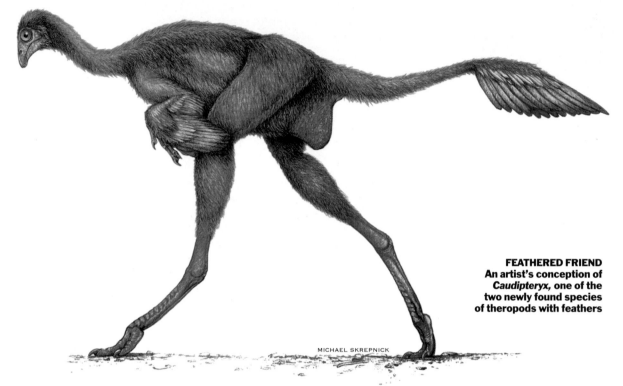

FEATHERED FRIEND
An artist's conception of
Caudipteryx, one of the
two newly found species
of theropods with feathers

MICHAEL SKREPNICK

FOR DINOSAUR LOVERS—AND THAT SEEMS TO BE JUST about everybody—1998 brought several major discoveries. Specimens found in Italy, China and Argentina gave us new insight into the way dinosaurs were born and how their internal organs worked—and provided further evidence of their link to modern birds.

DINOSAUR FEATHERS A team of paleontologists from China, Canada and the U.S. announced in June that they'd discovered two new species of a small theropod—a group of two-legged dinos that includes *T. rex* and velociraptors—each of which was clearly covered with feathers.

▶Did dinosaurs evolve to become birds, or did they both evolve from a common ancestor?

The specimens not only support the increasingly popular theory that birds are descended directly from dinosaurs; they also suggest that many kinds of dinosaur, including the vicious velociraptors of *Jurassic Park* renown, may have been festooned with a coat of colorful plumage.

Two turkey-size theropods found in 1997 at the Liaoning fossil beds in northeast China have feathers on their arms and tails and show evidence of body feathers as well. The discovery heated up a running controversy: Did dinosaurs evolve from birds, or did both evolve from a common ancestor? Critics of the direct link theory noted that the new fossils date from about 120 million years ago, making them some 30 million years younger than archaeopteryx, the oldest known bird.

DINOSAUR FLESH Examining for the first time a 9-in.-long dinosaur skeleton found outside Naples, Italy, about a decade ago, scientists found something remarkable: not only had the mini-dino's bones survived (save those of the lower legs and tail), but so had some of the tissues inside. The dinosaur, almost certainly a baby, has significant amounts of its intestines and liver still intact, along with muscles and the cartilage that once housed its windpipe—details of soft anatomy never seen previously in any dinosaur. As a result, the newly named *Scipionyx samniticus* may tell paleontologists more about the anatomy of theropods than they could ever learn from bones alone.

DINOSAUR EGGS In November a team of scientists revealed that they had stumbled upon the site of a doomed dinosaur rookery in central Argentina the prior year. They had found thousands of grapefruit-size, fossilized dinosaur eggs, including dozens of embryos, scattered over a square mile of parched Patagonian soil. The embryo dinosaurs had tiny, pencil-shaped teeth and miniature, lizard-like scales; they also had postage-stamp-size patches of fossilized embryonic skin—the first ever found. They were identified as a type of sauropod, kin to the huge *Apatosaurus* that is more familiarly known as *Brontosaurus*. ∎

I'M BACK: A wolf roams in Yellowstone

War of the Wolves

The 90 or so gray wolves who now roam through Yellowstone National Park are among the first of their species to tread the snows of the Wyoming park in 65 years. But they also make up one of the most lovingly tended—and now hotly debated— animal populations in the world. Hunted almost out of existence in the Western U.S., gray wolves have been making a triumphant comeback since the U.S. Fish and Wildlife Service re-introduced two groups into the park's 2.2 million acres and into another large patch of wilderness in nearby Idaho. In the three years since, con-servationists have nursed the nascent packs along in a highly successful

program. All that threatened to come to an end late in 1997, when a federal judge sided with local ranchers who don't like the predators, ruling that while the program's goals might be noble, its methods were illegal. The only solution, he said, was to remove the transplanted animals. In the cruel calculus of the wild, "remove" could mean "kill." Wolf-lovers vowed to fight the ruling to the Supreme Court.

Found: Neutrino Mass

Physicists love nothing more than announcing a discovery that rewrites the textbooks—unless, perhaps, it's a discovery that rewrites two textbooks at once. That's what happened in June at a scientific conference in Japan. An international team of 120 physicists reported that the neutrino, a subatomic particle long thought to be utterly without mass, actually weighs in at a tiny fraction of the mass of the electron (until now, the lightest particle known). For elementary-particle physicists, that means the basic tenets of the "standard model," which is the theoretical framework of all subatomic physics, will have to be rewritten; for astronomers, it means that the missing "dark matter," believed to pervade the cosmos and

far outweigh visible stars, may no longer be missing. It also suggests to cosmologists that the universe may collapse upon itself and end in a reverse Big Bang—the Big Crunch.

One Planet's Photo-Op

Astronomers have long believed the universe must be filled with planets orbiting faraway suns, but they didn't hope to photograph them until the next generation of super-powerful telescopes goes into space.

SAY CHEESE: First photo of a planet?

Yet in May NASA claimed that the Hubble telescope had snapped what they say is the first picture of a planet outside our solar system—a big, gaseous sphere twice as massive as Jupiter, some 450 light-years from Earth in the constellation Taurus. ∎

THE FIRE THIS TIME In one tropical land after another in 1998, flames went where they'd never gone before—into virgin, humid rain forests that have evolved without fire. To blame: human activity, which is literally paving the way for fire's intrusion. Roads into tropical forests provide access to loggers, ranchers and farmers, who then use fire to clear the land. Cutting the trees decreases rainfall, further drying an ecosystem not well adapted to recovery from major fires.

▶ Alternative medicine and herbal healing grabbed the headlines in 1998, but the hottest product of the year—the anti-impotence drug Viagra—arrived the old-fashioned way, from the laboratory. While genetic research seemed to speed ever forward, ethics struggled to keep pace

ALOE BARBADENSIS
This natural soother and other plant-based remedies continued their march into millions of medicine chests

HYPERICUM PERFORATUM

common name: St. John's wort **best-selling brands:** Sundown, Spring Valley, Your Life **what it does:** supports a healthy mood; helps relieve mild to moderate depression **precautions:** in high dosages may cause users to be extremely sensitive to sunlight **where it's grown:** Chile, Argentina

VACCINIUM MACROCARPON

common name: cranberry **best-selling brands:** Puritan's Pride, Nature's Resource **what it does:** helps prevent urinary infection **where it's grown:** Oregon, Massachusetts

GINKGO BILOBA

common name: ginkgo biloba **best-selling brands:** Sundown, Ginkoba, Spring Valley **what it does:** an antioxidant; increases blood circulation and oxygenation; improves memory **precautions:** do not use with blood thinners **where it's grown:** South Carolina

HYDRASTIS CANADENSIS

common name: goldenseal **best-selling brands:** Nature's Resource, Nature's Way **what it does:** antiseptic **precautions:** don't use when pregnant **where it's grown:** Wisconsin, Kentucky

PERHAPS YOU'VE NURSED A COLD WITH HOT TEA AND honey, jump-started the day with a cappuccino or soothed a sore throat with a mentholated cough drop. If so, you've practiced herbal medicine. These remedies are so much a part of our daily routine that no one thinks them flaky. Nor do most doctors mind that you use them—as long as you don't overdo it. So why are so many U.S. physicians reluctant to recommend herbal supplements? Is it just a matter of ignorance and provincialism?

No. Physicians have legitimate concerns about the safety, efficacy and potential misuse of the herbal products that their patients used—to the tune of $13 billion in 1998. More and more M.D.s, like their patients, accept that some herbal products may help when conventional treatments fail. The difference is that doctors are more demanding of proof. As Dr. Yank Coble of the American Medical Association puts it, "In God we trust. All others must have data."

Fortunately, those data are starting to trickle in. At the urging of its members, in one November week the A.M.A. for the first time devoted all its research publications, including the flagship *Journal of the A.M.A.*, to scientific studies on alternative, or complementary, medicine. As with conventional medicine, the results showed that some treatments work, whereas others don't.

One of the more intriguing studies, conducted in Australia, found merit in Chinese herbal treatments for irritable-bowel syndrome, a gastro-intestinal disorder that strikes 10% to 20% of the population in many industrialized countries and for which conventional medicine often offers only symptomatic relief.

Most of the other studies the A.M.A. reported on yielded mixed results. Researchers at St. Luke's–Roosevelt in New York City determined that *Garcinia cambogia* does not, by itself, help patients lose weight. A review of all the studies conducted on saw palmetto found significant improvement in urine flow in men with enlarged prostates. But the reviewers cautioned that the saw-palmetto studies were too hastily conducted to determine long-term results.

Because herbal remedies are not regulated in the U.S., consumers should read the best available studies before trying these medications. With a few notable exceptions, much of the information about herbs on the Internet is unreliable. But authoritative books are available from the

FLOWER
Herbs can both heal and harm.
Our advice: look before you leaf
POWER

American Botanical Council and the Medical Economics Co. Here are a few other tips:

▶ Don't assume that "natural" means safe. Folks have suffered liver damage from sipping teas brewed from comfrey, an herb that is used in poultices and ointments to treat sprains and bruises but should never be taken internally. Special note to pregnant women and nursing mothers: avoid echinacea, senna, comfrey and licorice.

▶ Make sure what you're taking is pure. In May 1998 the FDA verified industry reports that certain shipments of ginseng were contaminated with high levels of a fungicide. Some imported Chinese remedies have allegedly been doped with Valium or other prescription drugs.

▶ Look for standardized preparations to get the same product with each new bottle you buy. In November the U.S. Pharmacopeia, a nonprofit organization, published the first American standards for the potency of nine herbs. Manufacturers that adhere to those standards can add the letters NF, for national formulary, to their labels.

▶ Buy from companies that research their products. For example, most studies of ginkgo biloba, which appears to delay the progression of early Alzheimer's disease in some patients, have been conducted on an extract produced by Schwabe of Germany and distributed in the U.S. by Nature's Way (Ginkgold) and Warner-Lambert (the Quanterra line). The best-studied version of St. John's wort, which appears to work for mild to moderate depression, is Kira, produced by Lichtwer.

▶ Be sure to tell your doctor what you're taking. According to *J.A.M.A.*, 15 million Americans take herbs at the same time as prescription medications. Yet 60% of them don't inform their doctors, which would at least allow the physicians to watch for problematic drug-herb interactions.

▶ Don't let herbal preparations lull you into ignoring serious problems. "A lot of my patients with hepatitis C take milk thistle," says Dr. Melissa Palmer, a liver specialist in Plainview, N.Y. "It seems to normalize their liver-function tests, but it doesn't affect the underlying disease." Finally, don't expect a pill to make up for an unhealthy life-style. No herb can take the place of exercise and good nutrition. Among the most healthful plants you can consume are leafy green vegetables like broccoli and spinach. ■

VIM, VIGOR, VIAGRA

Y**ES, IT HAD A PHONY NAME, A FUNNY SHAPE AND AN UNAPPE**-tizing color—but that didn't stop Viagra, the pill that conquers impotence, from taking the public imagination by storm in 1998. Could there be a product more tailored to the easy-solution-loving, sexually insecure American psyche than this one? The drug, manufactured by Pfizer, went on sale in mid-April, finally giving talk-show hosts something other than President/intern escapades to crack smarmy jokes about.

Egged on, perhaps, by an advance avalanche of publicity, would-be patients besieged urologists' offices and sex clinics—men both genuinely dysfunctional and merely dissatisfied, intent on achieving "better" erections through chemistry. Cheap gas, strong economy, erection pills—what a time to be alive!

The very day Viagra became available, John Stripling, an Atlanta urologist, churned out 300 prescriptions with the help of a rubber stamp he had had the foresight to purchase. "It's the fastest takeoff of a new drug that I've ever seen, and I've been in this business for 27 years," said Michael Podgurski, director of pharmacy at the 4,000-outlet Rite Aid drugstore chain. Within weeks of its introduction, the drug was being prescribed at the rate of at least 10,000 scrips a day, outpacing such famous quick starters as the antidepressant pill Prozac (which went on to become one of the biggest-selling drugs in America) and the baldness remedy Rogaine (which has been something of a disappointment after its initial popularity). Pfizer stockholders celebrated, as the value of their shares jumped nearly 60%.

Amid the hubbub, even supporters of Viagra were worried about hyped expectations. "People always want a quick fix," complained Domeena

Sacre bleu! Romance is in the air as a new pill that counteracts impotence takes the country by storm

Renshaw, a psychiatrist who directs the Loyola Sex Therapy Clinic outside Chicago. "They think Viagra is magic, just like they thought the G spot worked like a garage-door opener." Initially the side effects of Viagra were reported as comparatively slight: chiefly headache, flushed skin, upset stomach and some vision distortions involving the color blue. But concerns soon arose concerning Viagra's safety: 16 users of the drug died in the first few months of sales. After investigating a number of the first cases, Pfizer said that the deaths had been caused by normal cardiovascular stress associated with sexual activity or by the use of Viagra in combination with nitrate heart medications, which its packaging advised against. The U.S. Food and Drug Administration concurred.

Viagra also sparked a new social debate: To what extent should the government and insurance companies fund sexuality? Viagra cost about $10 a pill; in June, Kaiser Permanente, America's largest nonprofit health maintenance organization, said it would not include Viagra in its prescription plans, saying to do so would cost it $100 million a year. The Clinton Administration informed states it planned to require that Medicaid reimburse its recipients for medically necessary uses of Viagra; some Governors strongly opposed the plan as too costly. By May an industry consulting company, IMS Health, found that nearly half of the 300,000 men taking Viagra weekly were reimbursed at least partially. Meanwhile, a number of women's groups argued that insurers who

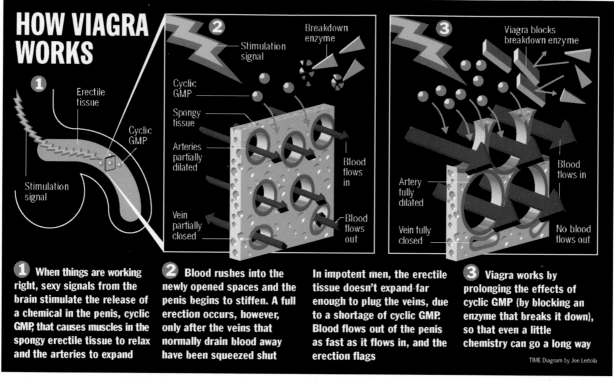

HOW VIAGRA WORKS

1 Erectile tissue

Cyclic GMP

Stimulation signal

2 Stimulation signal

Breakdown enzyme

Cyclic GMP

Spongy tissue

Arteries partially dilated

Vein partially closed

Blood flows in

Blood flows out

3 Viagra blocks breakdown enzyme

Artery fully dilated

Vein fully closed

Blood flows in

No blood flows out

1 When things are working right, sexy signals from the brain stimulate the release of a chemical in the penis, cyclic GMP, that causes muscles in the spongy erectile tissue to relax and the arteries to expand

2 Blood rushes into the newly opened spaces and the penis begins to stiffen. A full erection occurs, however, only after the veins that normally drain blood away have been squeezed shut

In impotent men, the erectile tissue doesn't expand far enough to plug the veins, due to a shortage of cyclic GMP. Blood flows out of the penis as fast as it flows in, and the erection flags

3 Viagra works by prolonging the effects of cyclic GMP (by blocking an enzyme that breaks it down), so that even a little chemistry can go a long way

TIME Diagram by Joe Lertola

provided some coverage for men's use of Viagra but no reimbursement for prescription contraceptives for women were guilty of discrimination. As with cloning, Viagra is a scientific advance that will require some social adjustment.

In the past decade there have been great strides in the treatment of impotence, which is now seen by most therapists, in most cases, as a physiological rather than a

> ### "Even if a man has an erection from floor to ceiling for an hour, it will not be pleasurable for a woman if he is not sexually literate."
> —DR. RUTH WESTHEIMER, sex adviser

psychological problem, rejecting the medical establishment's long-held view. The word impotence itself, like "frigidity" for women, is considered suspect in many circles; the more politically correct—or at least clinical—term is erectile dysfunction, or ED, as it is commonly abbreviated. Inspired by a 1992 National Institutes of Health conference and landmark 1994 study on the problem, the diagnosis has been defined more broadly, from the rather strict criterion of inability to get an erection, period, to the somewhat more elastic and subjective criterion of inability to get an erection adequate for "satisfactory sexual performance." This has led to a tripling of the number of men estimated to be impotent in this country—some 30 million according to the NIH, half of whom are thought to be under age 65. ED is associated with age; it affects about 1 in 20 men over the age of 40, 1 in 4 over 65.

From a drug manufacturer's point of view, this burgeoning of the potential market has coincided quite nicely with the development of pharmaceutical treatments. (At

least two more impotence pills are in the pipeline from different companies.) Before Viagra, the most promising therapies involved putting gel suppositories in the urethra and injecting drugs directly into the base of the penis. The downside is not hard to grasp. "You can imagine the look most patients gave when I told them they would have to stick a small needle into the most sensitive portion of their body," said University of Chicago urologist Gregory Bales. The good news is that the erections resulting from such injections can last an hour or more, even after orgasm, though depending on one's taste and circumstances, this too could be a downside. Other treatments, which involve vacuum pumps, penile implants and penis rings, are no less awkward or, to get to the heart of the matter, no more conducive to the spontaneous, unselfconscious, beautiful sex that Calvin Klein ads imply is everyman's daily right.

The promise of Viagra is its discretion and ease of use. Doctors recommend taking the pill an hour before sex, which might lead to some wastage among overly optimistic users but shouldn't otherwise interfere too greatly with the normal course of coital events. An even greater

> ### "It is frightening to be a male. Sex has always been to the woman's advantage. For sex to occur, all she really has to do is lie there."
> —NANCY FRIDAY, author of *The Power of Beauty* and *Men in Love*

advantage, or at least a more naturalistic one: unlike the injectable drugs, which when efficacious produce an erection regardless of context (famously proved by Dr. Giles Brindley, a leading British impotence researcher, who once demonstrated a successful experimental treatment by dropping his trousers in front of hundreds of astonished colleagues at a conference), Viagra merely paves the way for the possibility of arousal. Erections must still be achieved the old-fashioned way, whether through desire, attraction, physical stimulation, the guilty thrill of an illicit affair, page 27 of *The Godfather* or what have you.

Psychiatrist Renshaw offers the instructive example of a couple who came to see her the day after the man had taken Viagra for the first time: "They went to bed to wait

"[Men need Viagra] to bolster themselves ... to stiffen their erections. It's like the steel that they would get if they were at war."
—CAMILLE PAGLIA, postfeminist social critic

for something to happen and fell asleep while they were waiting. They forgot to have foreplay. They expected an instant erection." The next night, after Renshaw gently reminded them about the importance of stimulation, they had intercourse for the first time in three years.

During the drug's clinical trials, which as a rule tend to have rosier outcomes than real life, Pfizer reported a 60%-to-80% success rate, depending on the dosage (compared with a 24% success rate for placebos). The anecdotal evidence is even more compelling, if one can put up with a certain amount of crowing. Earl Macklin, a 59-year-old security guard in Chicago, has suffered from impotence on and off for 10 years as a result of diabetes. The first two times he tried Viagra, it produced minimal results; the third time he was able to have intercourse with his girlfriend for the first time in their four-month relationship.

"DO THOSE PILLS SEEM TO BE WORKING, SWEETIE?"

ILLUSTRATION FOR TIME BY PETER STEINER © 1998 THE CARTOON BANK

"I've been using it every day since then," he says (four days later) with a conspiratorial chuckle. "It makes me feel like I'm in my 30s again." Macklin's insurance company notified him that it wouldn't be reimbursing him, so, he said, "I'll limit myself to 20 pills a month."

Known to chemists by the less evocative name of sildenafil (the word Viagra, redolent of both "vigor" and "Niagara," had been kicking around Pfizer for years, a brand name in search of a product), the drug began life as a heart medication designed to treat angina by increasing blood flow to the heart. Sildenafil, it turned out, wasn't so good at opening coronary arteries, but happy test subjects did notice increased blood flow to their penises, a side effect brought to Pfizer's attention when the test subjects were reluctant to return their leftover pills.

The medication works by suppressing the effect of the naturally occurring enzyme phosphodiesterase type 5 (PDE5), which causes an erection to subside after orgasm by breaking down the body chemical known as cyclic GMP. It is cyclic GMP that initiates the muscular and vascular changes that lead to an erection. While PDE5 is always present in the penis, cyclic GMP is produced only during arousal. The catch in impotent men is that they may not produce enough cyclic GMP to "win out" temporarily over the PDE5. Thus the efficacy of Viagra: by strong-arming PDE5, it allows a little bit of one's cyclic GMP to go a long way.

"The penis is a weapon ... a lewdly lyrical thing. It is man's most honest organ. It is either up or down, and you can't lie about it."
—GAY TALESE, author of *Thy Neighbor's Wife*

One more nugget of crucial biochemistry: the erectile tissue in the penis has a finite number of receptors for cyclic GMP. This means that a normally functioning man with adequate levels of the chemical shouldn't get any more bang for his buck by gobbling Viagra. Still, it's hard to imagine that biochemical nitpicking is going to stop people from experimenting with this overhyped substance. Certainly it will be difficult for wet blankets and smarty-pants to compete with the siren calls coming out of sex clinics around the country from men "feeling 18 again." And what about a "Viagra jones"? According to Pfizer, there's no evidence that overeager users could develop a physical addiction to Viagra. But as for a psychological addiction, that is uncharted territory.

The Viagra craze should remind us that human sexuality is far too rich and complex for the entire subject to be balanced on the delicate fulcrum of an erection. Says Raymond Rosen, a professor of psychiatry at the Robert Wood Johnson Medical School in Piscataway, N.J.: "There's a danger that we could lose sight of the fact that a lot of sexual problems relate to poor relationships or poor self-esteem or anxiety, depression or other factors." Or, as James R. Petersen, who has written the *Playboy* magazine Advisor column for the past 22 years, puts it, "You can take an angry couple and give them Viagra, and then you have an angry couple with an erection." Oddly, that's reassuring. ■

Good News: Strokes

It's O.K. Go bananas. A major study discovered that men whose diets are loaded with potassium-rich foods—like bananas, tomatoes and oranges—may be able to cut their risk of stroke by one-third. But men, take precautions with potassium supplements: they may be harmful for those with kidney problems.

Bad News: Microwaves

Don't pop any old plastic container in the microwave. Federal health authorities say chemicals from some plastics may leach into food. To be safe, cook only in those containers labeled "microwave safe," don't nuke plastic wraps and don't recycle trays for microwavable entrées; they're made to be used only once.

Good News: Margarine

Healthy margarine? U.S. scientists confirmed that a margarine called Benecol, sold in Finland, reduces cholesterol. It's made with natural cholesterol-lowering compounds known as plant sterols. Just 1½ tsp. a day lowers total count and bad LDL cholesterols by 14%. The spread is scheduled to arrive in the U.S. in 1999.

Bad News: Black Smokers

Quitting smoking may be harder for African Americans. Studies showed black smokers have higher blood levels of cotinine (a chemical that indicates exposure to tobacco) than do white smokers—and that could possibly make smoking more addictive for blacks. It also might increase the risk to blacks of contracting lung cancer.

Bad News: Skin Cancer

Men and women with a history of basal-cell or squamous-cell skin cancers have a 20%-to-30% higher risk of dying from other types of cancer, including lung and prostate tumors. But there's no word yet on whether the link is a result of genetic or environmental factors.

To Your Good Health!

The good news in personal health, 1998? There was plenty of it, from nutrition tips to nifty new drugs. Sorry, but it's our job to break the bad news too

Good News: Caffeine

More evidence that caffeine may just be nature's perfect drug: a study of healthy coffee drinkers shows that fairly large doses of joe— three to four cups in one sitting—will not hurt your heart (sorry, no news on the effect on your bladder). While strong java can cause minor changes in one's heart rhythm, the fluctuations are entirely innocuous.

Good News: Prayer

A study of 4,000 elderly North Carolinians found that those who engaged in daily prayer or Bible study and attended church services weekly were less likely to suffer from high blood pressure than those who didn't. Greater exposure to religious radio or TV, however, upped blood pressure.

Bad News: AIDS

It was only a matter of time: researchers reported finding the first case of transmission of a strain of HIV that is resistant to all four protease inhibitors, the key to combination-drug therapy. However, they said, the combination program begun soon after HIV infection remains the best hope for keeping the virus at bay.

Good News: Birth Control

There's got to be a morning after—and it can be painful for those who don't plan ahead. But in 1988 the U.S. Food and Drug Administration approved a new "morning after" birth-control kit that can prevent pregnancy if taken within 72 hours after intercourse. Consisting of four pills taken in two doses spaced 12 hours apart, the treatment interferes with ovulation but has no effect if a woman is already pregnant.

Bad News: SUV Safety

Most guardrails lining U.S. roads were constructed 20 to 30 years ago—a time when your father's Oldsmobile rolled closer to the ground than today's high-riding sport-utility vehicles. The tires on the much taller SUVs and mini-vans have a tendency to snag the guardrails in a crash, often causing the vehicles to flip over. New computer models may lead to better rail design.

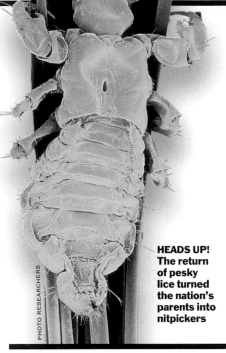

HEADS UP! The return of pesky lice turned the nation's parents into nitpickers

PHOTO RESEARCHERS

Gross! Head Lice Are Back!

Pediculus humanus capitis, the human head louse, returned at an alarming rate in school systems from New York to California in 1998. The sesame seed–size insects set up shop on human scalps and lay eggs, or nits, that they cement to hair shafts. Though head lice do not carry disease, they are tenacious and a nasty sight. The epidemic had nearly been stemmed decades ago by shampoos based on the chemical permethrin, but now the insect appears to be backed by a more potent force: evolution. As thousands of parents and school officials found that the standard arsenal of commercial lice-killing products was having little effect, scientists speculated that natural selection had bred lice immune to permethrin.

STROKED OUT: Parents in Miami learn the art of infant massage

CINDY KARP—BLACK STAR FOR TIME

Slaughter in Hong Kong

The world was appalled by a ghastly spectacle in Hong Kong early in 1998: more than 1 million chickens were gassed to death as officials desperately tried to avert the spread of the "bird flu"—a powerful strain of influenza identified in 1997 after it killed six people and left 18 seriously ill. Virologists say the decision to kill all the chickens in the former crown colony—widely derided at the time—was in fact the smartest thing that could have been done and that it may have prevented a widespread disaster. Indeed the "bird flu" seemed to have been quelled, even as

JOHN STANMEYER—SABA

TAINTED: They died to make men flu-free

public-health officials around the globe were quietly intensifying plans to cope with the next great global epidemic, or pandemic, which they say is inevitable.

Feel Me, Touch Me, Heal Me

Massage for infants? It sounds more like a New Age ritual than an internationally recognized alternative therapy. But studies at Florida's University of Miami Touch Research Institute have found that premature babies massaged three times a day for as few as five days consistently fare better than equally frail babies who don't get massages. Full-term infants and older babies also benefit. The International Association of Infant Massage estimates that 10,000 parents took training courses in 1997. New converts say massage helps babies sleep better, relieves colic and helps hyperactive children relax. ■

Calista Flockhart

Ally: The Skinny

Who knew? Apparently it *is* possible to be too thin in Hollywood. For proof, consider *Ally McBeal* star Calista Flockhart, who became the subject of rumors suggesting she is suffering from anorexia. Ally's famously skimpy skirts have always revealed an Audrey Hepburn–like reediness. But a skeleton-hugging sheath at September's Emmys strongly suggested a frame even more devoid of substance. In a PEOPLE magazine cover story, Flockhart insisted she is healthy and well fed.

A nonstory? No. The fact remains that 2 million Americans—most of them women and girls—suffer from eating disorders like bulimia (bingeing and purging) and anorexia. Doctors used to think such maladies were purely psychological. Now they're seeking biological factors. A 1998 study found abnormal levels of serotonin, a neurotransmitter in the brain, in women who had been free of bulimia for at least a year. That may help explain why drugs like Prozac and Zoloft, which affect serotonin, have allowed a lot of bulimics to stop bingeing. The bad news: the pills don't work as well for anorexics.

▶ All *Titanic,* all the time. So it seemed in 1998, when the costly romantic epic swamped box offices around the world, elevated theme-song warbler Celine Dion to diva divinity and made Leonardo DiCaprio the year's hottest poster boy. And in non-*Titanic* arts news? Uh ... let's see ...

NO MUTINY, MUCH BOUNTY
Titanic director James Cameron briefs White Star–crossed lovers Leonardo DiCaprio and Kate Winslet

FREEDOM AND POST-WAR MOBILITY: 1946–1958

Hog Heaven

A surprising show fills New York City's Guggenheim Museum with chrome, leather and wire-spoke wheels—and proves that art really does move in cycles

RANDY LEFFINGWELL—THE OTIS CHANDLER
MUSEUM OF TRANSPORTATION & WILDLIFE

VROOOOM!
TIME art critic Robert Hughes gets revved up on his Honda CB750 in 1971
Left: a 1957 Harley-Davidson Sportser XL

THE FACT THAT THE GREAT SPIRAL OF NEW YORK City's Solomon R. Guggenheim Museum was full of motorcycles in the summer of 1998 annoyed some critics. Not this one. If the Museum of Modern Art can hang a helicopter from its ceiling, why can't the Guggenheim show bikes? "The Art of the Motorcycle" might seem an opportunistic title until you actually saw the things. Design is design, a fit subject for museum consideration, and I'd rather look at a rampful of glittering dream machines than tasteful Scandinavian vases or floppy fiber art. My only regret is that the show didn't (so to speak) go the whole hog: with the exception of the iconic chopped Harley that Captain America rode in *Easy Rider*, everything in it was stock, so that it ignored the creative ingenuity that has gone into making the custom bike one of the distinctive forms of American folk art.

No matter. For personal reasons I probably couldn't have disliked this show if I tried. I have owned four large-bore bikes in my time, two of which (a Norton Commando and the great, purring, canonical 1970 Honda CB750) are in this show; and although I gave up riding after totaling a Kawasaki, and nearly myself, on a highway in Southern California some 25 years ago, I still rarely see a bike I don't like, and can't suppress a twinge of envy when some yuppie on a postmodernist Japanese burner splits the lanes of the Long Island Expressway and goes blasting past my sedate Volvo. Divided, I am reminded of a Japanese saying

MICHAUX PERREAUX STEAM VELOCIPEDE, 1868: The proto-motorcycle, a rudimentary engine jammed onto a bicycle

about the poisonous fugu blowfish, which, when prepared under license, becomes a gastronomic delicacy: "I want to eat fugu, but I want to live."

Bikes mean a lot of things, but the main one is raw, unprotected speed, and there is little point in owning one unless you are prepared to go somewhat out on the edge. Biking requires a special degree of both abandonment and focus, an unscrolling story line of concentration on intersecting factors that your average car driver is muffled from: road surface, camber, radius of curve, angle of attack, lean. It connotes a unique mixture of aggression and vulnerability, and to have owned a fast bike is, in some degree, to be inoculated against the bloated status envy that goes with the plushier forms of American motoring.

Bike manufacturers have gone to inordinate lengths in their attempts to make them seem respectable. "You meet the nicest people on a Honda" was the message of a brilliantly devised advertising campaign in the 1950s designed to counter the undoubted truth that you met some of the nastiest ones on a Harley or (as in *The Wild One*) a Triumph 650. But in essence, motorcycles are not respectable; and at heart, you wouldn't crave them if they were.

The proto-form of the motorcycle was simply a velocipede with a steam engine jammed in it, made in France in 1868. The first true serial production bike, with which the Guggenheim show began, was made in 1894 by the German firm of Hildebrand & Wolfmüller; its enormous engine—1,489 cc, the biggest that would be fitted to a production machine until the 1980s—chugged it along at 30 m.p.h. Motorcycle technology advanced so quickly under the spell of the fin-de-siècle obsession with heroic speed that only 13 years later, in 1907, the future aviation pioneer Glenn Curtiss was able to put an eight-cylinder engine in a truss frame of metal tubes and go rocketing through a measured mile in Florida at 136 m.p.h.

THE FIRST UNAMBIGUOUSLY BEAUTIFUL BIKE DEsign represented in the Guggenheim show was the 1915 Iver Johnson, with its arched frame and sculpted fuel tank (a feature that would become a near obsession with bike designers 75 years later). By the '20s and '30s, bike design was part of larger design fields. The 1923 BMW R32, with its clear, lean triangular geometry, is one of the most perfect expressions of Bauhaus sensibility. There were Art Deco machines too, with long swooping fenders, such as the 1922 Megola Sport and the mighty, lumbering 1948 Indian Chief. The BMW and the Indian are, in fact, the poles of motorcycle design: one stripped down, the other elaborately flared.

The chopped "outlaw" bike of the '60s represents, among other

▶ Cycles aren't respectable—and at heart, you wouldn't want them if they were

things, the desire to return to the raw purity of the early, "primitive" machine. On the other hand, motorcycle design in the '80s and '90s—especially in Japan—tended to enclose the machinery in baroque, forward-raked shells, bodywork that "floats" above the wheels and is loaded with sexual suggestion. Hence the argot for them: crotch rockets.

What began as a proletarian vehicle (cheap transport for folks who couldn't afford to purchase a car) has turned into an expensive, deliberate body metaphor. The automobile may be your wife/husband, but the bike is your Fatal Lover: if that weren't true, there would be no market for it. ■

FLYING MERKEL MODEL V, 1911: An expression of the century's love affair with speed

Wolfe's Latest? Just Dandy!

The journalist turned novelist has the write stuff in his bodacious best seller

THE MEGA-YIELD CRITICAL AND COMMERCIAL SUCCESS of *The Bonfire of the Vanities* in 1987 made Tom Wolfe a rich and very gratified author indeed. That big, boisterous novel, his first, proved a point that he had been arguing for years: American fiction could still portray the hectic complexities of contemporary social life if novelists would just leave their desks, maybe take a sabbatical from their professorships in creative writing, and go out and report on the fabulous stuff taking place all around them. But, Wolfe complained, most post-'60s U.S. novelists had simply abandoned the passing scene in favor of introspection or self-conscious artifice. They had ceded public reality to journalists, of whom Wolfe was a notable example (*The Electric Kool-Aid Acid Test, The Right Stuff*) before he invaded the House of Fiction and noisily threw open the windows.

After *Bonfire*, though, came the inevitable question: What next? The answers—all 1.2 million of them in the first printing, an astounding number for a novel not written by a Clancy or a Grisham—appeared in November in the form of *A Man in Full*. The novel quickly became the literary event of the year, thanks to its author's dandy way with public relations—and to the darts launched by writer John Updike, who called the book "entertainment, not literature" in a review in the *New Yorker* and then dissed Wolfe at the National Book Awards dinner (where Alice McDermott, not Wolfe, won the fiction award).

Wolfe admits that the risk of failing to top his first novel was high, but he found the challenge irresistible. "I thought the eight or nine years I'd spent on *Bonfire* had taught me what not to do the second time," he told TIME. "So, I proceeded to make every blunder a beginning writer could stumble into." As he lists them, it becomes clear why readers had to wait 11 years for *A Man in Full*. Among his mistakes, he claims, "was my feeling that I was obligated to write the biggest book in

A MAN IN WHITE: Wolfe is well suited to report on the well-to-do

MICHAEL O'NEILL FOR TIME

the world. So I spent 10 very expensive days in Japan looking for some way to get that country into the plot. And I also tried to work in some sort of television-news element and the life of an unsuccessful artist and the dealings of an unctuous insurance salesman, all of which required a lot of research and reporting and proved to be dead ends. I practically have bales of discarded manuscripts."

What remained constant in Wolfe's mind throughout this creative marathon was a tour two Atlanta friends had given him in 1989 of the plantations of southwest Georgia, immense tracts of property dotted with sumptuous homes, kept up at staggering expense by the superrich for the principal reason of shooting quail. "I look for milieu first," Wolfe says, "the setting of a story before the story itself, and I was astonished at those plantations, their psychological location in the past and the tremendous amount of conspicuous consumption required to maintain them. I thought they would make great material." And indeed, a fictional Georgia plantation is where *A Man in Full* begins.

Those expecting another *Bonfire* may have been disappointed—the new novel is better. It is not quite as glitzy and brash and hilariously in-your-face as its predecessor, but then Atlanta in the late '90s, where most of the action occurs, is a more well-mannered place than New York City was in the '80s. The same bloodlusts—sex, money, status—rage in the New South as they do everywhere else; it just takes a little more digging to find them. Wolfe does, of course, but among all the animal appetites that are slaked or comically thwarted during the novel there appears one new to Wolfe's fiction: his chief characters hunger for a code of conduct or a framework of beliefs that will make sense of their lives.

At its heart, *A Man in Full* is a cliff-hanging morality tale. It is alive with ethical nuances and hell-bent pacing; it offers social sweep and an intricate interweaving of private and public responsibilities; it is knowing in its electric sense of conveying current events and its portraits of people actually working. Call it entertainment or call it literature, Wolfe's novel is a dead-on account of America right now, a blink before the millennium. ∎

REEL WAR

Steven Spielberg directs a film about men at arms that shatters audiences with its intensity—as it reimagines war-movie stereotypes

FIRST, THERE'S THE FLAG. IT SNAPS BRAVELY ENOUGH IN the breeze blowing in off the sea. But there's something just slightly off about the image. Old Glory looks, well, old in this backlighted image—thin, faded, antique, like the unambiguous emotions it used to stir in an age less given to irony and selfishness than our own. In his brilliant film *Saving Private Ryan*, Steven Spielberg wants us to think about that, about how "the deep pride we once felt in our flag" has given way "to cynicism about our colors."

Then there's the memory of those distant days, now preserved by faltering old men. One such, accompanied by his anxious wife and middle-aged children, shuffles up the shady walk edging the military cemetery that stands where the guns once looked down on Omaha Beach, where American troops began the bloody business of liberating Europe in World War II. He makes his way through ranks of crosses, their fearful symmetry broken here and there by a Star of David. Finding the grave he seeks, he falls to his knees sobbing, overwhelmed by the flood of memories it is Spielberg's business to reimagine, then to incise on the minds of a generation dismayingly heedless of history.

Now comes the chaos that challenges patriotic fervor as well as the mind's capacity to comprehend horror—the D-day landing on Omaha: seasick soldiers slaughtered the

minute the ramps on their landing boats are lowered; the surf turning red with the blood of the butchered; some who make it to the narrow beach huddling immobilized yet pathetically vulnerable behind what little cover they can find. A few inch forward, hoping perhaps that being a moving target is safer than being a stationary one.

It makes no difference. Whether you live or die here is a matter of chance, not survival tactics. Spielberg's handheld cameras thrust us into this maelstrom, and his superb editing creates from these bits and pieces a mosaic of terror. We see as the soldiers see, from belly level, in flashes and fragments, none more vivid than the shot, rendered almost casually, of a soldier staggering along, carrying his severed arm—the struggle against mortality encapsulated in what amounts to a sidelong glance.

It is quite possibly the greatest combat sequence ever made, in part because it is so fanatically detailed, in part because the action is so compressed, in part because the horror is so long sustained, for more than 20 relentless minutes. "I wanted the audience in the arena, not sitting off to one side," says Spielberg. "I didn't want to make something it was easy to look away from."

But perhaps the most remarkable thing about this set piece is that it is not a virtuoso end in itself. For Spielberg it is something to build on, not build toward, in the delicately nuanced "morality play" that preoccupies the remainder of the film's nearly three-hour running time.

For throughout the battle on the beach (filmed in Ireland using some 3,000 performers), Spielberg has been introducing us to members of a small Ranger unit commanded by Tom Hanks' Captain Miller, in effect bonding us with them: feeling their fear, enduring their losses, sharing their weary triumph when they destroy a key enemy pillbox. And when they are assigned to find Private Ryan, the last survivor of four brothers sent to war from an Iowa farm family, we are ready to join them.

Now the film becomes a brilliant commentary on a certain kind of war movie, those depicting a small unit with a job to do. You know the drill: griping guys of disparate backgrounds do their duty—holding a vital position, taking a crucial hill—and in the process finding unity.

The eight questing men in Spielberg's film include a rebel (Edward

"I wanted the audience in the arena, not sitting off to one side. I didn't want to make something it was easy to look away from." —Steven Spielberg

Burns), an omnicompetent sergeant (Tom Sizemore) and, most important, Upham, an intellectual clerk-typist (Jeremy Davies), who learns more about himself than he will ever be able to confess in the book he wants to write. "He was me in the movie," says Spielberg. "That's how I would have been in war."

If Upham represents the unheroic realities of war, Hanks' character reminds viewers with long memories of figures like Robert Mitchum's stoic platoon leader in William Wellman's *The Story of G.I. Joe* or of the men of the PT-boat squadron grimly enduring decimation in the greatest of all paeans to American dutifulness, John Ford's *They Were Expendable.* Hanks is surely our age's Everyman, as compelling as any star of the classic era and for the same reason: the reserve beneath his openness, hinting at unspoken competencies that make us, like the troops he commands, willing to follow.

When he is found at last, Private Ryan (Matt Damon), refuses to be rescued. Like all infantrymen in Spielberg's view, he fights not for grand abstractions of policy and politics, but for his buddies, and the survival of the unit. In the film's final, heartbreaking passage at arms, where the losses are anything but acceptable, Ryan fights beside his would-be saviors.

Here Spielberg, the creator of *Schindler's List*, the film that more than any other justifies the justness of World War II, asks us to examine the war's morality in a different light. He is saying now that the lives that were given up in this conflict were every bit as valuable as the lives saved by those sacrifices. "Earn this," Captain Miller grunts to Private Ryan in that final fire fight.

Was he worth the price other men paid for him? We do not know. And that flag is impervious to the question. What we do know is that *Saving Private Ryan* is a war film that, entirely aware of the conventions of its genre, transcends them as it transcends the simplistic moralities that inform its predecessors, to take the high, morally haunting ground. ■

THE SCARLET LETTER: Spielberg directing Hanks. The film's realistic violence earned it an R rating—a rare occurrence for the director of *E.T.*

Critics' Choices

The Best of 1998

From Hannibal to Hepcat to Hedwig, TIME critics pick the year's ten best in design, movies, TV, music, theater and books

THE BEST OF 98 DESIGN

1 BORDEAUX RESIDENCE, FRANCE Has Rem Koolhaas reinvented the home? One architectural journal went so far as to call this "the best house in the world, ever." Yikes! Built for a wealthy client in a wheelchair who asked that it be made as complex as possible, the house has three stories, each having a 10-ft. by 10-ft. hole. The hole is filled only when the client's 10-ft. by 10-ft. elevator, which is also his office, is in that space. Get it? Instead of making allowances for the disabled owner, each floor is really complete only when he's there. Abled people are inconvenienced for him. But this is more than just a house

2 Jean-Marie Tjibao Cultural Center, Nouméa, New Caledonia
Never heard of Tjibao? Don't know New Caledonia from Old? Hardly matters. The silhouette of this arts complex is so eye

local building traditions, as wind shields and as thermal chimneys that promote airflow.

3 iMac Thank you, God or Steve Jobs or whoever is responsible, for the arrival of the iMac, a computer with color, a computer with fun translucent bits, a computer that looks like what a desktop computer for the home really is: a toy. And since the most fun thing about the computer is the Internet and the least fun thing is attaching all the ugly

TOM GRIFFITH—ESTO

catching that unlike much modern architecture, it doesn't need to be explained to be liked. But it helps to know that Renzo Piano designed the slatted wooden sails of the center as a tribute to the

cables, thank you for making it so easy to plug in. The two-tone keyboard! The adorable round mouse! The parabolic shape! Even the circuit boards, visible through the plastic sides, are alluring.

4 New Beetle Messing with a classic is dangerous, so when VW reintroduced the Beetle, it sprayed on the style with a fire hose. The Volks folks managed to make the car whimsical but not silly, ingenious but not too cutesy, sexy and sporty at the same time. Just as the old VW Bug inspires aging boomers to memories of more carefree days, the new Beetle suggests glad times ahead. Nothing—fenders, headlights, fuel tank—interrupts the curves of this happy hemisphere of color.

5 Bob Crowley's set designs Paul Simon's Broadway effort, *The Capeman*, may have been a turkey, but it was dressed like a peacock. Even bad plays look good when

HANS WERLEMAN

Christopher Reeve could use. The top floor is a concrete box that hangs implausibly over the column-free middle floor, as if two halves of an Eskimo Pie were held apart by nothing. The box is supported by a huge spiral-stair-filled column outside and anchored on one side by a vestigial-looking tendon that plunges into the ground. In the middle story, floor-to-ceiling windows slide away on hidden tracks to make the room disappear almost entirely. If that's not complex enough, there's a three-story-high bookcase, and the porthole-like windows of the bedrooms are angled to illuminate certain places. Absurd, wonderful, revolutionary.

designed by Crowley. Good plays, like *The Judas Kiss* and *Twelfth Night* (*below*), positively shimmer. Crowley knows how to stun and to enchant. He understands that showmanship need not be showy, and that one of the things drawing us to the stage is the way a good set mirrors and enhances a play, yet never overpowers it.

KEN HOWARD

6 The Proteus It's a bird! It's a plane! It's … O.K., it's a plane, named after the sea god who changed shape. This little flyer can too: the middle section and the wings can be adjusted according to the mission the plane is undertaking. And because Proteus can fly so high (about 65,000 ft.) and for so long, potential missions are manifold: atmospheric research, reconnaissance and—designer Burt Rutan hopes—launching vehicles for space tourism. Proteus has the body of an insect but the heart of a jumbo jet.

7 Felix Nussbaum Building, Osnabrück, Germany
This gallery, housing works of an artist who died in Auschwitz, is the first architectural theorist Daniel Libeskind, 52, has finished. Libeskind's ideas on the presence of absence—how to represent something that isn't there—and his fascination with layers and the fractured, broken and diagonal line make for some fabulously strange exhibition spaces (not to mention dangerous windows).

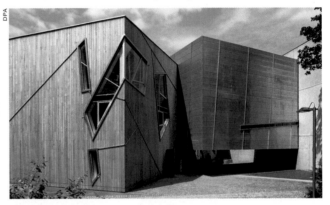
DPA

8 Hannibal tape dispenser
Cute, colorful and witty: Isn't this what the world has always wanted in a tape dispenser? Hannibal comes in bright colors and oh-so-1998 translucent plastic. He sits on your desk looking intimidatingly like his eponym, the guy who almost conquered Rome, until you need tape and then presto: as you fold his trunk out, he induces a mid-boring-office-chore smile. Only one flaw: Who pays $60 for a tape dispenser?

9 Dominus Winery, Napa, Calif.
It's a shed. A 300-ft.-long two-story shed sheathed in rocks that are held together with the gabion system—a technique used to hold up embankments on highways. But despite its stony visage, this winery, designed by Swiss architecture firm Herzog & De Meuron, is less brutal than brut-worthy and sits well in the Napa landscape. Once inside, visitors find that the stony exterior becomes a playful moiré that lets in shards of light. The stones are transformed, just like the grapes within each cask.

10 Mimid Miniature Mine Detector With 70 million land mines buried out there, this sleek, telescoping diviner with its Miesian line couldn't have arrived too soon. Created by Gerhard Heufler, its carbon and glass fiber–reinforced plastic body comes in basic G.I. Joe green, weighs 3 lbs. and quickly collapses into a small backpack for transporting to remote areas. The controls take just a few minutes to master. This is good design with a good purpose.

2 Decalogue A decade ago, Krzysztof Kieslowski made his 10-part cycle of short films, which dramatize the Ten Commandments in modern Poland. In their scope, wit, power and ethical poignancy, they stand even taller today. The series, though available in some video stores, still has not achieved U.S. release—a high crime against high artistry.

3 Shakespeare in Love Forbidden romance, raffish show-biz comedy, literary pranksterism and class warfare jostle joyously in this intricately imagined, exuberantly acted, cunningly directed tale of how the young, infinitely distracted Bard gets in touch with the genius he doesn't know he possesses. To Gwyneth Paltrow, muse of Miramax, we send our heart.

4 Happiness Todd Solondz sees the pursuit of happiness as a quest open to all souls, especially doomed ones. With unblinking wit and guile he paints hell as a place very like New Jersey, where an 11-year-old boy has several urgent sex chats with his loving father, who is a pedophile. Has tenderness ever been so frightening?

5 The Butcher Boy In a provincial 1960s Irish town, an emotionally starved child feeds his imagination on crud culture and warped religiosity, then innocently creates a miniholocaust. Arson, murder, madness—Neil Jordan

(*The Crying Game*) transforms it all into a bruising metaphor for the larger violence of our times.

6 The Thin Red Line Two great World War II epics in a year, and yet they are so different. This one, the first film directed by Terrence Malick since the 1978 *Days of Heaven*, imagines the battle for Guadalcanal as a standoff between man at his most frantic and nature at its most rapturous. In one embracing vision, Malick gives you Eden *and* the Fall. Welcome back, Terry.

7 Bulworth Just as Americans' disgust with our mendacious public life reaches critical mass, Warren Beatty imagines a U.S. Senator who starts telling the truth about the powerful. He's nuts, of course, but the star, director, co-writer and rapster is in a reckless mood. His maniacally skillful movie is that Hollywood rarity: political satire with real, wounding bite.

8 The Opposite of Sex A tramp, all of 16, seduces her gay half brother's lover, says she's pregnant and then steals $10,000. Don Roos'

Seven Characters in Search of a Spanking is pure modern romance: anguished, raunchy, caring. Praise be to the entire cast and, what the heck, a Nobel Prize to Lisa Kudrow as a twisted spinster looking for love.

9 Without Limits A portrait of the artist as a long-distance runner. Steve Prefontaine (well played by Billy Crudup) is a knothead and a hothead, determined to shape his life and race to his own vision. This biography, from director and

1 SAVING PRIVATE RYAN It is a measure of Steven Spielberg's maturity that by opening *Saving Private Ryan* with what may be the most unforgettably brutal sequence in the history of war movies—his astonishing re-creation of the Omaha Beach landing—he forces us to wonder if any cause can justify such carnage. The rest of his tense, brilliantly wrought epic puts men in mortal peril as they attempt to rescue a soldier whose life is no more valuable than theirs, then shows us how honor can be wrested from absurdity by common decency and modest dutifulness.

co-writer Robert Towne, is a sweet, sober meditation on winning, losing and the enduring enigmas of American maleness.

10 Live Flesh It could be a 1940s Hollywood melodrama or an 1840s French farce, but Pedro Almodóvar's gaudy thriller is as modern as Monica. His characters hurl themselves off fate's precipice to find love, lust, deliverance. A wise woman tells her beau that "making love involves two people." In this movie, that's right: delirious director, dazzled viewer.

1 LARRY SANDERS FINALE (HBO) When people say a TV show is "brilliant," what they usually mean is "brilliant—for a TV show." Yet some series are brilliant by any standard, and *The Larry Sanders Show,* which ended its six-year run in 1998, is one such rarity. Starring Garry Shandling as a talk-show host, *Sanders* sharply satirized show business and provided a unique celebrity frisson as it toyed with the images of its famous guests. But its humor arose equally from its deeply flawed, densely realized characters. The finale was a peak and included a sequence with Jim Carrey that should become television legend.

2 Jimmy Smits Farewell (ABC) *NYPD Blue* dispatched Detective Bobby Simone in four intensely moving episodes. Smits' low-key virility and Dennis Franz's emotionalism played perfectly in the tragic setting, and if you have to die, Kim Delaney is the woman—tender, beautiful—to have at your side.

3 Bill Clinton's Grand Jury Testimony An uncut four-hour videotape, taken by a motionless camera trained on one man talking. Disembodied background voices; absurdist dialogue about the word *is*—nothing so avant-garde has ever been broadcast before. Free of punditry, the Clinton Show was the highlight of Monica TV.

4 ER (NBC) O.K., maybe the new story line about Carter and his protégé is strained, but *ER* remains compelling week in and week out. It also remains atop the ratings, proving that quality and popularity can go together. As TV fragments, and another fall season comes to grief for the big networks, *ER* seems like the last universal hit.

5 Cold War (CNN) Any commercial network that dared to air a 24-part documentary on the cold war, no matter how dull, would deserve praise, but CNN went further, creating dramatic TV. Mixing rare footage and interviews with figures high and low, the series deftly told its grave story, while maintaining scholarly integrity.

6 Teletubbies (PBS) The most imaginative children's show to come along in years, *Teletubbies* features soft, bouncy creatures in an odd green world and seems like a perfect projection of the toddler sensibility. Its greatest brainstorm: repeating films immediately after showing them, just as a two-year-old wants. "Again, again!"

7 Sports Night (ABC) Of all the shows that premiered this season, only this one was at all intriguing. Set at a fast-paced cable show, *Sports Night* is a sort of *ER* with jokes—the camera work, the dialogue and the conflicts are similar to those of TV dramas, but it offers wry comedy and could lead sitcoms in a welcome new direction.

8 An Evening with the Rat Pack (TV Land) This amazing artifact tape captures Sinatra, Martin and Davis in 1965, at the height of their joint fame. With Johnny Carson as emcee, the avatars of cool sing for typical burgher fans. Ringleader Frank is a bit stiff, but Dean performs with oozing plushness, while Sammy winces at some racial cracks.

9 AMC Although its library is inferior to that of Turner Classic Movies, AMC is more fun to watch. Here you see the unfamiliar Jeff Chandler or Virginia Mayo films that are often deliciously bad but can be crudely fascinating and say much about the times in which they were made. All this, and George Clooney's dad Nick as a host too.

10 The Baby Dance (Showtime) Weepy, female-skewed movies almost never get respect, but this one deserves a lot on account of its craft and emotional truth. Stockard Channing's character contracts to adopt the baby Laura Dern is carrying. They seesaw between distrust and affection, and of course it all ends in tears. In this case, they are fully earned.

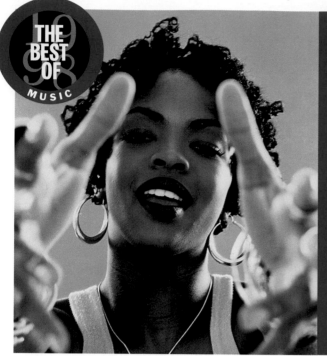

MARC BAPTISTE—OUTLINE

1 LAURYN HILL *THE MISEDUCATION OF LAURYN HILL* (Ruffhouse) Hill has given hip-hop the gift of her own heart: bruised, but still beating strong. She's shown that the genre can reach down deeper than bravado, deeper than rage, and dare to reveal an artist's emotional insecurities and romantic failings. Hill blends neo-soul vocalese and rap rhymes, all powered by hip-hop beats. Inspired by the old masters, she soars beyond easy sampling and mere pastiche: her songs are of the moment, but built to last. Listen to her voice and hear a new world.

2 **Seal** *Human Being* (Warner Bros.) The man sometimes called the British Marvin Gaye lends intelligence and panache to the often juvenile world of pop R. and B. Seal's majestic, soulful voice has never been more expressive, and his songwriting, always pensive, now reaches deeper into the mysteries of love. Who will save soul? Seal will.

3 **Chucho Valdés** *Bele Bele en La Habana* (Blue Note) A native of Cuba, this fleet-fingered performer is one of the world's finest pianists. Mixing jazz with traditional Afro-Cuban musical forms such as *son, danzón* and *mambo*, he creates ferociously cerebral songs that break boundaries, cross oceans and are too spirited for any embargo to contain.

KEN FRANCKLING—CORBIS

4 **Aretha Franklin** *A Rose Is Still a Rose* (Arista) In her latest album, Franklin teams up with some of the hottest producers in pop, including Sean ("Puffy") Combs, Dallas Austin and Jermaine Dupri. The rejuvenating cross-generational collaborations are more than a marketing move: this is Franklin's most rewarding album in more than two decades. The queen's long reign continues.

5 **Stephen Hough** *New York Variations* (Hyperion) England's most imaginative pianist pays tribute to America's finest solo piano music, including Aaron Copland's *Piano Variations*, composed 68 years ago but still as up to date as a news flash, and the debut recording of George Tsontakis' *Ghost Variations*, a forceful, boldly conceived virtuoso showpiece headed for a concert hall near you.

6 **Deana Carter** *Everything's Gonna Be Alright* (Capitol) A queen of the four-minute soap opera sings about lovers and losers—her people are both—in a strong set that blends country, rock and power pop. In songs of dreams without fulfillment, hurt without despair, Carter makes a hard life sound beautiful.

7 **Hepcat** *Right on Time* (Hellcat) This nine-member band plays old-school ska with sweet vocals and warm, gentle horns. The songs, many of them genial ballads and jazzy instrumentals, breeze by, carefree but never insubstantial. This is an album that will have you dreaming of the Caribbean, or of dancing under starlight, or perhaps both.

8 **Jewel** *Spirit* (Atlantic) Jewel has come up with a beautifully calibrated set of songs that honors and builds on her folk roots, using a framework of light rock that gives her music a robust new feel and builds a bridge to what looks like a bright future for this talented troubadour.

9 **Hole** *Celebrity Skin* (DGC) Much has been made of band-leader/provocateur Courtney Love's musical makeover. Her group's previous albums were raw and ragged, but this latest is shiny, sometimes

STEVE MARCUS—REUTERS

slick. Still, bleached hair has dark roots: beneath the polite production, this CD boasts galvanizing moments of rude, undeniable beauty.

10 **Danilo Perez** *Central Avenue* (Impulse) Perez, a pianist, is after a kind of musical Creole, mixing straight-ahead bop with motifs from Cuba, Brazil and his native Panama—all at once! *Central Avenue* may not be the year's most coherent album, but it's emblematic of the new eclectic brand of fusion that's enriching jazz in the late '90s.

2 **Cabaret** Remember when Joel Grey was considered seedy? Alan Cumming gave Grey's *Wilkommen* a sinister new twist as the androgynous emcee; Natasha Richardson embodied a defiantly deglamorized Sally Bowles; and British director Sam Mendes made the terrific Kander and Ebb musical even more terrific.

CAROL ROSWEGG

3 **Hedwig and the Angry Inch** John Cameron Mitchell, who co-wrote this off-Broadway hit, also plays the "internationally ignored" song stylist who changed sexes to escape East Germany. Part nightclub monologue, part drag musical, the show has a score that outrocks *Rent* and a script that is by turns funny, outrageous and poignant.

4 **Not About Nightingales** Looking back, Tennessee Williams probably found his early, unproduced play crude and lacking in poetry. Both are true. But Trevor Nunn's intense production (which had its U.S. debut at Houston's Alley Theatre) also shows off the raw power of a dramatist on the verge of greatness.

5 **Corpus Christi** Pity the play that doesn't live up to its advance controversy. Terrence McNally's recasting of Christ as a contemporary homosexual might have drawn more fans had it really been a gay *Godspell*, as some sniffed. Instead it's a sober, impassioned work, given great force by Joe Mantello's clean and clever staging.

6 **Trainspotting** The Scottish slackers of Irvine Welsh's novel are even grungier and sadder in Harry Gibson's stage adaptation than they were onscreen.

The off-Broadway production is stripped down, but rich dialogue and fine acting turn it into a memorable trip to the lower depths. Including that infamous toilet bowl.

7 **Forbidden Broadway** You had to look hard for good entertainment on Broadway this year, but the latest version of Gerard Alessandrini's perpetually updated

CAROL ROSWEGG

1 THE BEAUTY QUEEN OF LEENANE For the first few minutes, it seems like a typical slice of Irish local color, full of overripe characters and accents you can barely decipher. But Martin McDonough's extraordinary play, about a mother and daughter testing each other's patience in a bleak corner of rural Ireland, gradually displays an imposing arsenal of playwrighting weapons: a well-made plot that keeps bending in unexpected ways; flashes of sardonic comedy; and a sense of tragic inevitability that Ibsen might have admired. Flawlessly performed by the original London cast (three of the four won Tonys), it is one of the major theatrical experiences of the '90s.

satirical revue certainly found it. From the ragged sets of *Titanic* to the titanic ballads of *Ragtime*, this show has got Broadway's number— and makes the invalid fabulous fun.

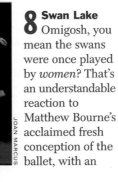

JOAN MARCUS

8 **Swan Lake** Omigosh, you mean the swans were once played by *women*? That's an understandable reaction to Matthew Bourne's acclaimed fresh conception of the ballet, with an

all-male corps of swans. This is no cross-dressing stunt but a visually luscious and dramatically convincing reinterpretation. But will the Tony Awards notice?

9 **The Magic Fire** In Péron's Argentina, a family of refugees from Hitler's Europe is jolted into a realization that history may be repeating itself. Lillian Garrett-Groag's play, staged at Washington's Kennedy Center by the Oregon Shakespeare Festival, combines warm family comedy and savvy political melodrama with rare skill.

10 **Wit** In this off-Broadway gem, a woman dying of ovarian cancer spends her last hours telling us about her life. The subject may be familiar, but one cannot remain unmoved by Margaret Edson's well-crafted play and the toughness of Kathleen Chalfant's starring performance.

THE BEST OF 98 THEATER

N O N F I C T I O N

1 KING OF THE WORLD: THE RISE OF MUHAMMAD ALI A book about a boxer would seem to lack, well, social significance. Not true here. David Remnick takes off from the 1964 bout in which a brash Cassius Clay dethroned the menacing heavyweight champ Sonny Liston. That fight changed Clay into Muhammad Ali and created a new sort of black athlete. Remnick's account of the aftershocks packs a punch too.

ROBERT GOMEL—LIFE

2 Pillar of Fire: America in the King Years 1963-65 Taylor Branch's second installment of his trilogy on the life of Martin Luther King Jr. covers but three complex and fateful years. L.B.J. ascended to the White House and rammed through the Civil Rights Act of 1964, a triumph for King. But his doctrine of nonviolence was being challenged by Malcolm X. Branch's book is an eerie chronicle of deaths foretold.

3 Lindbergh His 1927 solo flight across the Atlantic made him, at 25, the most famous person on the planet. A. Scott Berg records what happened to the aviator before, during and after his moment of glory. The later life proves especially poignant, not only because of his child's murder. Lindbergh came to dislike commercial aviation and was accused of pro-Nazi sympathies. A hero who flew so high became a troubled human back on the ground.

4 Titan: The Life of John D. Rockefeller, Sr. The man who made his surname synonymous with limitless riches was reviled and caricatured during his life, and posterity has not been too much kinder. Biographer Ron Chernow's account portrays both the thin-lipped skinflint and the philanthropist who gave away hundreds of millions of dollars to worthy enterprises. With monopolies back in vogue, the old man must be smiling—wherever he is.

5 Slaves in the Family Sullivan's Island, across the bay from Charleston, S.C., was once a major docking point for incoming African slaves. Journalist Edward Ball grew up on the island; his family in the area stretches back to 1698 and includes generations of slaveowners. Ball's research into the past is not a guilt trip but a journey of discovery.

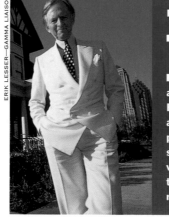
ERIK LESSER—GAMMA LIAISON

F I C T I O N

1 A MAN IN FULL Tom Wolfe's long-awaited successor to *The Bonfire of the Vanities* lives up to all the hype, and then some. Big, overflowing with the author's keen and boisterous prose and encyclopedic in its scope, Wolfe's cross sectional view of today's Atlanta proves that novels can still hold a mirror to the way we live now.

2 Paradise Toni Morrison's first novel since she won the 1993 Nobel Prize for Literature tells a haunting tale. After the Civil War, nine ex-slaves move their families to the Western territories to found a new community and new lives. Nearly a century later, some of their descendants jointly commit a violent crime. Why?

What happened to the dream of paradise? Morrison's soaring, incantatory prose provides the rich, unforgettable answers.

3 Charming Billy The title character, Billy Lynch, has just been buried when this shrewd, elegiac novel opens. Alice McDermott shows Billy's family and friends in a Bronx bar, hoisting a few drinks to the memory of the deceased, a hopeless alcoholic. The author does not underscore this irony; she lets her characters talk, to each other and themselves, and turns in a clear-eyed portrait of Irish-American life.

4 I Married a Communist Iron Rinn, né Ira Ringold, is a prominent radio actor during the late '40s and early '50s whose career collapses when his estranged wife writes a book titled, quite accurately, *I Married a Communist.* Philip Roth filters the story of Rinn's downfall through the memories of two men who loved and admired him. The mania of the Red-baiting days is recorded with perfect pitch. Roth's look at the past is harrowing and mesmerizing.

5 Cloudsplitter Was John Brown, the antislavery revolutionary who led the famous 1859 raid at Harpers Ferry, W. Va., a visionary or a madman? In an imaginative leap, Russell Banks frames this question in a furious, sprawling drama narrated by Brown's real-life son Owen.

THE BEST OF '98 FOR THE RECORD

Nobel Prizes

Peace
John Hume and David Trimble, *for their efforts to find a peaceful solution to the conflict in Northern Ireland*

Literature
José Saramago, *Portuguese novelist, whose fables and parables mix magic realism with historical criticism*

Economics
Amartya Sen, *for contributions to the economics of welfare*

Physiology & Medicine
Robert F. Furchgott, Louis J. Ignarro and Ferid Murad, *for research on nitric oxide as a signaling molecule in the cardiovascular system*

Physics
Robert B. Laughlin, Horst L. Störmer and Daniel C. Tsui, *for discovery of a new form of quantum fluid*

Chemistry
Walter Kohn, *for development of the density-functional theory,* and John A. Pople, *for computational methods in quantum chemistry*

Tony Awards

Play
Art

Musical
The Lion King

Actress, Play
Marie Mullen
The Beauty Queen of Leenane

Actor, Play
Anthony LaPaglia
A View from the Bridge

Actress, Musical
Natasha Richardson, *Cabaret*

Actor, Musical
Alan Cumming, *Cabaret*

Best-Selling Fiction

1. *Memoirs of a Geisha,* Arthur Golden
2. *Cold Mountain,* Charles Frazier
3. *Message in a Bottle,* Nicholas Sparks
4. *The Street Lawyer,* John Grisham
5. *Summer Sisters,* Judy Blume
6. *Black and Blue,* Anna Quindlen
7. *A Widow for One Year,* John Irving

8. *I Know This Much Is True,* Wally Lamb
9. *Rainbow Six,* Tom Clancy
10. *Paradise,* Toni Morrison

Best-Selling Nonfiction

1. *Tuesdays with Morrie,* Mitch Albom
2. *Conversations with God: Book I,* Donald Neale Walsch
3. *Angela's Ashes,* Frank McCourt
4. *The Millionaire Next Door,* Thomas Stanley
5. *The Man Who Listens to Horses,* Monty Roberts
6. *Midnight in the Garden of Good and Evil,* John Berendt
7. *A Walk in the Woods,* Bill Bryson
8. *The Gifts of the Jews,* Thomas Cahill
9. *A Pirate Looks at Fifty,* Jimmy Buffett
10. *Talking to Heaven,* James VanPraagh

Academy Awards

Picture
Titanic

Director
James Cameron
Titanic

Actress
Helen Hunt
As Good as It Gets

Actor
Jack Nicholson
As Good as It Gets

Supporting Actress
Kim Basinger
L.A. Confidential

Supporting Actor
Robin Williams
Good Will Hunting

Hollywood Films

Domestic box office
1. *Titanic*
2. *Armageddon*
3. *Saving Private Ryan*
4. *There's Something About Mary*
5. *The Waterboy*
6. *Doctor Dolittle*
7. *Deep Impact*
8. *Godzilla*
9. *Good Will Hunting*
10. *Rush Hour*

Sports Champions

Baseball
▶ *World Series*
  New York Yankees
▶ *College World Series*
Southern California Trojans

Basketball
▶ *NBA* Chicago Bulls
▶ *NCAA Women* Tennessee Lady Vols
▶ *NCAA Men* Kentucky Wildcats

Football
▶ *Superbowl XXXII* Denver Broncos
▶ *College* Tennessee Volunteers

Hockey
▶ *Stanley Cup*
  Detroit Red Wings

Horse Racing
▶ *Kentucky Derby*
  Real Quiet

James Cameron

▶ *Preakness Stakes*
  Real Quiet
▶ *Belmont Stakes*
  Victory Gallop
▶ *Breeder's Cup Classic*
  Awesome Again

Golf
▶ *Masters* Mark O'Meara
▶ *LPGA* Se Ri Pak
▶ *U.S. Open* Lee Janzen
▶ *U.S. Women's Open* Se Ri Pak
▶ *British Open* Mark O'Meara
▶ *PGA* Vijay Singh

Tennis
▶ *Australian Open*
  Martina Hingis
  Petr Korda
▶ *French Open*
  Arantxa Sánchez Vicario
  Carlos Moya
▶ *Wimbledon*
  Jana Novotna
  Pete Sampras
▶ *U.S. Open*
  Lindsay Davenport
  Patrick Rafter

Top-Rated Television

1. *ER*
2. *Friends*
3. *Frasier*
4. *Veronica's Closet*
5. *NFL Monday Night Football*
6. *Jesse*
7. *Touched by an Angel*
8. *60 Minutes*
9. *CBS Sunday Movie*
10. *NYPD Blue*

REED SAXON—AP/WIDE WORLD

SOURCES: FACTS ON FILE (NOBELS);
SIMBA INFORMATION FROM NEW YORK TIMES
BEST-SELLER LISTS (BOOKS);
BASELINE II (FILMS);
NIELSEN MEDIA RESEARCH (TELEVISION)

Cartoon Insects: Incestuous?

Sometimes it really is a small, small world. DreamWorks—the studio founded by Steven Spielberg, Jeffrey Katzenberg and David Geffen—released its first cartoon feature, *Antz*, in early October. The computer-animated story of life in an ant colony, *Antz* features the voices of Woody Allen and Sharon Stone. In November, Pixar, the creator of *Toy Story*, and Disney, the studio where Katzenberg was chairman for 10 years, released *A Bug's Life*, which also happens to be the computer-animated story of life in an ant colony. Coincidence? That depended on whom you asked. Pixar head Steven Jobs complained that Katzenberg swiped the idea for *Antz* from Disney. Meanwhile, Katzenberg put *Antz* on a rush schedule to get it out early— and beat *A Bug's Life* into theaters.

Jerry Springer

SNAPSHOT

Squalid Mr. Springer

The rise of *The Jerry Springer Show* was one of the wonders of the age. As recently as early 1997, its ratings were mediocre, but by February 1998 it had become TV's first syndicated talk show to beat *Oprah* since 1987. What explains his success? Well, maybe it's the live fights that occurred among the parade of low-lifes who graced Springer's stage. Even after 16 former "guests" on the show claimed on the TV show *Extra* that the stories they told and the fights they engaged in were faked, the public couldn't get enough. A *Springer* video showing back-to-back fights, along with cursing and nudity censored from the show, sold hundreds of thousands of copies. Springer, 54, launched his talk show in 1991, having served as mayor of Cincinnati in his early 30s and then anchoring a local news show there. At year's end he starred in a movie, *Ringmaster,* loosely based on his show; he was a man at the peak of his career. Well, the pay was good.

Jack the Dripper

That's what TIME once called Jackson Pollock; the pioneer of action painting was not amused. Now Robert Hughes said that a major retrospective at New York City's Museum of Modern Art proved that "Pollock was a great painter; at least he painted some great pictures, which changed the face of American art, and look ... fresh and strong today."

Below, *Blue Poles: Number 11* (1952)

ANTZ: DreamWorks got to theaters first

A BUG'S LIFE: Disney got the last laugh

And what about those of us who care more about movies than the machinations by which they're produced? TIME critic Richard Schickel hailed the "dark-toned computer animation" of *Antz;* fellow TIME critic Richard Corliss said *A Bug's Life* was "rich and rewarding" with "stellar" design. Moviegoers, who vote with dollars, liked both: *Antz* took in a strong $17 million on its first weekend, while *A Bug's Life* scored $46 million in its five-day Thanksgiving weekend opening.

Tubbies Tops with Tube Tots

Just when you thought television couldn't get any more puerile, along came a Teletubby. Was it Laa-Laa? Po? Dipsy? Tinky Winky? Who knew—or cared? Presumably the target audience did, for *Teletubbies* was the first show explicitly designed for the one-to-two-year-old set. The British import centers on the comical activities of four fuzzy creatures who speak in baby talk, eat Tubby Custard ("Tubby Tustard!"), share "big hugs" and have TV antennas on their heads and TV screens on their stomachs that transmit short film clips showing real children. In other words, this is a TV show about infants, for infants, that extols the

TELETUBBIES: King George III's revenge?

RAGDOLL PRODUCTIONS & THE ITSY BITSY ENTERTAINMENT COMPANY

wonders of, among other things, television. How could it fail? About 2 million people in Britain have watched it daily since its launch in 1997; after its U.S. premiere on PBS in April 1998, it swiftly landed alongside *Barney* and *Sesame Street* in the top five of kids' shows on the network. But don't worry about the nation's infants: *Teletubbies* was a surprise hit with the college audience.

Playboy of the Western World

Playwright Martin McDonagh may or may not be the greatest, but he is certainly the freshest, most confident new voice in the theater to come along in years. The Irish writer, only 28, was the talk of London, where four of his plays were staged to wide acclaim in 1996 and 1997. In 1998 he conquered America. *The Beauty Queen of Leenane,* TIME critic Richard Zoglin's selection as best play of the year (*see* The Best of 1998), opened off-Broadway and drew such ecstatic reviews that it moved to Broadway and became a hit. When *The Cripple of Inishmaan* opened at New York City's Public Theater, Zoglin hailed the second play as a "work of surprises and unexpected depths." ■

Fresh Face of '98

There's surely something about Cameron Diaz; everyone's crazy about her. Maybe it's the throaty laugh, the sinewy silhouette, the radiant smile that seems to wonder at the edges if you really think she's all that gorgeous. Well, she is—and a fine comic actress too. In *My Best Friend's Wedding* in 1997, Diaz, 26, out-dazzled and outcuted Julia Roberts, no contest. In 1998 she had five men—four pathetic losers and N.F.L. quarterback Brett Favre—drooling over her in Peter and Bobby Farrelly's latest assault on the already benumbed

Cameron Diaz

taste buds of the American moviegoer, *There's Something About Mary.* The gross-out fest was a surprise hit, perhaps because it offered the chance to see Diaz in giggly, gangly bloom. In the fall she starred alongside Christian Slater in an over-the-top black comedy, *Very Bad Things.* And in one of the surest signs of Hollywood beatification, in its 1998 Hall of Fame issue *Vanity Fair* magazine presented Diaz as the year's official model turned actress, dubbing her a "Tweety Bird with sex appeal."

▶ **Set 'em up, Joe. In 1998 we toasted the memories of a skinny kid from Hoboken, a sprinter with a heart (and medals) of gold, and a pair of beloved cowboys. Here's to the father of *West Side Story*, the godfather of conservatives — and the grandfather who helped raised us all**

THE SECRET SHARER
Frank Sinatra's intimate way
with a lyric linked songwriter,
singer and listener in a
fraternity of yearning

The Music Man

Frank Sinatra: 1915-1998

FRANK SINATRA'S PASSING WASN'T IN character. It should have been quick, furious, defiant. Instead, when he died of a heart attack on May 14 at 82, it was lingering, pernicious, sad. He last performed in the winter of 1995, but he was unsteady on his feet, and lyrics he'd known for years eluded him. A last triumph, a standoff against encroaching fate, would have rounded memory with a perfect dramatic closure. Too much to expect perhaps, but in a sense that was Sinatra's own fault. Too much, he had taught us, was the least we could expect from him. So much heart, so much sorrow, such delicacy and such braggadocio, all for the music he made indelible, with enough to spare so that it spilled over into his life and into all the public refractions of it.

He sang songs so personally that he was remade in the image of the music, and the image shifted with each new generation. In the 1930s he quickly left his skeptical parents behind to

AT EASE: Sinatra at a 1953 recording session. His supple lyrical delivery belied the intensity he put into his singing

launch a career based on iron self-confidence. In the '40s, husband to his doting first wife Nancy, he was the heartthrob balladeer who sang *I'll Be Seeing You* to World War II G.I.s and their sweethearts. In the '50s the persona went to war with the man. Sinatra at ballad tempo was the soul-sick, lovelorn, solitary man who closes down a midtown saloon. Up-tempo, and increasingly in his life, he was the unapologetic and (some said) unconscionable swinger, the ring-a-ding ringmaster of a million all-night parties. Which was the real Sinatra, the reveler or the lost man?

If the question ever bothered him, he never let on. He could walk the sunny side of the street as well as the boulevard of broken dreams, snap brim tilted off the right side of his head, raincoat slung over his shoulder like an open bandolier. The proud champion of classic American pop fought a pitched battle against the tide of rock in the '60s. Became music's elder statesman in the '70s. Then the resurgent master of the '80s. And—at last, at the end of his days—the icon who could be forgiven anything for a song.

He passed songs along like pieces of a shared life, an intimacy between himself and whoever was listening. You could play a Sinatra album all alone or hear him in a stadium. Either way, it was always the same: a one-on-one experience, the song a shared secret between the singer and you. Only you.

He knew your hidden heart. Did anyone know his? He sang and made us all believe we did. And then, just when we had his assurance, he changed and kept us guessing. How could the guy who made an album as naked and forsaken as *Only the Lonely* get into all that Rat Pack hugger-mugger, knocking back drinks with Dean Martin and Sammy Davis Jr. and flattening intrusive photographers? How could the exuberance of *Come Fly with Me*, the joyful, rapturous carnality of *I've Got You Under My Skin*, the sinuous *Summer Wind* match up with the temperament of a tempestuous loner who traveled with a squadron of pals and protectors, who swung on the gents of the press and who declined to forswear certain companions—Vegas oddsmakers and knee breakers, sharply tailored gentlemen in New York City and Chicago like Sam Giancana—in whom the law retained an inveterate interest?

Sinatra's attitude about all this was simple enough. He was responsible to the world for his music, but for his life answerable only to himself, and to hell with the rest of you. There was, all through him, a kind of animating anger, an Italian street-kid swagger that made good cover for his black-and-blue soulfulness. But that attitude was a dodge, barbed wire for the unwary, protecting his private preserve of deepest feeling and experience, saving it for where it was needed most: the songs.

He was a formidable public personality and retained an outspoken interest in politics. He was, at the start and for a long time, an out-front liberal. Surely swayed by charm and power, he passed along a Mob-linked mistress to his pal President John F. Kennedy, who used her but eventually froze Sinatra out of Camelot. Sinatra responded bitterly and swung right. He golfed with Spiro Agnew, sang (wonderfully) at the Nixon White House, partied with the Reagans.

He was natural tabloid fodder, doing the clubs with Ava Gardner (wife No. 2) and Juliet Prowse, and courting Mia Farrow, who became, fleetingly, wife No. 3. He was a superb actor, but he pretended not to take acting seriously. Yet in a film career that spanned some 40 years, he gave an impressive number of unforgettable performances: *On the Town, From Here to Eternity, The Man with the Golden Arm, Some Came Running, Pal Joey, The Manchurian Candidate.* These are not the credits of a dabbler. Despite his professed approach to the craft, which was breezy to the point of gale force, he met with junkies for *Golden Arm* and hung around with cops whenever he had to play on the cool side of the law. He did his homework. He just didn't want anyone to see his notes.

Notes were for singing, and on the subject of music, Sinatra could write a book. He was generous to other singers, maybe because he knew he had no serious rival, but also out of a genuine respect for musicianship. He talked about music as he sang it: with diligence and a passion that left no doubt that this above all was what mattered most. Not only does his music define the time and temper of the American decades in which it was made, but his singing moves those songs out of time into something indistinct, everlasting. In Sinatra's music, there is no past tense. ∎

COLUMBIA PICTURES

ONSCREEN: Emoting with Montgomery Clift in 1953's *From Here to Eternity*

BOB WILLOUGHBY—MPTV

ONSTAGE: Rat-packing in Las Vegas with Dean Martin, Sammy Davis Jr. and friends

UPI—CORBIS-BETTMANN

ON HAND: Partying with John Kennedy, before Sinatra was exiled from Camelot

Conscience of a Curmudgeon

Barry Goldwater: 1909-1998

AMERICANS LIKE THEIR CONSERVATIVES TO BE CURMUD-geonly—irascible, unblinkered, plain-talking tellers of uncomfortable truths, with a keen eye for hypocrisy. Curmudgeons are amusing, colorful and, most impor-tant, utterly harmless. Barry Goldwater's public career spanned 40 years, and for most of them he managed to be thought curmudgeonly—almost universally enjoyed, like a prickly old teddy bear you can't help hugging.

But it was not always so for Mr. Conservative. For the first dozen years of his career, from his arrival in Washington as the upset winner of a 1952 race for the Senate to his climactic run for the presidency in 1964, he was notorious for casting lone-ly and unpopular votes—against the 1963 Test Ban Treaty, for example, and against the Civil Rights Act a year later. For his offenses against progressive opinion, he was variously de-scribed as "dangerous," "psychotic," "a Hitlerite," "fascistic" and a "rallying point for racists." Even now, in a political era supposedly debased by attack ads, the vilification of Goldwa-ter in the 1964 campaign seems astonishing. We are used to politicians accusing rivals of heartlessness or racial insensitiv-ity, but Goldwater's opponents made a weightier claim. They said he wanted to destroy the world.

President Lyndon Johnson's infamous daisy ad, in which a cute little girl pulled petals off a flower until the eruption of a mushroom cloud broke her reverie, was only one example. *Fact* magazine came out with a 64-page "psychological study," purportedly a survey of professional shrinks, that showed Goldwater was "psychologically unfit" to be President. The candidate's slogan, "In your heart, you know he's right," was transformed into a snicker: "In your guts, you know he's nuts."

How did the conservative psycho become the prickly ted-dy bear? Simple: Goldwater lost, and lost big—so big that no one could seriously entertain the idea that he would ever become President or even lead his party. Declawed, he returned to Capitol Hill, free to make his caustic comments. Richard Nixon, he said, was "the most dishonest individual I have ever met in my life." After Iran-*contra*, he said Ronald Reagan—a famed Goldwaterite—must be either "a liar or an incompetent."

But there was no such thing as a Goldwaterite. There was only Goldwater, sui generis. He remained an individualist, and the right passed him by. In his last years his libertarian-ism hardened. Now it was conservatives who thought he was nuts. He came out for gay rights, including in the military, and opposed controls on abortion. When Republicans attacked President Clinton about Whitewater, Goldwater told them to "get off his back and let him govern." During the ascendancy of the religious right, Goldwater said, "Every good Christian ought to kick Jerry Falwell in the ass." In his curmudgeon's heart, Barry Goldwater knew he was right, and more often than not he was. ■

PRICKLY PAIR
The crusty Southwesterner savored a dustup—first with the left and, in his final years, with the right

Repentant Rebel

George Wallace: 1919-1998

FLIP SCHULKE—BLACK STAR

ONCE UPON A TIME, YOUNG GEORGE WALLACE WAS a racial moderate. But this child of rural southeast Alabama burned with pugnacious ambition, a flame as pure as rage. After a fiercer segregationist, John Patterson, outdueled him for the governorship in 1958, Wallace declared he would never be "outniggered" again. At his inauguration as Governor in 1963, he ended with a cry: "Segregation now, segregation tomorrow, segregation forever!" A few months later, he stood in the schoolhouse door to block two black students from enrolling at the University of Alabama. The Justice Department overrode him with bayonets.

Wallace was one of the great political arsonists; no material in America was more flammable than race. He took his magnificent sneer and slurring menace up North to Rust Belt, hard-hat country, where he scorched the earth with a message of racial contempt and populist economic grievance. In the 1968 presidential election, he took 13% of the popular vote. Shot down and crippled by a deranged gunman in the 1972 campaign, Wallace lived to repent: years later, he wheeled himself before the Southern Christian Leadership Conference, apologized to the assembled black elders and begged forgiveness. They seemed to grant it. ∎

NATE THAYHER—TOM KELLER & ASSOCIATES LLC

Tiller of the Killing Fields
Pol Pot: c. 1925-1998

OW WE WILL NEVER KNOW WHY: WE STAND mute before genocide, when women's throats are slit with sharp palm leaves, when children's heads are smashed against tree trunks, when men are slaughtered with the crack of a hoe. These things happened every day in Cambodia for 3½ terrible years under Pol Pot's regime.

The conundrum of this man who butchered his own people is that he did not seem savage at all. Before fleeing into the jungle in 1963, the French-educated son of prosperous landowners, born Saloth Sar, taught school in Phnom Penh, and his former students remembered him as a soft-spoken, even-tempered man. Yet when the communist guerrilla took power in April 1975, he vowed to turn back the clock to "Year Zero." In the name of a bizarre blend of peasant romanticism and radical Maoism, his Khmer Rouge conducted a reign of terror intended to give birth to an agrarian utopia.

Elusive and mysterious throughout his life, Pol Pot slipped just as stealthily into his grave. The teenage guerrillas of the Khmer Rouge who had kept the 73-year-old under "house arrest" since his surprising reappearance at a 1997 show trial blandly informed the world that he died peacefully of a heart attack. Now we will never know why. ∎

The Good Doctor
Benjamin Spock: 1903-1998

MARVIN KONER—BLACK STAR

D R. BENJAMIN SPOCK SINGLE-HANDEDLY CHANGED the way today's parents raise their children. He preached, albeit gently, that what infants need most from their mothers and fathers is love. Babies are not, he argued (against the prevailing wisdom of the times), little savages who must be broken in to adult schedules as quickly as possible. Don't rush them, he urged; cherish them. Small wonder that for millions of parents who followed Dr. Spock's advice with their children, who then did the same with theirs, news of his death felt like a loss in the family.

A book doesn't always reflect its author's personality, but Spock's *Common Sense Book of Baby and* *Child Care* did. He was as he seemed: modest, funny, empathetic, confident enough in his own knowledge not to be stuffy about it. And he was something else: a most unlikely revolutionary.

In the 1960s, when Spock and the first generation he had helped raise noisily protested the war in Vietnam and nuclear proliferation, critics blamed Spock's "permissive" book for the uproar. "People who call the book permissive never use the book," he replied. He had a point. For all his emphasis on love, Spock stressed parents' obligations to set limits for their children, to teach them by example and precept "what's right and proper." Good prescription, Doc. ■

KEN REGAN—CAMERA 5

Speeding Beauty

Florence Griffith Joyner: 1959-1998

EULOGY WHEN YOU THINK OF FLORENCE GRIFFITH Joyner, you think of beauty, style, long fingernails and speed. But she was so much more. I first met Florence in 1984 and was captivated not only by her beauty but also by her grace and the patience of her character. In 1996 at the Olympic Games in Atlanta, Florence came to my room before the 100-m final to give me words of encouragement. "All right, Gail," she said, "go make history."

On and off the track, Florence gave gold-medal performances. She inspired and motivated many people through her speech and words. How many people's lives make us stand back in awe? In 38 years Florence accomplished what would take others three lifetimes to do. She was a wife, a mother, an actress and a poet; she ran, she taught, she loved. Although she retired from track and field in 1989, she left a lasting mark. She raised the standard of competition and at the same time brought femininity to our sport. She showed by example that when you look great, you feel great—and when you feel great, you perform great. Florence brought to track a unique flair, style and grace, and added to them gold medals and world records. She was unquestionably the fastest woman in the world.

—Gail Devers

Adios, Amigos!

Gene Autry: 1917-1998   Roy Rogers: 1911-1998

PHOTOFEST (2)

NOW AND THEN, DESTINY HAS A SENSE OF SYMMETRY; in 1998 death took two beloved icons of the big-sky country—and the big-screen country. Texas born and Oklahoma raised, Gene Autry was Hollywood's first singing cowboy. He set out to play baseball; instead he entered show business, heeding the advice of Will Rogers, who recommended a radio career after hearing Autry, on break from a job as a telegrapher at a train station, sing and play his guitar. His first hit, 1931's *That Silver-Haired Daddy of Mine*, was followed by TV and radio shows, almost 100 films and 635 recordings—including *Rudolph the Red-Nosed Reindeer* and *Back in the Saddle Again*. "I got better as I went along," said the self-effacing star. "I couldn't get any worse." He ended up indulging his passion for baseball as owner of the California Angels.

Autry's counterpart was Roy Rogers, who wore a white hat and sang in more than 90 westerns; the uncomplicated "King of the Cowboys" was a beloved public figure in the decades after World War II. His strong supporting cast included wife Dale Evans, sidekick Gabby Hayes—and his famous steed, Trigger. A canny businessman, he founded the Roy Rogers fast-food chain. Happy trails, Roy and Gene. ■

"Light This Candle!"

Alan Shepard: 1923-1998

RALPH MORSE—LIFE

EULOGY ALAN SHEPARD WAS MANY THINGS. HE was a patriot, a leader, a competitor, a hero, a friend. When we seven were named America's first astronauts, Al stood out. I had first met him when we were test pilots, but not until the Mercury program did I see the determination, toughness and courage of Alan Shepard.

Remember, it was the depths of the cold war. After Sputnik, our technological superiority was questioned; we were being beaten by a country that bragged, "America will sleep under a Russian moon." But Al brought us back. He brought us back by car-

rying the American questing spirit on his shoulders into the heavens. He brought us back because he took the Soviet challenge not only as a patriot—he took it personally.

All seven of us saw the failures in those early Redstone rocket tests, but that didn't deter us—especially not Al. Waiting in his capsule through yet another delay before his historic mission, we heard him bark, "Why don't you fix your little problem and light this candle?" That moment says more about Alan Shepard than anything else.

—John Glenn

GJON MILI—LIFE

Native Dancer
Jerome Robbins: 1918-1998

THE CURTAIN OF NEW YORK CITY'S METROPOLITAN Opera House rose to reveal a seedy-looking bar as three male dancers in bell-bottom trousers charged onstage. One of them was a 25-year-old choreographer from New Jersey, starring in the premiere of his first ballet, a breezy tale of girl-crazy sailors on shore leave that he called *Fancy Free*. At a time when most Americans thought ballet meant women in tutus acting like birds, *Fancy Free* looked more like Fred Astaire than *Swan Lake*; it had MADE IN THE U.S.A. stamped on every move. Jerome Robbins took two dozen curtain calls that night in 1944, and never looked back.

In the '50s and '60s, Robbins worked mainly on Broadway, staging such landmark productions as *Gypsy* and *Fiddler on the Roof*; he made Mary Martin fly in *Peter Pan* and taught the Jets and the Sharks how to rumble in *West Side Story*, his theatrical masterpiece. But classical dance was his true love, and in 1969 he decided to devote himself solely to George Balanchine's New York City Ballet, for which he made a string of masterworks—above all, *Dances at a Gathering*, a garland of sometimes sentimental, sometimes intensely romantic dances set to Chopin—that secured his standing as America's first great native-born ballet choreographer. ■

BRIAN BRAKER—RAPHO/GAMMA LIAISON

The Dream Shaper
Akira Kurosawa: 1910-1998

EULOGY AKIRA KUROSAWA WAS ONE OF THE TOWER-ing figures of world cinema. His work—31 movies made over 50 years—is one of the great treasures of film history. Kurosawa introduced Japanese cinema to the West in 1950 with *Rashomon*, a work of tremendous moral and cinematic force whose influence on Western filmmakers is immeasurable. This was the first in a series of Kurosawa masterpieces in the '50s and '60s, one more startling than the other: *Ikiru, The Seven Samurai, Throne of Blood, The Hidden Fortress, Yojimbo, High and Low;* in his work, the frame always threatens to explode with odd tensions and latent energies.

It is perhaps *Ikiru*, about a man with cancer who searches for meaning in life, that had the greatest impact on me. Seeing this film was one of the most intense emotional experiences of my teenage years. From then until the time, many years later, when I played a small part in his film *Dreams*, my admiration for the mental agility and physical energy of this great master (who at 82 was still climbing ladders on the set) never waned. While it saddens me that he is gone, I know that his genius—which allowed him to achieve much, much more than most of us could ever hope for—will live on forever in his films.

—*Martin Scorsese*

General Sani Abacha, 54, Nigerian dictator who wrested power in a 1993 coup and kept his grip on Africa's most populous and oil-rich nation by canceling free elections and imprisoning or executing critics.

Bella Abzug, 77, milliner's friend and champion of women, labor, blacks and all underdogs. Declaring "This woman's place is in the House—the House of Representatives," she won a seat in Congress in 1970.

Clayton ("Peg Leg") Bates, 91, tap dancer who refused to let an accident that severed his leg at the age of 12 stay his art. Wearing a wooden limb outfitted with metal taps, he hoofed from the 1920s to 1989, making more than 20 appearances on *The Ed Sullivan Show.*

Otto Bettmann, 94, excavator of the past and refugee from Hitler's Germany who accumulated 5 million images in the archive of photographs that bore his name.

Lloyd Bridges, 85, actor and patriarch of a Hollywood dynasty, whose myriad roles ranged from the dramatic (*High Noon*) to the slapstick (*Airplane!*) to the adventurous (*Sea Hunt*).

Harry Caray, 83, irrepressible baseball announcer. "Holy cow!"—he spent nearly 60 years behind the mike, the last 27 at Chicago's Wrigley Field.

Betty Carter, 69, boldly idiosyncratic jazz singer and nurturer of young jazz talent, who won a National Medal of Arts award in 1997.

Carlos Castaneda, 72 (maybe), mystery man who was either an unfairly vilified anthropologist or a wildly inventive novelist, depending on whether his accounts of mind-bending sessions with a Yaqui Indian sorcerer are taken as fact or fiction.

Eldridge Cleaver, 62, prophet of black power. While serving a jail term for

assault, Cleaver penned *Soul on Ice,* his 1968 polemic on black rage. He joined the Black Panther Party on his release. Two years later, after a gunfight with police in Oakland, he fled the U.S. to live in exile for eight years. Crack addiction and petty crimes followed his return.

Clark Clifford, 91, consummate Capitol insider. Tall and elegant, he advised four Democratic Presidents, advocating causes from civil rights to the environment. His involvement in the B.C.C.I. banking scandal led to 1992 criminal charges that were dropped because of his age.

Marjory Stoneman Douglas, 108, vigilant empress of the Florida Everglades, who led a half-century crusade to preserve the watery wilderness.

Brief farewells to Tarzan's Jane, Betty Boop's voice, Howdy Doody's dad and Lamb Chop's mom, a tap dancer with one leg and the Empress of the Everglades

Clark Clifford, 1948   Carlos Castaneda, 1973

Fred Friendly, 82, broadcasting pioneer and former president of CBS News whose early documentary work set the standard for journalistic integrity.

Martha Gellhorn, 89, war correspondent, novelist and Ernest Hemingway's third wife. Her dispatches from the Spanish Civil War, World War II and Vietnam focused on the ordinary and the powerless.

Brendan Gill, 83, urbane man of letters who began and ended his career at the *New Yorker* as a columnist and critic—of architecture and everything else. He wrote poetry, novels, plays, biographies and even a best seller: *Here at the New Yorker.*

Ted Hughes, 68, British poet laureate who had a stormy marriage to tormented American poet Sylvia Plath. Acclaimed for his unsentimental poetry filled with violent images of

nature, Hughes also wrote a number of poems and stories for children.

Bob Kane, 83, creator of the comic-book icon Batman in 1939. The strength and creativity Kane bestowed on his superhero allowed Batman to leap from comics to a 1960s TV series to the movies.

Denise Levertov, 74, activist-poet who meditated on the politics of the home and state, writing such fierce antiwar collections as *To Stay Alive.*

Shari Lewis, 65, puppeteer who animated both her inquistive sidekick Lamb Chop and the quest for quality children's TV. A talented musician, conductor and dancer, she wrote 60 children's books and won 12 Emmys during her 40-year career.

Sid Luckman, 81, brainy Chicago Bears Hall of Fame quarterback who perfected the T-formation offense, changing the way the game was played. He led an All Star line-up, dubbed the Monsters of the Midway, to four NFL championships in seven years.

E.G. Marshall, 84, Emmy-winning actor whose resonant voice and stoic demeanor led him to portray a succession of authoritative and trustworthy characters. Perhaps best known for his role on *The Defenders,* Marshall also starred in films and appeared in the 1956 Broadway premiere performance of *Waiting for Godot.*

Linda Eastman McCartney, 56, fetching photographer of '60s rockers who wed one of her dreamiest subjects, Beatle Paul. Their 29-year union was the rule-proving exception to short-lived celebrity marriages. She was a tireless champion of animal rights as well as vegetarianism.

James McDougal, 57, eccentric Arkansas banker and erstwhile friend of Bill and Hillary's, who snitched on his business dealings with the Clintons and sparked the Whitewater investigation. He died in prison in Texas.

Roddy McDowall, 70, child star who went on to become a versatile actor. After playing sensitive-boy roles in the '40s (including *Lassie Come Home* and *How Green Was My Valley*), he played such adult parts as Octavian in *Cleopatra* and chimp Cornelius in the *Planet of the Apes* series.

Cary Middlecoff, 77, dentist who traded in his drill to become a top golfer and the leading money earner on the PGA Tour in the 1950s, winning two U.S. Opens and the Masters.

Helen Wills Moody (Roark), 92, imperturbable tennis ace. "Little Miss Poker Face" won 31 major championships—eight at Wimbledon.

Archie Moore, 84, champion light-heavyweight boxer; he was the only man to fight both Rocky Marciano and Muhammad Ali— but he lost both matches.

Wright Morris, 88, writer-photographer of the Middle-American gothic, who spun tales of small-town strangeness about his native Nebraska.

Maureen O'Sullivan, 87, demure silver-screen actress who originated Tarzan's sarong-clad jungle-gal Jane and was the mother of a brood of seven—including actress Mia Farrow.

Octavio Paz, 84, Mexico's prolific, Nobel-winning man of letters, who plumbed his country's psyche in more than 40 volumes of poems and essays. His hybrid heritage (part Spanish, part Indian) informs his seminal *The Labyrinth of Solitude*.

Carl Perkins, 65, the Big Daddy of rockabilly, whose *Blue Suede Shoes*, *Matchbox* and *Honey Don't* helped teach the Beatles rock 'n' roll.

Ferdinand Porsche, 88, who helped his father engineer the Volkswagen Beetle (at Hitler's behest) and later created the popular, profitable, eponymous German sports car.

Lewis Powell, 90, the Burger court's balanced conservative who was appointed in 1971 by Richard Nixon. His 1978 *Bakke* opinion barred racial quotas but opened the door for affirmative action.

Mae Questel, 89, helium-toned actress who gave voice to the sexy Betty Boop and Popeye's sexless Olive Oyl.

Dan Quisenberry, 45, relief pitcher and three-time All Star for the Kansas City Royals, whose wit was as devastating as his unique sinker ball.

James Earl Ray, 70, criminal who con-

Helen Wills, 1926   James Earl Ray, 1977   Flip Wilson, 1972

fessed to killing Martin Luther King Jr. His prison term was marked by botched jailbreaks and his steady insistence that he had only been the fall guy in a larger conspiracy to slay King—a claim that received the unlikely backing of the King family.

"Buffalo Bob" Smith, 80, revered TV icon and host of the medium's first smash hit, *The Howdy Doody Show*. Starting in 1947, the avuncular would-be cowboy cheerfully presided over Doodyville U.S.A. for 13 years.

Kay Thompson, in her 90s, a successful nightclub performer who starred in the movie *Funny Face*. But her most enduring character was Eloise, an irascible six-year-old who lived in New York City's Plaza Hotel.

Kwame Ture, 57, American revolutionary, a.k.a. Stokely Carmichael, who popularized the term "black power."

In 1969 he moved to Guinea, severing ties with the Black Panthers, whom he deemed too timid.

J.T. Walsh, 54, character actor and specialist in obdurate personae who stood out in nearly 60 films.

Dorothy West, 91, sole surviving voice of the Harlem Renaissance. West was just a teen when she tied with Zora Neale Hurston for second place in a short-story contest, winning swift admission into the gifted clique of black intellectuals.

Carl Wilson, 51, a founder of America's quintessential pop group, the Beach Boys, and the youngest and most level-headed of the band's Wilson brothers. Carl's smooth pitch is heard in lead vocals on such classics as *Good Vibrations* and *God Only Knows*.

Flip Wilson, 64, caricaturist. Creator of such pop-cultural icons as Geraldine—the sassy black woman who warned "What you see is what you get!"—Wilson was the first African-American to host a variety show.

Tammy Wynette, 55, country music's down-home diva. A beautician turned songstress, she wailed plaintive ballads that traced her life story: five marriages, bankruptcy, a painkiller addiction and a kidnapping.

Frank Yankovic, 83, a.k.a. America's Polka King, maestro of Midwestern dance halls for seven decades.

Robert Young, 91, TV's benevolent authority figure on *Father Knows Best* and *Marcus Welby, M.D.* His serene characters belied a troubled offscreen life; Young struggled with alcoholism and depression.

Henny Youngman, 91, motor-mouth comic who was once clocked at 250 one-liners in 45 minutes. One favorite standby: "Take my wife—please!" ■